ACKNOWLEDGEMENTS

I would like to thank Abhijit Mukhopapdhyay, Leslie Machado, Sanjay Mishra, Asha Shetty, Parsana Joshi, Sudha Shah, Mehernosh Randeria, Balwant Gajdhar and Major Ramesh Sharma, all of whom provided invaluable research support. A huge thank you is also due to Nick Daws of My Writers Circle, Diana Nadin of the Writers Bureau, my writing mentor, and G. S. Sauhta, my boss, who circulated a virtual 'Do Not Disturb' sign throughout the organisation when I went underground to write.

I would also like to thank Dr. Joseph Gama, my father, who 'loaned' me his 'secret room' in his Portuguese villa; Noemia Gama, my mother, who cheered me on and pampered me with her Indo-Portuguese food; Rocky III, our German shepherd dog and faithful companion; and last, but not least, my wife, Louella and my boys, Noah and Leo, for putting up with my 'absences'.

Others who deserve my gratitude include the publisher for giving me the opportunity to write this book, Joe Laredo, my long-suffering editor, Peter Read for additional editing and proof-reading, Sara Letts for final checks and editing, Di Tolland for DTP and photo selection, and Jim Watson for the cover design and maps. Finally a special thank you to all the photographers (listed on page 222) – the unsung heroes – whose beautiful images add colour and bring India to life.

THE AUTHOR

Noël Gama trained as a copywriter and is also an HR professional with over 25 years' experience. He has authored corporate manuals and edited corporate newsletters, besides being a columnist for a national news magazine in India, where he lives in the former Portuguese enclave of Daman. Noël's passion is the study of cultures and his trademark Blog2Book projects caught the attention of a Consul General of Portugal in India, who recently launched one of his projects on Indo-Portuguese culture, which is now being turned into four books. Noël was the winner of the 'Writer of the Year 2007' award from the Writers Bureau (UK) and the American Writers & Artists Institute (USA). Culture Wise India is his first book.

What readers & reviewers have said about Survival Books:

'If you need to find out how France works then this book is indispensable. Native French people probably have a less thorough understanding of how their country functions.'

Living France

'It's everything you always wanted to ask but didn't for fear of the contemptuous put down. The best English-language guide. Its pages are stuffed with practical information on everyday subjects and are designed to compliment the traditional guidebook.'

Swiss News

'Rarely has a 'survival guide' contained such useful advice – This book dispels doubts for first-time travellers, yet is also useful for seasoned globetrotters – In a word, if you're planning to move to the US or go there for a long-term stay, then buy this book both for general reading and as a ready-reference.'

American Citizens Abroad

'Let's say it at once. David Hampshire's Living and Working in France is the best handbook ever produced for visitors and foreign residents in this country; indeed, my discussion with locals showed that it has much to teach even those born and bred in l'Hexagone – It is Hampshire's meticulous detail which lifts his work way beyond the range of other books with similar titles. Often you think of a supplementary question and search for the answer in vain. With Hampshire this is rarely the case. – He writes with great clarity (and gives French equivalents of all key terms), a touch of humour and a ready eye for the odd (and often illuminating) fact. – This book is absolutely indispensable.'

The Riviera Reporter

'A must for all future expats. I invested in several books but this is the only one you need. Every issue and concern is covered, every daft question you have but are frightened to ask is answered honestly without pulling any punches. Highly recommended.'

Reader

'In answer to the desert island question about the one how-to book on France, this book would be it.'

The Recorder

'The ultimate reference book. Every subject imaginable is exhaustively explained in simple terms. An excellent introduction to fully enjoy all that this fine country has to offer and save time and money in the process.'

American Club of Zurich

'The amount of information covered is not short of incredible. I thought I knew enough about my birth country. This book has proved me wrong. Don't go to France without it. Big mistake if you do. Absolutely priceless!'

Reader

'When you buy a model plane for your child, a video recorder, or some new computer gizmo, you get with it a leaflet or booklet pleading 'Read Me First', or bearing large friendly letters or bold type saying 'IMPORTANT - follow the instructions carefully'. This book should be similarly supplied to all those entering France with anything more durable than a 5-day return ticket. – It is worth reading even if you are just visiting briefly, or if you have lived here for years and feel totally knowledgeable and secure. But if you need to find out how France works then it is indispensable. Native French people probably have a less thorough understanding of how their country functions. – Where it is most essential, the book is most up to the minute.

Living France

A comprehensive guide to all things French, written in a highly readable and amusing style, for anyone planning to live, work or retire in France.

The Times

Covers every conceivable question that might be asked concerning everyday life – I know of no other book that could take the place of this one.

France in Print

A concise, thorough account of the Do's and DONT's for a foreigner in Switzerland – Crammed with useful information and lightened with humorous quips which make the facts more readable.

American Citizens Abroad

'I found this a wonderful book crammed with facts and figures, with a straightforward approach to the problems and pitfalls you are likely to encounter. The whole laced with humour and a thorough understanding of what's involved. Gets my vote!'

Reader

'A vital tool in the war against real estate sharks; don't even think of buying without reading this book first!'

Everything Spain

'We would like to congratulate you on this work: it is really super! We hand it out to our expatriates and they read it with great interest and pleasure.'

ICI (Switzerland) AG

CONTENTS

Golden Temple, Amritsar, Punjab

INTRODUCTION

If you're planning a trip to India or just want to learn more about the country, you'll find the information contained in *Culture Wise India* invaluable. Whether you're travelling on business or pleasure, visiting for a few days or planning to stay for a lifetime, Culture Wise guides enable you to quickly find your feet by removing the anxiety factor when dealing with a foreign culture.

Adjusting to a different environment and culture in any foreign country can be a traumatic and stressful experience, and India is no exception. You need to adapt to new customs and traditions and discover the Indian way of doing things - whether it's sharing the afternoon *chai* and *samosa* with neighbours or toasting a work colleague's success with Indian Made Foreign Liquor (IMFL), learning Hindi or deciphering Hinglish, dancing the Dandya Ras or performing a graceful *namaste*, your personal experience of 'Incredible India' will be unique.

India is a land of contrasts and contradictions: where foreigners are welcomed as honoured guests despite the huge cultural divide; where people are prejudiced against the West yet obsessed with it; where there's drought and floods simultaneously in different parts of the country; where people are spiritual yet materialistic; where bovine traffic enjoys right of way while luxury cars totter over potholes; where the obscenely rich minority flaunt their wealth and flout the rules, while the impoverished majority stoically trust in fate. The 'India Shining' reflects all this and shines on.

Culture Wise India is essential reading for anyone planning to visit India, including tourists (particularly travellers planning to stay a number of weeks or months), business people, migrants, retirees, holiday homeowners and transferees. It's designed to help newcomers avoid cultural and social gaffes; make friends and influence people; improve communications (both verbal and non-verbal); and enhance your understanding of Indian and the Indian people. It explains what to expect, how to behave in most situations, and how to get along with the locals and feel at home – rather than feeling like a fish out of water. It isn't, however, simply a monologue of dry facts and figures, but a practical and entertaining look at life in India.

A period spent in India is a wonderful way to enrich your life, broaden your horizons, and hopefully expand your circle of friends. We trust this book will help you avoid the pitfalls of visiting or living in India and smooth your way to a happy and rewarding stay.

Shubh Kaamna! (good luck!)'

Nöel Gama
February 2009

peacock, India'a national bird

1.

A CHANGE OF CULTURE

With almost daily advances in technology, ever-cheaper flights and knowledge about almost anywhere in the world at our fingertips, travelling, living, working and retiring abroad has never been more accessible, and current migration patterns suggest that it has never been more popular. However, although globalisation means the world has in effect 'shrunk', every country is still a 'world' of its own with a unique culture – and India is certainly no exception.

> 'There are no foreign lands. It is the traveller only who is foreign.'
> Robert Louis Stevenson (Scottish writer)

Some people find it impossible to adapt to a new life in a different culture – for reasons which are many and varied. According to statistics, partner dissatisfaction is the most common cause, as non-working spouses frequently find themselves without a role in the new country and sometimes with little to do other than think about what they would be doing if they were at home. Family concerns – which may include the children's education and worries about loved ones at home – can also deeply affect those living abroad.

Many factors contribute to how well you adapt to a new culture – for example, your personality, education, foreign language skills, mental health, maturity, socio-economic conditions, travel experience, and family and social support systems. How you handle the stress of change and bring balance and meaning to your life is the principal indicator of how well you'll adjust to a different country, culture and business environment.

INDIA IS DIFFERENT

Many people underestimate the cultural isolation that can be experienced in a foreign country, particularly one with a different language. Even in a country where you speak the language fluently you'll find that many aspects of the culture are surprisingly foreign, despite the cosy familiarity engendered by cinema, television and books. India is perceived by many foreigners – particularly the British – as a relatively easy option because English is widely spoken, it has traditional links with Britain, it's a multicultural society, and there are well established foreign communities in the major cities.

However, when you move to India you'll be faced with a host of challenges

– possibly including a new job, a new home and a new physical environment – which can be overwhelming – and all this before you even encounter the local culture! You may have left a job in your home country where you held a senior position, were extremely competent and knew everyone. In India, you may be virtually a trainee and not know any of your colleagues, and the sensation that you're starting from scratch can be demoralising.

India has many extremes of climate and weather, and you mustn't underestimate the effects that this can have on you. Extreme conditions of heat (and humidity) can lead to a lack of energy, poor sleep and dehydration. In the summer in most parts of India, 24-hour air-conditioning is common and if you aren't used to this it can be draining.

Even if you move to a major city, many things that you're used to and take for granted in your home country may not be available in India, e.g. certain kinds of food, opportunities to enjoy your favourite hobby or sport, books and television programmes in your language. Even 'Indian English' takes some getting used to. This lack of 'home comforts' can wear you down. You'll also have to contend with the lack of a local support network. At home you had a circle of friends, acquaintances, colleagues and relatives you could rely on for help and support. In India there's no such network, which can leave you feeling lost.

The degree of isolation you feel usually depends on how long you plan to spend in India and what you'll be doing there. If you're simply going on a short holiday you may not even be aware of many of the cultural differences, although if you are, it will enhance your enjoyment and may save you from a few embarrassing or confusing moments. However, if you're planning a business trip or intend to spend an extended period in India – perhaps working, studying or even living there permanently – **it's essential to understand the culture, customs and etiquette at the earliest opportunity.**

> 'If you reject the food, ignore the customs, fear the religion and avoid the people, you might better stay at home.'
>
> James A. Michener (American writer)

CULTURE SHOCK

Culture shock is the term used to describe the psychological and physical state felt by people when arriving in a foreign country or even moving to a new environment in their home country (where the culture, and in some cases language, may vary considerably by region and social class). Culture shock is a common experience among those who travel, live, work or study abroad, when in addition to adapting to new social rules and values, they may need to adjust to a different climate, food and dress. It manifests itself in a lack of direction and the feeling of not knowing what to do or how to do things, not knowing what's appropriate or inappropriate. You literally feel like a 'fish out of water'.

Culture shock is precipitated by the anxiety that results from losing all familiar rules of behaviour and cues to social intercourse: when to shake hands and what to say when you meet people; how to buy goods and services; when and how much to tip; how to use an ATM or the telephone; when to accept and refuse invitations; and when to take statements seriously and when not to.

These cues, which may be words, gestures or facial expressions, are acquired over a lifetime and are as much a part of our culture and customs as the language we speak and our beliefs. Our peace of mind and social efficiency depend on these cues, most of which are unconsciously recognised.

The symptoms of culture shock are essentially psychological. However, there are also physical symptoms including an increased incidence of minor illnesses (e.g. colds and headaches) and more serious psychosomatic illnesses brought on by depression. Culture shock can even cause physical pain. You shouldn't underestimate the consequences of culture shock, although the effects can be lessened if you accept the condition rather than deny it.

Stages of Culture Shock

Severe culture shock – often experienced when moving to a country with a different language – usually follows a number of stages. The names of these may vary, as may the symptoms and effects, but a typical progression is as follows:

1. **Honeymoon stage** – The first stage, commonly known as the 'honeymoon' stage, usually lasts from a few days to a few weeks after arrival (although it can last longer, particularly if you're insulated from the usual pressures of life). This stage is essentially a positive (even euphoric) one, when you find everything an exciting and interesting novelty. The feeling is similar to being on holiday or a short trip abroad, when you generally experience only the positive effects of a change of culture (although this depends very much on where you're from and the country you're visiting – see box).

2. **Rejection or distress stage** – The second stage is usually completely opposite to the first and is essentially negative and a period of crisis, as the initial excitement and 'holiday' feeling wears off and you start to cope with the real conditions of daily life – except of course that life is nothing like anything you've previously experienced. This can happen after only a few weeks and is characterised by a general feeling of disorientation, confusion and loneliness. Physical exhaustion, brought on by a change of time zone, extremes of hot or cold, and the strain of having hundreds of settling-in tasks to accomplish, is a symptom of this stage.

You may also experience regression, where you spend much of your time speaking your own language, watching television and reading newspapers from your home country, eating food from home and socialising with expatriates who speak your language. You may also spend a lot of time complaining about the host country and its culture. Your home environment suddenly assumes a tremendous importance and is irrationally glorified. All difficulties and problems are forgotten and only the good things back home are remembered.

3. **Flight stage** – The third stage is often known as the 'flight' stage (because of the overwhelming desire to escape) and is usually the one that lasts the longest and is the most difficult to cope with. During this period you may feel depressed and angry, as well as resentful towards the new country and its people. You may experience impatience and frustration at not being understood and discontentment, sadness and incompetence. These feelings are inevitable when you're trying to adapt to a new culture that's very different from that of your home country, and they're exacerbated by the fact that you can see nothing positive or good about the new country, but focus exclusively on the negative aspects.

You may become hostile and develop an aggressive attitude towards the country. Other people will sense this and in some cases either respond in a confrontational manner or try to avoid you. You may have difficulties with the language, your house, job or children's school, transportation ... even simple tasks such as shopping

may be fraught with problems, and the fact that local people are largely indifferent to these problems only makes matters worse. Even if they try to help, they may be unable to understand your concerns, and you conclude that they must be insensitive and unsympathetic to you and your problems.

Transition between your old culture and customs and those of your new country is a difficult process and takes time, during which there can be strong feelings of dissatisfaction. The period of adjustment can last as long as six months, although there are expatriates who adjust earlier and (although rare) those who never get over the 'flight' stage and are forced to return home.

4. **Recovery or autonomy stage** – The fourth stage is where you begin to integrate and adjust to the new culture, and accept the customs of the country as simply another way of living. The environment doesn't change – what changes is your attitude towards it. You become more competent with the language and you also feel more comfortable with the customs of the host country and can move around without anxiety. However, you still have problems with some of the social cues and you don't understand everything people say (particularly colloquialisms and idioms). Nevertheless, you've largely adjusted to the new culture and start to feel more at home and familiar with the country and your place in it, realising that it has its good as well as bad points.

5. **Reverse culture shock stage** – The fifth stage occurs when you return to your home country. You may find that many things have changed (you'll also have changed) and that you feel like a foreigner in your own country. If you've been away for a long time and have become comfortable with the habits and customs of a new lifestyle, you may find that you no longer feel at ease in your homeland. Reverse culture shock can be difficult to deal with and some people find it impossible to re-adapt to their home country after living abroad for a number of years.

The above stages occur at different times depending on the individual and his circumstances, and everyone has his own way of reacting to them, with the result that some stages last longer and are more difficult to cope with than others, while others are shorter and easier to overcome.

> The whole object of travel is not to set foot on foreign land; it is at last to set foot on one's own country as a foreign land.'
>
> G. K. Chesterton (English writer)

Reducing the Effects

Experts agree that almost everyone suffers from culture shock and there's no escaping the phenomenon; however, its negative effects can be reduced considerably and there are a number of things you can do before leaving home and immediately on arrival:

● **Positive attitude** – The key to reducing the negative effects of culture shock is to have a positive attitude towards India (whether you're visiting or planning to live there). If you don't look forward to a trip or relocation, you should question why you're going. There's no greater guarantee of unhappiness in a foreign environment than taking your prejudices with you.

It's important when trying to adapt to a new culture to be sensitive to the locals' feelings, and try to put yourself in their shoes wherever possible, which will help you understand why they react as they do. Bear in mind that they have a strong, in-bred cultural code, just as you do, and react in certain ways because they're culturally 'programmed' to do so. If you find yourself frustrated by an aspect of the local culture or behaviour, the chances are that your attitudes or behaviour will be equally puzzling to the natives.

> **'Travellers never think that THEY are the foreigners.'**
>
> Mason Cooley (American aphorist)

● **Research** – Discover as much as possible about India before you go, so that your arrival and settling-in period doesn't spring as many surprises as it might otherwise.

Reading up on India and its culture before leaving home will help you familiarise yourself with the local customs and make the country and its people seem less strange on arrival. Being aware of many of the differences will make you better prepared to deal with them. You're less likely to be upset by real or imaginary cultural slights, or to offend the locals by making cultural gaffes. Being prepared for a certain amount of disorientation and confusion (or worse) makes it easier to cope with it.

● There are literally hundreds of publications about India as well as dozens of websites for expatriates (see **Appendices B** and **C**). Many sites provide access to expatriates already living in India who can answer questions and provide useful advice. There are also 'notice boards' on many websites where you can post messages or questions. Try to find people in your area who have visited India and talk to them about it. Some companies organise briefings for families who are about to relocate abroad.

● **Visit India first** – If you're planning to live or work in India for a number of years or even permanently, it's important to visit the country before making the leap to see whether you think you'll enjoy living there and be able to cope with the culture. Rent a property before buying a home and don't burn your bridges until you're certain that you've made the right decision.

● **Learn Hindi** – As well as adopting a positive attitude, overcoming the language barrier will be your greatest weapon in combating culture shock and making your time in India enjoyable. The ability to speak Hindi (or local language) and understand the local vernacular (see **Chapter 5**) isn't just a useful tool that will allow you to buy what you need, find your way around, etc., but the key to understanding India and its culture. If you can speak Hindi, even at a basic level, your scope for making friends is immediately widened. You may not be a natural linguist, and learning Hindi can take time and requires motivation. However, with sufficient perseverance virtually anyone can learn enough Hindi to participate in the local culture.

● **Be proactive** – Join in the activities of the local people, which could be a carnival, a religious festival or some sporting activity. There are often local clubs where you can play sport or keep fit, be artistic, learn to cook local dishes, etc. Not only will this fill some of your spare time, giving you less time to miss home, but you'll also meet new people and make friends. If you feel you cannot join a local club – perhaps because your Hindi isn't good enough – you can always participate in activities for expatriates, of which there are many in the major cities.

Look upon a period spent in India as an opportunity to acquire new skills, attitudes and perspectives. A change of culture can help you develop a better understanding of yourself and stimulate your creativity.

● **Talk to other expatriates** – Although they may deny it, many expatriates have been through exactly what you're experiencing, and faced the same feelings of disorientation. Even if they cannot provide you with advice, it helps to know that you aren't alone and that it gets better over time.

However, don't make the mistake of mixing only with expatriates, as this will alienate you from the local culture and make it much harder to integrate.

● **Keep in touch with home** – Keeping in touch with your family and friends at home and around the world by telephone, email and letters will help reduce and overcome the effects of culture shock.

● **Be happy** – Don't rely on others to make you happy, or you won't find true and lasting happiness. There are things in life which only you can change. Every day we're affected negatively by things over which we have little or no control, but to complain about them only makes us unhappier. So be your own best friend and nurture your own capacity for happiness.

Culture shock is an unavoidable part of travelling, living and working abroad, but if you're aware of it and take steps to lessen its effects before you go and while you're abroad, the period of adjustment will be shortened and its negative and depressing consequences reduced.

FAMILIES IN INDIA

Family life may be completely different in India and relationships can become strained under the stress of adapting to culture shock. Your family may find itself in a completely new and possibly alien environment, your new home may scarcely resemble your previous one (it may be much more luxurious or significantly smaller) and the climate may differ dramatically from that of your home country. If possible, you should prepare your family for as many aspects of the new situation as you can, and explain to your children the differences they're likely to encounter, while at the same time dispelling their fears.

> 'And that's the wonderful thing about family travel: it provides you with experiences that will remain locked forever in the scar tissue of your mind.'
>
> Dave Barry (American writer & humorist)

Culture shock can affect non-working spouses and children more than working spouses. The husband (the breadwinner is usually the husband) has his work to occupy him, and his activities may not differ much from what he had been accustomed to at home. On the other hand, the wife has to operate in an environment that differs considerably from what she's used to. She will find herself alone more often – a solitude intensified by the fact that there are no relatives or friends on hand. However, if you're aware that this may arise beforehand, you can act on it and reduce its effects.

Working spouses should pay special attention to the needs and feelings of their non-working partners and children, as the success of a family relocation depends on the ability of the wife and children to adapt to the new culture.

Good communication between family members is vital and you should make time to discuss your experiences and feelings, both as a couple and as a family. Questions should always be invited and, if possible, answered, particularly when asked by children. However difficult the situation may appear at the beginning, it helps to bear in mind you're by no means unique, and that most expatriate families experience exactly the same problems, and manage to triumph over them and thoroughly enjoy their stay abroad.

MULTICULTURALISM

Coined in Canada in the '70s, multiculturalism is the term used for an ideology advocating that immigrants integrate into society while retaining and valuing the most important elements of their own culture (including speaking their own language and teaching it to their children).

India is a tolerant, multicultural society, where people from over 100 nationalities live, work and play together in harmony. This has not only greatly enriched the Indian way of life and added to its range of foods, religions, businesses and ideas, but makes it much easier for immigrants to integrate into society. Virtually all ethnic groups in India maintain clubs and societies to which newcomers are warmly welcomed.

In India, migrants are encouraged to maintain their culture and ties with their homeland – rather than abandon them – while being urged to embrace Indian values. Consequently, the country has a low level of inter-ethnic conflict and high levels of cooperation. However, marriage between different ethnic groups isn't common.

A NEW LIFE

Although you may find some of the information in this chapter a bit daunting, don't be discouraged by the foregoing catalogue of depression and despair; the negative aspects of travelling and living abroad have been highlighted simply in order to help you prepare for and adjust to a new life. The vast majority of people who travel and live abroad naturally experience occasional feelings of discomfort and disorientation, **but most never suffer the most debilitating effects of culture shock.**

As with settling in and making friends anywhere, even in your home country, the most important thing is to be considerate, kind, open, humble and genuine – qualities that are valued the world over. Selfishness, brashness and arrogance will get you nowhere in India – or any other country. Treat India and its people with respect and they will reciprocate.

The majority of foreigners in India would agree that, all things considered, they love living there – and are in no hurry to return home. A period spent in India is a wonderful way to enrich your life, broaden your horizons, make new friends and maybe even please your bank manager. We trust that this book will help you avoid the pitfalls of life in India and smooth your way to a happy and rewarding future in your new home.

> '**Twenty years from now you'll be more disappointed by the things you didn't do than by the ones you did do. So throw off the bowlines. Sail away from the safe harbour. Catch the trade winds in your sails. Explore. Dream. Discover.**'
>
> Mark Twain (American writer)

Sadhu (holy man)

2.

WHO ARE THE INDIANS?

Disembark at any airport, railway station, bus station or dock in India, and it hits you. No, not the heat or dust, but the mass of humanity – homogeneous yet unimaginably diverse: seven religions, at least 30 ethnic groups and over 300 languages, the result of millennia of migration and invasion.

> 'I had no shoes and complained, until I met a man who hd no feet'
>
> Indian Proverb

The world's largest democracy, with a population – rapidly growing – of over a billion, is a major player in the global economy, ranking fourth in terms of purchasing power, according to the IMF and the World Bank, with an annual GDP of US$3.8 trillion. This call-centre superpower carries out back-office processing for over 40 per cent of the world's top 500 corporations.

With a middle class as numerous as the population of the US and degree-holders outnumbering that of France, India, currently the world's twelfth-largest consumer market, is predicted to be the fifth-largest by 2025 (McKinsey Global Institute). According to Visa, the world's largest retail electronic payment network, annual commercial spending in India was US$2.3 trillion in 2007, an increase of almost 25 per cent over 2006.

However, despite the economic and technological advances of recent decades, the world's oldest civilisation (albeit with the youngest population) has remained culturally little changed for thousands of years, enticing today's sophisticated travellers as it once did intrepid explorers and conquerors such as Alexander the Great, Marco Polo and Vasco da Gama.

To help you familiarise yourself with India and the Indians, this chapter provides information about its history, the Indian character and the country's cultural icons.

TIMELINE

The history of India is as colourful as its women's clothing and food. Listed below are the important events that not only shaped its history but also had a profound impact on Indian culture.

First Arrivals

400,000 years ago – *Homo sapiens* began to spread throughout a large part of the Indian subcontinent (which now includes Bangladesh and Pakistan as well as India) in wave after wave of migration from what is now Iran. Archaeological excavations have unearthed Mesolithic sites in the Chotta Nagpur area of central

---

Demographics

Population: 1.15bn.

Population density: 349 inhabitants per km² (903 per mi²), but Delhi has a density of 9,340 inhabitants per km² (24,172 per mi²), Mumbai (Bombay) 21,880 inhabitants per km² (56,645 per mi²) and Kolkata (Calcutta) a huge 24,760 per km² (64,100 per mi²).

Largest cities: Mumbai (18mn), Kolkata (12.9mn), Delhi (11.7mn), Hyderabad (6.8mn), Chennai/Madras (6.6mn), Bangalore (5.5mn).

Foreign population: 335,000.

Largest expatriate groups: Americans, British, Germans, French, Swedish.

State religion: India is a secular country.

Most followed religions: Hinduism (81.3%), Islam (12%), Christianity (2.3%).

India and south of the Krishna River. The Bhimbetka caves near Bhopal are famous for their Mesolithic paintings.

2500BC – Excavated tablets and pottery depicting animals and ornately coiffed women, as well as elaborate jewellery, indicate a sophisticated artisan society in the cities of Harappa and Mohenjo-daro in the Indus River valley, regarded as the cradle of Indian civilisation.

1700BC – The Indus valley civilisation falls to tectonic upheavals, which cause a series of floods.

1700-200BC – Aryan (or Vedic) warriors sweep in from the northern Steppes to conquer India (as they have Persia and elsewhere) but end up mixing with the indigenous population.

326BC – Alexander of Macedon ('Alexander the Great') crosses the Indus and wins the epic Battle of Hydaspes against local ruler Raja Puru (Porus). Two years later he withdraws from India, his soldiers pleading to return home.

Empires & Dynasties

321BC – Chandragupta Maurya creates an empire in the vacuum left by Alexander's retreating army, ruling (by force) over the whole of the Indus Valley.

273BC – Emperor Ashoka (Chandragupta Maurya's grandson) leads the Mauryans in their occupation of most of what is modern India. For the next 37 years Ashoka governs the largest area under a single 'ruler' until the British occupation, etching his principles on magnificently sculpted pillars and boulders – the first written language in India since that of the ancient city of Harappa – before dying in 232BC.

155-130BC – After the brief rule of the Maurya dynasty, the Greeks return and expand their power into the Punjab, resulting in greater contact between India and the Mediterranean world.

320AD – The Gupta dynasty revives many of Ashoka's principles and makes vast leaps in architecture, sculpture, painting and poetry. The period is considered a Golden Age in Indian history.

Fifth century – Huns, Turks and Mongols begin infiltrating India via Afghanistan.

800 – Arabs begin settling (for trading purposes) on the Malabar Coast in the south of India.

1210-1526 – There's continuous Muslim rule, known as the Delhi

Jai Mahal 'Water Palace', Jaipur

Sultanate, mostly in the south of the country.

1398 – The Turkish army under Timor invades India from Samarqand and plunders Delhi.

1497 – The Portuguese come to Goa (now a state) and remain until 1961, integrating into the life of the state, including its enclaves in Daman and Diu (now union territories), with the result that the culture of these areas is quite different from that of the rest of the country.

1526 – The Delhi Sultanate is overcome by Zahiruddin Babur. He establishes the Moghul Empire, the greatest of its rulers being Akbar the Great, who fosters the arts. In the 17th century, the Marathas, led by Shivaji, weaken Moghul rule, the Rajputs openly revolt and by the end of the century, the Moghul Empire collapses.

The British

1600 – Queen Elizabeth I grants a charter to the East India Company (originally intended to trade with the East Indies) to trade with India. The Company (later to merge with its principal rival and, in 1708, renamed

the United Company of Merchants of England Trading to the East Indies, but known as the Honourable East India Company) creates a network of roads, canals and railways, introduces a legal system, administrative procedures and an education system, whereby knowledge of English literature and science is to be imparted to the native population through the medium of the English language. The indigenous mercantile capitalist economy is restructured to serve the interests of the British, and many local religious, cultural and military centres are dismantled, thereby reducing levels of literacy.

1757 – Although the British have ruled the areas surrounding the East India Company's factories since 1600, Robert Clive's ('Clive of India') victory at the Battle of Plassey is often regarded as the beginning of British rule.

1857 – The 'Indian mutiny' is triggered by the rumour that rifle cartridges were greased with cow and pig fat (abhorrent to Hindus and Muslims respectively) but is suppressed by the British.

1858 – The mutiny prompts the British to buy out the East India

Company and add the purchase price to the public debt. India therefore comes under direct rule of the British crown and 'pays for itself' in becoming a British colony.

1885 – The Indian National Congress is founded as a forum for emerging nationalist feeling.

1920-22 – Nationalist figurehead Mahatma Gandhi launches an anti-British civil disobedience campaign.

1942-43 – Congress launches the 'Quit India' movement.

1947 – British rule is brought to an end and the subcontinent divided into (mainly Hindu) India and (mainly Muslim) Pakistan, comprising East Pakistan and West Pakistan. The remaining large and unwieldy bureaucracy turns corrupt.

1947-48 – Hundreds of thousands die in widespread fighting resulting from partition.

1948 – Gandhi is assassinated by a Hindu extremist. India goes to war with Pakistan over the disputed territory of Kashmir.

1950 – India becomes a republic within the British Commonwealth after promulgating its Constitution on 26th January 1950.

Modern India

> '**If I were asked under what sky the human mind has most fully developed some of its choicest gifts, has most deeply pondered on the greatest problems of life, and has found solutions, I should point to India.**'
>
> Max Mueller (German philologist & orientalist)

1951-52 – The Congress Party wins the country's inaugural general election Jawaharlal Nehru becomes its first Prime Minister.

1962 – India loses a brief border war with China.

1964 – Nehru dies.

1965 – India wages a second war with Pakistan over Kashmir.

1966 – Indira Gandhi (Nehru's daughter) becomes Prime Minister.

1971 – A third war with Pakistan breaks out over the creation of Bangladesh, formerly East Pakistan.

1974 – India explodes its first nuclear device in an underground test.

1975 – Indira Gandhi declares a state of emergency after being found guilty of electoral malpractice, bestowing on herself the power to rule by decree, thus suspending elections and civil liberties.

1977 – Morarji Desai becomes Prime Minister, heading the Janata Party, an amalgam of five opposition parties.

1979 – Desai's government crumbles and Charan Singh forms an interim government.

1980 – Indira Gandhi returns to power heading a Congress party splinter group, known as Congress (Indira) or Congress (I).

1984 – Troops storm the Golden Temple (the Sikhs' most holy shrine) to flush out Sikh militants pressing for self-rule. Indira Gandhi is assassinated on 31st October by her Sikh bodyguards. Her son, Rajiv, is chosen by Congress (I) to take her place.

1989 – The Janata Dal, a union of opposition parties, joins the Hindu-nationalist Bharatiya Janata Party (BJP) on the right and the Communists on the left to form the government. This loose coalition collapses in November 1990, and the Janata Dal, supported by

nationalist BJP emerges as the largest single party.

1998 – BJP wins 182 seats in a general election and forms a coalition government under Prime Minister Atal Behari Vajpayee and India carries out nuclear tests, leading to widespread international condemnation.

1999 – Prime Minister Vajpayee makes a historic bus trip to Pakistan in February, to meet Premier Nawaz Sharif and to sign the Lahore peace declaration, but tension in Kashmir leads to a brief war with Pakistan in May. In October, a cyclone devastates the eastern state of Orissa, leaving at least 10,000 dead.

21st Century

India marked the birth of its billionth citizen in May 2000.

2000 – US President Bill Clinton makes a groundbreaking visit to improve ties.

2001 – In January, massive earthquakes hit the western state of Gujarat, leaving at least 30,000 dead.

2001 – In December, a suicide squad attacks the parliament building in New Delhi, killing several policemen, and India imposes sanctions on Pakistan to force it to take action against the two Kashmiri militant groups blamed for the attack. Pakistan retaliates with similar sanctions. The two countries mass troops on their border amid mounting fears of a looming war.

2002 – In January, India successfully test-fires 'Agni,' a nuclear-capable ballistic missile, off its eastern coast.

2002 – In February, 57 Hindu volunteers are burnt to death on a train when returning from Ayodhya, sparking

Congress (I), come to power for a short period, with Chandra Shekhar as Prime Minister. That alliance also collapses, resulting in national elections in June 1991.

1991 – Rajiv Gandhi is assassinated on 27th May by Tamil extremists from Sri Lanka.

1991 – Congress (I) wins 213 parliamentary seats and returns to power at the head of a coalition, with P. V. Narasimha Rao as Prime Minister. He serves a full five-year term and initiates a gradual process of economic liberalisation and reform, opening the Indian economy to foreign trade and investment.

1992 – Hindu nationalists supportive of the BJP agitate to build a temple on a disputed site in Ayodhya, destroying the 17th century Babri mosque there and sparking widespread religious riots in which thousands are killed.

1996 – Congress (I) suffers its worst ever electoral defeat as the Hindu anti-Muslim riots throughout Gujarat which leave over 900 people dead and 100,000 homeless.

2002 – In July, retired scientist and architect of India's missile programme, APJ Abdul Kalam, is elected president.

2003 – In August, 50 people are killed in two simultaneous bomb blasts in Mumbai.

2003 – In November, India matches Pakistan's declaration of a Kashmiri ceasefire.

2004 – The Congress Party wins a surprise victory in the general election. Manmohan Singh is sworn in as Prime Minister.

2004 – Thousands are killed on 26th December when a tidal wave (*tsunami*), caused by a powerful undersea earthquake off the Indonesian coast, devastate coastal communities in the south and on the Andaman and Nicobar Islands.

2005 – Prime Minister Singh and President Bush sign a strategic partnership agreement on 18th July 2005.

2006 – President Bush visits India to anchor the US-India partnership.

2007 – India's first commercial space rocket is launched in April, carrying an Italian satellite.

2007 – Pratibha Patil is sworn in as country's first woman president on 25th July.

2008 – In July, a series of explosions kills 49 in Ahmedabad, in Gujarat state. The little-known group Indian Mujahideen claims responsibility. The same group carries out attacks in Bangalore in the same month and in Delhi on September 13th.

2008 – In October, President Bush signs a deal which ends a three-decade ban on US nuclear trade with Delhi.

India launches its first unmanned lunar spacecraft from Andhra Pradesh. It enters the lunar orbit on November 8th

2008 – In November, some 200 people are killed and hundreds injured in a series of co-ordinated attacks by gunmen on the main tourist and business area of India's financial capital, Mumbai. India blames militants from Pakistan for the attacks and demands that Islamabad take firm action against those responsible.

THE PEOPLE

> **'The Brahmins are fair, the Kshatriyas are reddish, the Vaishyas yellow and the Sudras are black.'**
>
> excerpt from the *Mahabharata*, one of the two great Sanskrit epics of ancient India, the other being the *Ramayana*/

India's 5,000-year history of invasion and immigration, her varied geography and her sheer size have contributed to the diversity of her people, who are made up of over 30 ethnic groups and more than a hundred subgroups. Technically, 72 per cent of the population (mostly in the north, west and centre of the country) are Indo-Aryan and 25 per cent (mainly in the south) Dravidian; the remaining 3 per cent. largely in the northeast, include Negroids in the Andaman and Nicobar Islands. This means that Indians' appearance varies from tall and fair-skinned (e.g. in Punjab) to dark-skinned (e.g. the Tamils) and oriental (in the states bordering Bhutan, China and Nepal).

Not surprisingly, Indians' customs, dress, food, language, and even names are equally diverse. However, in spite of the many outward differences, there's a distinct cultural homogeneity about Indians, often referred to as 'unity in diversity', and most have a surprising number of similar characteristics.

Collectivism & Patriarchy

Indians aren't individualistic and privacy isn't important. They rarely act on their own initiative but rather consult elders, relatives and friends, and major decisions in life are made only after taking lots of advice. It's a family-oriented and patriarchal society, with great respect accorded to age and tradition, and priority in all things given to males.

Family units include both sets of grandparents, uncles, aunts and cousins – first cousins are called 'cousin-brothers' or 'cousin-sisters'. The older members of a family, and of society as a whole, are deferred to. In particular, the father (or the oldest male in the house) is the head of the family. Elderly women (finally) achieve equality with men and do little or nothing to conceal their age.

Collectivism is further fostered by various pledges of brotherhood and patriotism, and children are encouraged to take part in a number of group activities, such as school trips and summer camps.

Despite their regional and local differences and occasional internal riots, Indians have repeatedly shown their solidarity in the face of adversity – in the aftermath of the many terrorist attacks, floods, earthquakes and border conflicts they've suffered. Peaceful demonstrations, rallies and protest marches (*morcha*) by tens of thousands, including schoolchildren and senior citizens, are a common sight in major cities. Massive fund/food collection drives are recurring phenomena in the wake of natural catastrophes such as the tsunami in December 2004.

Karma & Reincarnation

Indians believe in and follow the 'law of karma'. Literally, karma means 'fate', but it isn't fate in the Western sense – something that controls your life over which you have no influence. The law of karma is that your actions determine your past, present and future, that you're responsible for your own fate. If you do good things, good things will happen to you; if you do bad things, bad things will happen.

> 'In India, I found a race of mortals living upon the Earth, but not adhering to it, inhabiting cities, but not being fixed to them, possessing everything, but possessed by nothing.'
>
> Apollonius Tyanaeus (first-century Greek traveller)

The law of karma applies even beyond your present life. Hindus believe that humans go through a repetitive cycle of birth and death, which is intended to improve their spiritual state, until they reach oneness with God. What you've done in your previous life or lives affects your present life and what you do in this life affects subsequent lives. In July 2007, a leading national newspaper carried a story of a four-year old girl believed to be the reincarnation of astronaut Kalpana Chalwla who died in the Columbia space shuttle crash two months before the girl's birth.

Contradictory to the law of karma is Indians' belief in astrology, many of them relying on its predictions even in business and politics. Auspicious days (and auspicious times of the day) for a particular endeavour, determined by astrologers based on the positions of the stars and planets, are carefully chosen. Roadside fortune-tellers and tarot card readers – assisted by their parrots – abound, and both men and women wear rings with gemstones prescribed by their astrologer, as good luck charms.

Double Standards

The karma/astrology contradiction is just one of many double standards employed by Indians, not only in the family, community and society, but particularly in business government and law-enforcement agencies, whose high-minded laws (based on British models) are often poorly implemented. This is because actions are justified not in absolute terms, but with reference to their context.

On the one hand, Indians generally live a simple life, even when they can afford opulence, as they believe in the purity of the soul, which is tainted by trappings. On the other, they can be shockingly ambitious, often using dishonest means to attain their goals. Status is measured in terms of money, and there's an innate disposition to collude with the rich and powerful rather than stick to principles. In the interest of self-preservation, the pursuit of wealth and power is legitimate – and the end may justify the means.

The only acceptable substitute for money is rank, and Indians (particularly those without money) cling to titles and designations even after they've left office. Retired army officers, judges, government officials and business executives cannot do without their visiting cards, which prominently state who they once were.

Hospitality & Accommodation

To foreigners, Indians' hospitality can be overwhelming. Even total strangers will often invite you to their home, persisting until you accept and then showering you with food, drink and endless questions. If you wish to decline such an invitation, it's best to respond with a "We'll come one day," a promise that you aren't expected to keep.

Indians usually refrain from a straightforward 'no' in response to a request for a commodity or service, even if it's beyond his means to supply it. Instead they will suggest an alternative arrangement. Indians are accommodating in more ways than one.

> When trying to find a place, it's wise to ask at least two people, because even those that have no inkling where it is will try to be helpful by pointing one way or another.

Indians invest time in building relationships, whether personal or business. Unlike in the West, it's 'pleasure before business', because it's important for an Indian to know who he's dealing with before he enters into any kind of relationship of trust. Business partners will even go to the extent of inviting you home for dinner to get to know you better and observe how you interact with members of their family.

Democracy & Regionalism

Indians are proud of the fact that their country is the world's largest democracy, but they aren't democratic by temperament. On the contrary, according to *The Indians: Portrait of a People* by psychoanalyst and cultural commentator Sudhir Kakar and anthropologist Katherina Kakar, Indians are possibly the world's most undemocratic people.

Although every adult has the right to vote, the country is run by the rich, and the poor are either exploited or ignored altogether. Politics are seen largely as a means to upward mobility rather than as a way of making India a better place for its billion-plus citizens to live.

While Indians are patriotic, they tend to be more loyal to their native states than to the country as a whole. If forced to live in a state other than the one in which they were born, they often associate mainly with other people from their home state and even buy fruit and vegetables imported from that state, irrespective of the quality and price of what is available locally.

This 'statism' inevitably leads to antagonism between people from different parts of the country. It's at its fiercest among the Maharashtrians, who resent the fact that numerous migrants from neighbouring Gujarat have come to dominate the commercial world of 'their' capital, Mumbai. More generally, northern Indians look down on southerners – largely for purely for racial reasons.

SENSE OF HUMOUR

Although the British governed India for several hundred years, their subtle, dry wit failed to rub off on the natives, whose sense of humour is at the opposite extreme – loud and

unsophisticated to the extent of being crude. Even middle-aged men will laugh noisily on seeing an unfortunate pedestrian slip and fall.

Just as the British deride the supposed stupidity of the Irish, and the French mock the Belgians, Indians (for some reason) make fun of the Poles. A popular cartoon is of a mock advertisement for Polish Airlines showing a grounded plane full of passengers and an air hostess walking up and down outside waving a placard with a picture of blue sky, clouds and birds. Similar jokes are made at the expense of Sikhs, who are known as Sardars. The stock characters in Sardar jokes are Banta Singh and Santa Singh.

Sardar Joke

Santa Singh and Banta Singh board a double-deck bus in Bombay but are separated in the crush, Santa on the lower deck and Banta on top. As passengers alight, Santa goes upstairs to find his friend, who is trembling and clutching the seat in front of him with both hands. 'What's wrong, Banta Singh? Why are you scared? I was enjoying my ride down there.' 'Yeah,' replies the terrified Banta, 'but you've got a driver.'

But Indians seldom laugh at themselves – the true test of humour. Even among English-speaking Indians, you'll find that they tend to lapse into Hindi or another native language in order to share a joke, as they feel it would be lost in translation.

Joking about respected people and national icons is in bad taste, although politicians are often the butt of jokes at parties. Derisive remarks about deities and religions are strictly taboo, and could get you into serious trouble.

Although humorous literary works are generally regarded as frivolous and suitable only for children, two authors are noted for their 'adult' humour: R K Laxman, India's leading cartoonist best known for his daily strip entitled *You Said It*, featuring *The Common Man*, a caricature of the archetypal aspiring but troubled Indian; and Mario Miranda, known for his cartoon characters Miss Fonseca, the buxom secretary to the Boss, and Godbole, the clerk who is constantly, but fruitlessly, angling for her.

THE CASTE SYSTEM

India's caste system (*jati*) is among the most rigid and pernicious 'class systems' in the world and it persists despite attempts to outlaw it. Simply put, the caste system ranks people according to their occupation into a four-layer hierarchy: Brahmins (priests and teachers) at the top, then Kshatriyas (rulers and warriors), Vaishyas (merchants and cultivators) and, at the bottom, Shudras (labourers and servants), who are considered 'unclean' by members of the upper castes.

There is, however, a fifth 'class', the notorious 'untouchables', whose duties involve contact with dirt and death and who are therefore considered too lowly even to be included in the caste system. Although 'untouchability' has been abolished by law, it still exists in practice. Mahatma Gandhi

evidence in rural areas, where inter-caste marriages, while not officially outlawed, are still discouraged (particularly in North India). The matrimonial pages of Indian newspapers (where people advertise for marriage partners) invite replies from people, not only of a particular caste, but often of a particular skin colour (see **Racism** below). There are even occasional reports of fathers killing their daughters for eloping with a lower-caste lover.

One way for Hindus to erase their low-caste stigma is to convert to Buddhism, Christianity or Islam, but even these communities have become stratified into hierarchies, and some observers regard such conversions as 'forced' – part of a devious Western plot to Christianise India.

re-named the untouchables *harijans*, meaning 'children of God', but they prefer to emphasise their plight by calling themselves *dalits* ('the oppressed').

Officially, the lower castes are known as the 'Scheduled Castes' or 'Scheduled Tribes' and 'Other Backward Castes,' written as SC/ST and OBC in government publications, but commonly referred to collectively as the 'underprivileged classes'.

An affirmative government intervention to accelerate upward mobility has been the reservation of a percentage of university admissions as well as job quotas for the underprivileged classes of Indian society.

While caste barriers have largely been eradicated in the major cities, where people from most castes can be found in most trades and professions, and where a Westernised 'class system' has established itself, they're still much in

On the positive side, the caste system, like any class structure, provides a sense of community and belonging.

> The Sanskrit word for caste is *varna*, meaning colour, and the caste system evolved from the 'simple' racial discrimination of invading fair-skinned Aryans against the dark-skinned natives of the Indus Valley into a more complex kind of apartheid based on heredity, marriage, custom, profession and economic standing.

CHILDREN

Population growth is a major concern in India, but government intervention has so far been limited to an 'awareness campaign' and the provision of free condoms and contraception clinics. While the middle and upper classes generally stick to having two children, as recommended by the Family Welfare Department, the lower classes continue to have as many as five children or even more, and the current birth rate is 22.8 (i.e. there are 22.8 births per 1,000 head of population per year – an annual total of some 25m births), compared, for example, with 14.8 in the US and 10.65 in the UK.

There isn't only a numerical imbalance between the classes. The children in middle- and upper-class families have a privileged position and are pampered by their elders with expensive toys, 'designer' clothes and lavish birthday parties, whereas lower-class children are often deprived of their childhood and education, and made to work to augment the family income.

Paradoxically, this motivates poor couples to procreate.

Indian children are generally noisy and unruly, not only at play but even in school, and, if reprimanded, seldom pay heed. They know that childhood is a time of indulgence and they will be forgiven almost anything. However, while boys may be treated like royalty, girls are generally regarded as a burden.

Another paradox of Indian society is that children are in some ways treated like adults, and in other ways prevented from 'growing up'. They're normally allowed to stay up late and accompany their parents to restaurants, performances, parties and other events, rather than being left at home with a babysitter. But they must sleep with their parents until they're around five years old, after which they will have to share a bedroom with older siblings. Children aren't taught to be independent. For example, they don't usually bathe themselves until they're almost ten. They tend to play with their siblings and cousins rather than friends, and contact between the sexes is restricted, which is often frustrating for teenagers – and arranged marriages only add to their sense of oppression.

Indians don't generally leave their parents' home until they're married, and men often remain with their parents even after marriage, their wives and children merely 'extending' the family and making their contribution to household income and duties.

ATTITUDES TO FOREIGNERS

Most Indians use the word 'foreigner' to refer to white people from the developed world. All blacks are referred to as 'Africans' and Mongolians as 'Asians'. Having been swept by waves of marauding and interfering peoples, including Mongols, Turks, Greeks, Moghuls, Dutch, French, Portuguese and British, the Indians might be expected to harbour a measure of hostility towards foreigners, particularly whites. However, there isn't just a surprising absence of malice – on the contrary, Indians are xenophiles (attracted to foreigners and foreign ideas) rather than xenophobes.

> **Although the British ruled India, they enjoy more respect than most other foreigners. The memory of the 'Raj' (British rule) is not only alive but fond, as is clear from the courtesy and hospitality generally bestowed on visiting and expatriate Britons.**

On spotting a foreigner looking lost, an Indian will be the first to strike up a conversation and offer help, even inviting the visitor to his home. Neither class nor creed gets in the way of such encounters, and Indians are more adept at bridging the cultural gap between Westerners and themselves than the other way around.

Racism

Indians perceive themselves as victims rather than perpetrators of racism due to their colonial past. However, racism is rife, although it's generally 'disguised' by caste discrimination: dark skin is equated with the lower castes and light skin with their superiors (see above). Such is the Indian obsession with colour that 'fairness creams' and hair dyes are top-selling items in the cosmetic market,

not to mention cosmetic contact lenses to lighten the colour of the eyes. Most matrimonial advertisements specify that brides should be 'fair' (which doesn't refer to their equanimity).

African immigrants reportedly find it difficult to obtain housing and entry into certain restaurants and are often referred to as 'scary' and 'dirty' even in cosmopolitan cities. Whites, in contrast, are generally treated with deference.

NATIONAL ICONS

Every country has its icons – people, places & structures, symbols, flora and fauna, and food and drink – which are revered or unique to that country and have special significance to its inhabitants. The following is a list of some of India's most cherished icons. (The author apologises for the absence of many notable Indians – it's a tribute to India that it has so many people worthy of the title 'icon'.)

Icons – People

Akbar (1542-1605) – Akbar 'the Great', conventionally described as the glory of the empire, reigned for almost 50 years from 1556 until his death, and extended his empire as far to the west as Afghanistan, and south to the banks of the Godavari river. The Mughal architectural style began as a definite movement under Akbar's rule, whose most ambitious and magnificent architectural undertaking was the new capital city that he built on the ridge at Sikri near Agra.

Viswanathan Anand (b 1969) – Four times world chess champion (2000, 2001, 2007 and 2008) , Anand is one of only four players in history (the others being Garry Kasparov, Vladimir

Kramnik and Veselin Topalov) to break the 2800 mark on the Elo (or FIDE) rating system. He has been among the top three ranked players in classical time-control chess continuously since 1997.

Sri Aurobindo (1872-1950) – An Indian nationalist, scholar, poet, mystic, philosopher, yogi and guru, and one of the leaders of the early movement for the freedom of India from British rule. Aurobindo turned to the development and practice of a new spiritual path, called 'integral yoga', the aim of which was to further the evolution of life on earth by establishing a high level of spiritual consciousness (the 'Supermind') that would represent a divine life free from physical death.

Amitabh Bachchan (b 1942) – Known as the Big B, Bachchan reigned supreme in Bollywood from the '70s to the mid-'80s and continues to be the *Badshah* (literally 'great king' but used in the sense of 'veteran') of Indian showbiz. He was voted the 'Greatest Star of the Millennium' by a BBC online poll in 1999 and in 2000 became the first living Asian to have been immortalised in wax at Madame Tussauds.

Annie Besant (1847-1933) – President of the Theosophical Society of India, Besant (who was born in London of Irish origin) founded the Home Rule League in 1916, which demanded self rule for India. She became the first woman president of the Indian National Congress in 1917 and was a prominent theosophist, social reformer, political leader, women's rights activist, writer and orator.

Asha Bhosle (b 1933) – Grammy nominee for the Best Contemporary World Music Album award in 2006, Bhosle is best known as a Bollywood playback singer, with a career spanning six decades. She has collaborated with Boy George and Code Red, among others.

Subhas Chandra Bose (1897-1945) – Generally known as Netaji (literally 'respected leader'), Bose was one of the most prominent and highly respected leaders of the Indian Independence Movement against the British Raj. He strongly disagreed with Gandhi over his non-violence movement and was an advocate of violent resistance to British rule, and led the Indian National Army into battle against the British in Imphal and Burma during the Second World War.

Nirad C. Chaudhuri (1897-1999) – India's most distinguished writer of English prose in the 20th century, Chaudhuri was also one of his country's most controversial commentators since its independence. He wrote many books in English and Bengali, the most famous of which is his first, *The Autobiography of an Unknown Indian*, a memoir of his childhood and youth.

Kapil Dev (b 1959) – One of the greatest cricket all-rounders, he was

Mahatma Ghandi

named as the 'Indian Cricketer of the Century' in 2002 (the 20th century, that is, not the 21st) by *Wisden* for captaining India to their Cricket World Cup in 1983 and holding the world record for the most Test match wickets from 1994 until 1999.

Indira Priyadarshini Gandhi (1917-84) – The Prime Minister of India for three consecutive terms from 1966 to 1977 and for a fourth term from 1980, Indira Gandhi was the country's first and (to date) only female Prime Minister. Born into the politically influential Nehru dynasty – her father was Jawaharlal Nehru – she was assassinated by her own Sikh bodyguards in 1984.

Mohandas Karamchand (Mahatma) Gandhi (1869-1948)

Perhaps the most famous of all Indians, Mahatma Gandhi was a major political and spiritual leader of India and the Indian independence movement. He was the pioneer of *satyagraha* – resistance to tyranny through mass civil disobedience, founded upon *ahimsa* or non-violence – which led India to independence and inspired movements for civil rights and freedom across the world. Gandhi is commonly known in India and throughout the world as Mahatma ('great soul' in Sanskrit) and as *bapu* ('father'), and in India is officially accorded the honour of 'Father of the Nation'.

Rajiv Gandhi (1944-91) – The son of Indira Gandhi, Rajiv became the youngest Prime Minister of India upon the death of his mother in 1984 and made a valuable contribution to modernising India. Like his mother, he was assassinated while Prime Minister. His wife, Sonia Gandhi (see below), is the President of the Indian National Congress.

Sonia Gandhi (b 1946) – The Italian-born leader of India's most powerful political party, the Indian National Congress, which won the general election in May 2004, Gandhi was at the time ranked the third most powerful woman in the world by *Forbes*. In her plain white sari, she has became a role model for Indian women.

Sunil Gavaskar (b 1949) – Regarded as India's greatest-ever opening batsman, 'Sunny' Gavaskar played in 125 test matches and scored 10,122 test runs (including a record 34 centuries), becoming the first batsman to pass the 10,000 mark.

Indian gods – Although Hinduism is a monotheistic religion with one god, Brahman – the Supreme Being that permeates everything but is both impersonal and impossible to describe – the Hindu pantheon of gods is vast. Through Ganesh, Krishna, Lakshmi, Parvati, Shiva and Vishnu, devotees can see, touch and feel Brahman, each representing one tiny aspect of Brahman; for example, Shiva takes on Brahman's destructive power, while Vishnu preserves the order of the universe.

The Hinduja Brothers – One of the wealthiest Indian business families, consisting of four brothers, Ashok (b 1950), Srichand (b 1935), Gopichand (b 1940) and Prakash, who are based in London, Geneva and Mumbai. They're involved with various multi-national businesses including finance, telecommunications, film and oil (Gulf Oil) and are together worth an estimated £6bn.

Maqbool Fida (M F) Husain (b 1915) – Financially, India's most successful painter. His *Battle of Ganga and Jamuna: Mahabharata 12* was sold for US$1.6m, a world record for contemporary Indian art, at an auction by Christie's in March 2008. Husain's work has incurred the wrath of hardline Hindu groups for depicting Indian goddesses in the nude.

Madhur Jaffrey (b 1933) – A noted actress, Jaffrey is more famous internationally as the food writer who introduced the Western world to the many cuisines of India.

Shabuddin Mohammed Shah Jahan (1592-1666) – Shah Jahan 'the Magnificent' was the fifth ruler of the Mughal Empire (after Babur, Humayun, Akbar and Jahangir), which lasted from 1628 to 1858. His name is Persian for 'King of the World' and it was during his reign that the Mughals reached their greatest prosperity and influence. He was the most prolific builder in Indian history (responsible for modern-day Delhi) and his legacy includes the world's most famous and beautiful mausoleum, the Taj Mahal, where he's buried next to his beloved Mumtaz Mahal.

Jahangir (1569-1627) – Ruler of the Mughal Empire from 1605 until his death in 1627, when he was succeeded by Shah Jahan. Jahangir ('Conqueror of the World') was susceptible to the influence of others, a weakness that was exploited by many, not least his wife Nur Jahan (whom he married in 1611) who soon became the real power behind the throne.

Muhammad Ali Jinnah (1876-1948) – A contemporary of Mahatma Gandhi, Jinnah was a celebrated attorney and outspoken champion of Muslim rights in India. When India achieved independence from the British in 1947, it was Jinnah who formed the two new lands for the Islamic people of India: West and East Pakistan. He is revered in Pakistan as *Baba-e-Qaum* ('Father of the Nation') and *Quaid-e-Azam* ('Great Leader').

Jiddu Krishnamurti (1895-1986) – A writer and speaker on fundamental philosophical and spiritual subjects. His subject matter included the purpose of meditation, human relationships, and the improvement of society. His talks and dialogues have been compiled and published in over 50 books, translated into as many languages. His work continues through the Krishnamurti Foundation of America and a number of independent schools in India, England and the US.

Cenotaphs, Rajasthan

Kishore Kumar (1929-87) – Indian film playback singer ('the Everlasting Voice') and comic actor, who also achieved success as a lyricist, screenwriter, composer, producer and director.

Lata Mangeshkar (b 1929) – One of the foremost Indian vocalists of all time and known as the 'Nightingale of India', Mangeshkar began her career in 1942 and is still active. She has recorded songs for over 1,000 Bollywood movies, has sung in over 20 Indian languages (she has been recognised by the *Guinness Book of World Records* for making 'the most recordings in the world') and is one of only two Indian singers to have received the Bharath Ratna, India's highest civilian honour.

Zubin Mehta (b 1936) – Though fans of classical music are few and far between in India, this orchestral conductor has achieved iconic status, regularly appearing in advertisements.

Lakshmi Narayan Mittal (b 1950) – Mittal is a London-based Indian billionaire industrialist and the wealthiest man in the United Kingdom and the fifth-richest person in the world, with a personal fortune of over US$50bn. His company, Arcelor Mittal, is the world's largest producer of steel with plants throughout the world.

Narayana Murthy (b 1946) – Indian industrialist and software engineer, Murthy is the brains behind Infosys Technologies, a global consulting and IT services company based in India, which is considered the jewel of India's IT crown.

Rasipuram Krishnaswami Iyer Narayanaswami (1906-2001) – R.K. Narayan, as he's popularly known, is the most widely read Indian novelist writing in the English language. His sensitive and graphic portrayals of 20th-century Indian life are set mostly in the fictional South Indian town of Malgudi.

Pandit Jawaharlal Nehru (1889-1964) – Political leader of the Indian National Congress and a pivotal figure in the Indian independence movement and the India-Pakistan partition, Nehru became the first Prime Minister of independent India. Popularly referred to as *Panditji* ('Scholar'), Nehru was the patriarch of the Nehru-Gandhi family, one of the most influential forces in Indian politics.

Indra Krishnamurthy Nooyi (b 1955) – Chairman and chief executive officer of PepsiCo (the world's fourth-largest food and beverage company) since 2006, Nooyi was named as the world's most powerful businesswoman in 2006 and 2007 by *Fortune* magazine.

Lord Swaraj Paul (b 1931) – One of the most famous Indian-born entrepreneurs in Britain, Paul is the founder of multinational company Caparo, a UK-based steel and engineering group. He was knighted by the Queen in 1978 and became Lord Paul of Marylebone and a member of the House of Lords.

Aishwarya Rai (b 1973) – Crowned Miss World 1994, Rai has become the most successful female Bollywood actor of all time.

Bhagwan Shree Rajneesh (1931-90) – Osho, as he preferred to be called, was one of India's most popular and flamboyant 'export gurus' and undoubtedly the most controversial. He followed no particular religion, tradition

or philosophy, and his advocacy of sex as a path to enlightenment outraged his Indian critics and earned him the epithet 'sex guru' from the Indian press.

Chandrasekhara Venkata Raman (1888-1970) – C V Raman was awarded the 1930 Nobel Prize for Physics for his work on the molecular scattering of light and for the discovery of a phenomenon now named after him, the 'Raman effect'.

Satyajit Ray (1921-92) – Bengali filmmaker regarded as one of best of the 20th century, Ray directed 37 films, including feature films, documentaries and shorts. His first film, *Pather Panchali*, won 11 international prizes, including 'Best Human Document' at Cannes.

Arundhati Roy (b 1961) – A novelist and social activist, Roy came to prominence in 1997 when she won the British Booker Prize for her first novel *The God of Small Things*. She was awarded the Sydney Peace Prize in 2004.

Salman Rushdie (b 1967) – An Anglo-Indian novelist and essayist, Rushdie achieved fame with his second novel, *Midnight's Children* (1981), which won the Booker Prize, but is best known for his fourth, *The Satanic Verses* (1988). Accused of insulting Islam, Rushdie was the 'victim' of a *fatwa* (religious edict) issued by Ayatollah Ruhollah Khomeini, the Supreme Leader of Iran, calling for his murder, which led to death threats and police protection. He was knighted for 'services to literature' in 2007.

Vikram Seth (b 1952) – Indian poet, novelist, travel writer, librettist, children's author, biographer and memoirist, Seth is most famous for his novel *A Suitable Boy* (1993), an epic of Indian life.

Geet Sethi (b 1961) – Four-times world billiards champion and generally acknowledged to be one of the greatest players of all time, Sethi is a recipient of India's highest sporting award, the Rajiv Gandhi Khel Ratna, besides making it into the *Guinness Book of Records* as the youngest amateur ever to make the maximum snooker break of 147.

Ravi Shankar (b 1920) – Dubbed the 'Godfather of World Music' by George Harrison, the legendary sitarist and composer is India's most esteemed musical ambassador.

Lal Bahadur Shastri (1904-66) – A man of vision and of supreme patriotism, Shastri was the second Prime Minister of India after Jawaralal Nehru. He was a devout Gandhian and advocated social reform as a means to achieving self-reliance and land reform through land donations (*bhudaan*). He gave away his wealth and died in mysterious circumstances on a peace mission to the Soviet Union.

Rabindranath Tagore (1861-1941) – Also known by the sobriquet Gurudev, Tagore was a Bengali poet, philosopher, visual artist, playwright, novelist and composer, whose works re-shaped Bengali literature and music in the late 19th and early 20th centuries.

He became Asia's first Nobel laureate when he won the 1913 Nobel Prize for Literature.

Jamsetji Tata (1839-1904) – A pioneer in the field of modern industry, Tata founded what would later become the Tata Group of companies, India's largest conglomerate (famous for their trucks), and is generally acknowledged as the 'father of Indian industry'.

Sachin Tendulkar (b 1973) – One of the word's greatest batsmen (dubbed the 'modern Bradman'), 'the Little Master' was the first player to score 10,000 runs in one-day cricket (now 16,422 runs). At the time of writing he had scored 12,429 test runs and 41 test centuries, both world records.

Mother Teresa (1910-97)

An Albanian-born Catholic nun, Mother Teresa founded the Missionaries of Charity in Kolkata in 1950 and devoted herself to working among the poorest of the poor in the city's slums. She was an inspiration for people throughout the world and was honoured with the Nobel Prize for her work in 1979 and beatified by Pope John Paul II on 19th October 2003 with the title 'Blessed Teresa of Calcutta'.

Maharishi Mahesh Yogi (b 1917) – Founder of Transcendental Meditation (TM) and related programs and initiatives, including schools and a university with campuses in the United States and China.

Icons – Places & Structures

Agra fort – The foundation of this majestic citadel was laid by Emperor Akbar – it's surrounded by a 70-foot high wall with two gates, the Delhi Gate and Amar Singh.

Ajanta caves – Dating back to the second century BC, the paintings and sculptures on these cave walls are considered masterpieces of Buddhist religious art.

Bhimbetka – This 10,000-year-old 'art gallery' comprises over 400 paintings on the walls and ceilings of rock shelters spread over a 10km^2 area near Bhopal. The paintings were made at various times, from the Upper Palaeolithic Age to the Middle Ages.

City Palace – In the centre of the Pink City of Jaipur, enclosed by high walls and set amidst fine gardens and courtyards, the City Palace was built by Jai Singh in 1728 and was the principal residence of the Maharajas of Jaipur.

Elephanta caves – The 'City of Caves', on an island in the Sea of Oman close to Mumbai, contains a collection of 'rock art' (larger-than-life paintings on rock formations) which has made it a UNESCO World Heritage Site.

Ellora caves – Comprising 34 monasteries and temples spread over 2km and dug into the wall of a high basalt cliff near Aurangabad, Maharashtra, Ellora immortalises ancient Indian civilisation.

Golden Temple – The exterior of this beautiful 16th-century Sikh temple in the Punjab is decorated with intricate tracery and embossed in gold.

Hampi City – Founded in 1336 and an important city of the Vijayanagara empire for over two centuries, Hampi (near Bangalore) was left in ruins after the battle of Talikota in 1565 but remains of great architectural interest – especially its huge statues

Lotus Temple, New Delhi

of Hindu deities. The setting for Jackie Chan's *The Myth* in 2004-05, Hampi is now a UNESCO World Heritage Site.

Hawa Mahal – Also known as 'The Palace of the Winds', this five-storey palace (in Jaipur, Rajasthan – see page 174) in pink sandstone was built by Maharaja Sawraj Pratap Singh in 1799. Its hundreds of screened windows were designed so that the women of the royal family could view ceremonial processions without themselves being observed.

Jaisalmer – Known as 'The Golden City', Jaisalmer (the 'Hill Fort of Jaisal') in Rajasthan is named after its founder Rawal Jaisal. It's built of yellowish sandstone and crowned by a fort containing the palace and several ornate Jain temples.

Kailash Temple – This ancient temple is the world's largest monolithic rock sculpture, having been carved in the wall of a basalt cliff amid the Ellora caves near Aurangabad. The work, which took hundreds of years, involved the removal of an estimated 200,000 tonnes of rock.

Khajuraho – Hovering between architecture and sculpture, the 20 remaining ancient temples of Khajuraho are among the greatest masterpieces of Indian art.

Lotus Temple – Located in Delhi, the Lotus Temple is made from 10,000m³ of marble quarried from the Mount Pentilekon mines in Greece and cut and shaped in Italy.

Mysore Palace – One of the largest palaces in the country, also known as Amba Vilas, Mysore was the residence of the Wodeyar Mahararajas of the Mysore state. The original wooden palace burned down in 1897 and the present edifice was built for the 24th Wodeyar Raja in 1912. Designed in Indo-Saracenic style by the British architect, Henry Irwin, it's a treasure house of exquisite carvings and works of art from all over the world.

Nalanda – This fifth-century residential university, spread over an area of around 14 hectares (35 acres) near Patna in Bihar, was the first of its kind in the world. The remains of several red brick edifices, divided by a central walkway, can still be seen.

Qutab Minar – This 72m (239ft) sandstone and marble structure in Delhi is the highest stone tower in India.

Red Fort – The Red Fort (*Lal Qil'ah* or *Lal Qila*) in Delhi was constructed by the Emperor Shah Jahan in 1639 as the palace for his new capital,

Shahjahanabad. It gets its name from its massive red-sandstone walls (2.5km/1.5m in length), which vary in height from 16m (60ft) on the river side to 33m (110 ft) on the city side. It's a UNESCO World Heritage Site.

Shravanabelagola – At over 17m (57ft) in height, this tenth-century statue of Bahubali in Karnataka (previously Mysore) is considered to be the largest monolithic stone statue in the world.

The Sundarbans – The world's largest network of mangrove swamps and forests, in the Ganges delta, is the habitat of a number of rare or endangered species of aquatic mammals, birds and reptiles, as well as tigers.

Taj Mahal

Voted into the 'official' list of the New Seven Wonders of the World in July 2007, the Taj Mahal is the most visited monument in India, attracting around 3mn visitors a year. It's an immense mausoleum of white marble, built in Agra between 1631 and 1648 by the Moghul emperor Shah Jahan in memory of his favourite wife, Mumtaz.

Icons – Symbols

Amar Chitra Katha – India's favourite comic books, depicting Indian history and culture, Hindu mythology and biographies, have sold over 86mn copies in 40 years.

Bharat Natyam – A classical dance form whose distinctive feature is its expressive hand gestures.

Bindi – An auspicious mark worn by girls and women, *bindi* is derived from *bindu*, the Sanskrit word for dot. It's usually a red dot between the eyebrows made with vermilion powder. Considered a symbol of the goddess Parvati, a *bindi* signifies female energy and is believed to protect women and their husbands. Traditionally a symbol of marriage, it has also become decorative and is also worn today by unmarried girls and women.

Bollywood – The world's largest film industry is the Indian answer to Hollywood. It gets the 'B' from the name of the city formerly known as Bombay (Mumbai), where its studios are located.

Dabbawallas – Enterprising teams of people who deliver freshly cooked food from homes to Mumbai office workers at lunchtime. They're so efficient that they've achieved '6 Sigma' (the highest quality level an organisation can achieve). Prince Charles not only visited them during his visit to India, but also invited their representatives to his wedding with Camilla.

Garlanding – Flower garlands are generally offered as a mark of respect and honour to welcome visitors or to honour the gods and goddesses. They're generally made with white jasmine and orange marigold flowers.

Henna – Indian women celebrate happy occasions by applying designs to their hands and feet using *mehndi*, a paste made by grinding the leaves of the henna tree, sold in markets throughout India.

Kama Sutra – The seminal Sanskrit work on the art of love and sexual behaviour, the *Kama Sutra* is attributed to Nandi, the sacred bull and Shiva's doorkeeper, who overheard the lovemaking of the god and his wife Parvati and later recorded his utterances for the benefit of mere mortals.

Mangalsutra – The Indian equivalent of the Western wedding ring, the *mangalsutra* is a necklace made of black beads, worn by women to signify that they're married.

Namaskar & Namaste – Popular forms of greeting in India, used both as a welcome and a farewell (see **Chapter 8** for details).

National Emblem – A pride of four lions seated back to back, a replica of the Lion Capital constructed in the third century BC at Sarnath in North India at the behest of Emperor Ashoka.

Swastika – Deriving from the Sanskit *svastika*, meaning any lucky or auspicious object and in particular a mark made on people and things to denote good luck, this ancient symbol was widely used in religions including Hinduism, Buddhism and Jainism, before being appropriated by the Nazis.

Tilak – A ritual mark on the forehead that has many significances, including blessing, greeting or auspiciousness. It's made with a red vermilion paste (*kumkum*) which is usually a mixture of turmeric, alum, iodine, camphor and other ingredients, but can also be made from sandalwood paste (*chandan*) blended with musk.

The Times of India – The world's largest-selling English-language broadsheet newspaper.

Udipi – A highly successful chain of vegetarian fast-food restaurants, serving dishes from South India.

Icons – Flora & Fauna

Ashoka – India's most revered tree on account of the fact that the Buddha is said to have been born under one.

Banyan – The national tree of India, the banyan has the widest-reaching roots of all known trees; they can cover several acres and send up shoots, so that a single tree can become a forest. The banyan figures prominently in many of India's oldest stories.

Cobra – Found throughout India, the Indian cobra has 'spectacle' marks on the back of its hood and is respected as much as it's feared. The Hindu God Shiva is often depicted with a cobra coiled around his neck. Cobras are worshipped during the Hindu festival of *Nag Panchami*. Flute-playing snake charmers with cobras emerging out of wicker baskets, seemingly swaying to the soulful tunes, are a common sight in India.

Cow – The Vedic scripture teaches that cows are to be treated with the same respect 'as one's mother' because of the milk they provide. Indians have traditionally found it economically wise to keep cattle for their milk rather than consume their flesh at a single meal – which is why in India the cow is sacred, though not worshipped. Even non-vegetarian Hindus don't eat beef, and cows, unlike humans, are exempt from road traffic laws.

Elephant – Found in southern India and Assam, Indian elephants are distinguished from their African counterparts primarily by their smaller, more pointed ears, but they also have greyer skin, a more rounded back, a flatter, taller forehead and shorter tusks. They are used as beasts of burden, in circuses and in religious processions in South India.

Gharial – Found in deep Indian rivers, notably the Bhima, Brahmaputra, Ganges and Irrawady, this crocodilian reptile inspires fear in people travelling by foot because of human remains and jewellery found in their stomachs. However, these come mainly from scavenging on corpses tipped into the rivers according to the funeral practices in such regions, and the gharial rarely attacks living people.

Lotus – Hindus associate the lotus with creation – the emergence of its pure beauty from mud represents a spiritual promise, its unfolding petals suggesting the expansion of the soul – and it has become the national flower of India.

Mango – A fleshy fruit, eaten ripe or used unripe in pickles, the mango is the national fruit and has been cultivated in India since ancient times. The poet Kalidasa sang its praises and Alexander savoured its taste, as did the Chinese pilgrim, Hieun Tsang. There are over 100 varieties of mango, which come in many sizes, shapes and colours.

Peacock – Perhaps nothing symbolises India more accurately or completely than its national bird, its clashing colours representing the 'unity in diversity' characteristic of the country; and its poses echoed in the classical dance form *Bharat Natyam*, the poise of its head in the *namaste* greeting (see **Chapter 8**). Not surprisingly, this non-migratory bird is found in zoos, parks and gardens all over the world – India's *de facto* international ambassador.

Royal Bengal Tiger

The proper name of the 'Indian tiger', the national animal. Though it's found throughout the country (except in the northwest), it's facing extinction despite Project Tiger, which has set up 27 reserves covering an area of 37,760km² (14,750mi²).

Tulsi – Literally meaning 'the incomparable one' (in Sanskrit), *tulsi* is a kind of basil which is venerated by Hindus as a goddess and is used medicinally in *Ayurveda*, the ancient Indian philosophy on health and well-being.

Water buffalo – Symbolising Yama, the Hindu God of death, the Indian water buffalo live in wet grasslands and swamps, and around lakes and rivers. Herds are made up of family clans, each consisting of around 30 related females and their young, headed by an older female. Adult males form small groups of up to ten, while ageing males go solo.

Icons – Food & Drink

Amul – The world's best-selling vegetarian cheese brand, known as the 'Taste of India'.

Basmati rice – A variety of long-grain rice that's famous for its fragrance and delicate flavour. Its name means 'the fragrant one' in Hindi, but can also mean 'soft rice'.

Biryani – An all-in-one meal, generally consisting of rice, meat, vegetables, yogurt and spices. The recipe varies from region to region, the Hyderabad *biryani* being by far the most popular.

Chai – India's favourite drink is in essence, spiced tea. It's prepared by boiling tea leaves in a pot with a pinch of *chai masala* (powdered spices) – or any combination of cardamom, cinnamon, cloves, dry ginger and peppercorns – and adding milk and sugar to taste.

Curry – The first thing that comes to many Western minds at the mention of India is 'curry', although there's no such dish and the word isn't used in India, where the key ingredient of what Westerners call 'curry' is the *kadipatta* (literally 'sweet leaf').

Fenny – This heady Indian liquor, a product of Goa, is distilled from coconut palm sap or the juice of the cashew apple. (Unusually, cashew nuts grow outside the apple.)

Jal Jeera – A concoction of powdered cumin (*jeera* in Hindi), rock salt and mint in water (*jal*), generally served cold before meals.

Lassi – A yogurt drink, sweetened with sugar and served chilled.

Nan – Round flat bread made from white flour, resembling pita bread, nan (also written 'naan') is usually leavened with yeast, although unleavened dough is also used. It's cooked in a *tandoor* (see below) and is a staple accompaniment to hot meals in India. It can be eaten plain or filled with meat or vegetables.

Pani puri – A mouth-watering snack sold by hawkers which resembles a ping-pong ball (made from dough) 'injected' with a tangy concoction. The ball is popped whole into the mouth, where it 'explodes'.

Papadum – However you spell it (and there are many versions), a poppadom is a thin wafer, sometimes described as a cracker or flatbread, and an important part of Sindhi cuisine. Recipes vary from region to region and family to family, but it's typically made from lentil, chickpea, black gram (urad or bean) or rice flour.

Shrikhand – Served chilled, this thick and creamy Indian dessert is made from strained yogurt, sugar, cardamom powder and saffron, and often garnished with mango pulp (the pulverised flesh of the fruit).

Papadum

Tandoor – A cylindrical clay oven in which food is cooked over a charcoal fire in temperatures of up to 480°C (900°F). It's also known as a *bhatti*, after the Bhatti tribe of the Thar Desert of north-western India. Typical food cooked in a *tandoor* (and therefore known as *tandoori*) includes chicken and bread varieties such as *nan* and *roti*.

Spices

An integral part of food preparation in India, spices are used to enhance the flavour and aroma of a dish (and, traditionally, to conceal the poor quality of the main ingredients). They're often heated in a pan with oil to intensify their flavour before other ingredients are added. The most frequently used spices in Indian cuisine are asafoetida (*hing*), black mustard seed (*rai*), chili pepper (*mirch*), cumin (*jeera*), fenugreek (*methi*), garlic (*lassan*), ginger (*adrak*) and turmeric (*haldi*).

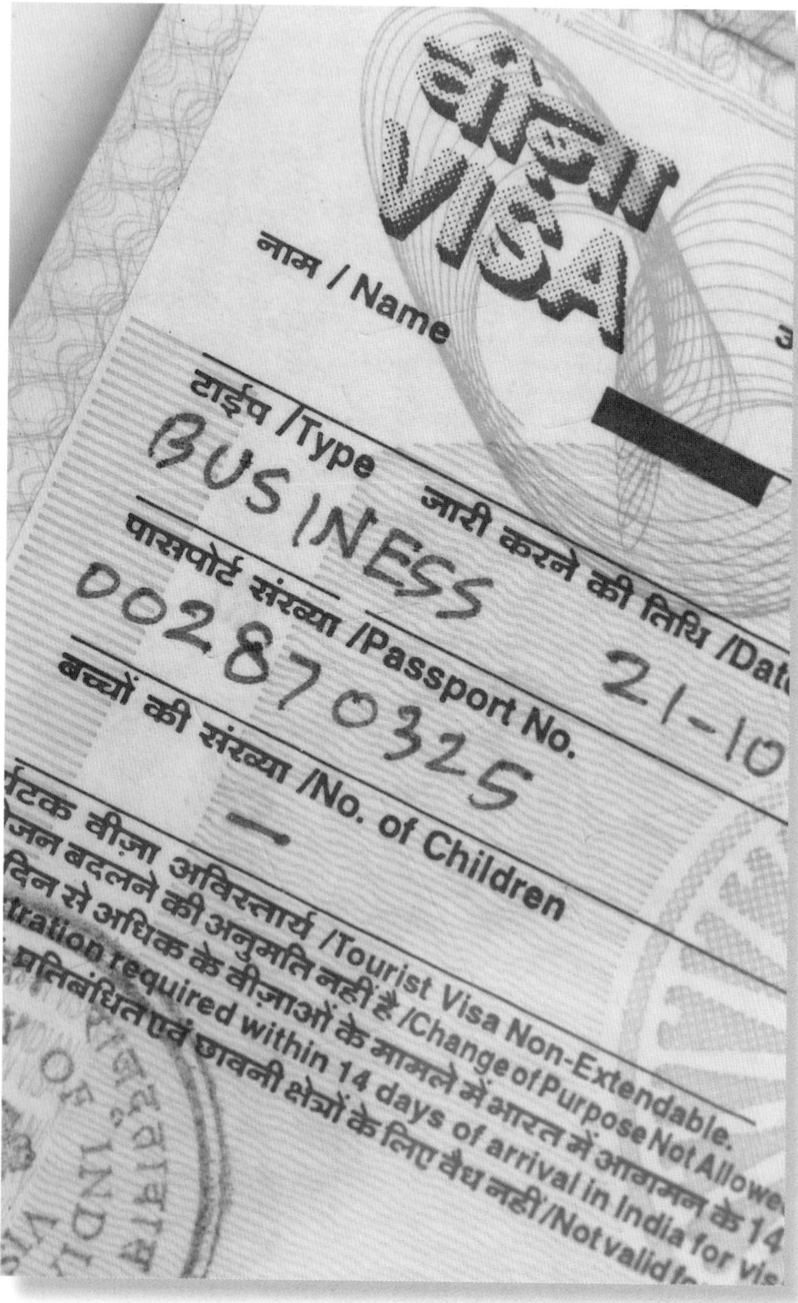

वीज़ा / VISA

नाम / Name

टाईप /Type
BUSINESS   जारी करने की तिथि /Date

पासपोर्ट संख्या /Passport No.
00287 0325   21-10

बच्चों की संख्या /No. of Children
—

पर्यटक वीज़ा अविस्तार्य /Tourist Visa Non-Extendable.
प्रयोजन बदलने की अनुमति नहीं है /Change of Purpose Not Allowed.
दिन से अधिक के वीज़ाओं के मामले में भारत में आगमन के 14
...tration required within 14 days of arrival in India for Vis...
...प्रतिबंधित एवं छावनी क्षेत्रों के लिए वैध नहीं/Not valid f...

3.

GETTING STARTED

Change is always a challenge and the first step in the process of adjusting to change is the hardest. This chapter will prepare the way for you and smooth your transition from newcomer to resident by providing you with the information required to overcome hurdles such as obtaining the right visa, finding accommodation, renting or buying a car, opening a bank account, registering for taxes, obtaining healthcare, council services and utilities, finding schools for your children, getting online, staying informed and dealing with the omnipresent Indian bureaucracy.

It's easier to find your way through the Sundarbans jungle than through the mazes and tangles of Indian rules and regulations.

IMMIGRATION

All foreigners need a visa to enter India and there's no provision for obtaining a 'visa on arrival', therefore you need to ensure that you have a valid visa before departure. The purpose of your visit determines the type of visa you need; the most common categories are listed below:

- **Tourist visa:** Valid for six months from the date of issue (not from the date of travel or arrival in India) and can routinely be extended for three months;

- **Business visa:** For people exploring business opportunities or setting up business ventures in India; usually valid for a year but can be granted for up to five years. Applications for business visas should be accompanied by a letter from your employer stating the purpose of your visit.

- **Employment visa:** For people taking up employment in India, in either a foreign or an Indian company;

- **Entry visa:** Issued to people of Indian origin and people whose spouses are posted to India on company business. Normally valid for a year and extendable in India, but can be granted for up to five years.

- **Student visa:** Valid up to five years. You need to present a letter of admission from a recognised school/institution, either in India or abroad, and evidence of finance to cover your stay in India. You may also need a letter of approval from the Ministry of Health, Government of India (for admission to medical or para-medical courses) or a letter of approval from the Ministry of Human Resources Development (for admission to technical institutes or to graduate or post-graduate courses in engineering).

It's best to check your visa category with the Indian Consulate in your home country. Whatever category of visa you need, it's also best to opt for multiple-entry, as it doesn't entail an extra fee.

If you're white, getting through immigration control when you arrive in India usually poses even fewer problems than for a non-resident Indian. Your passport and visa will be checked and stamped on arrival and your luggage may be searched. Africans and travellers from the Middle and Far East may be searched by customs officials for illegal drugs.

Immigration officials and customs officers are generally polite, though not necessarily helpful, and it's advisable to be cooperative, however long the entry procedure may take.

A stay of more than six months requires you to register with the local Foreigners' Registration Office (in most large cities) or at the local police station (elsewhere). You must go in person and will be issued with a document or booklet that acts as proof of residence. If possible, ask a colleague to accompany you. If you stay more

than two years, you must undergo a test for HIV at a government hospital. The registration certificate must be surrendered at the time of your final departure from India.

> **There are restricted areas in India, including the borders with China and Pakistan, the Union Territories of Andaman, the Nicobar and Lakshadweep islands, parts of Uttar Pradesh and Rajasthan, and the north-eastern frontier states of Arunachal Pradesh, Assam, Manipur, Meghalaya, Mizoram, Nagaland, Tripura and scenic Sikkim (which boasts Mount Kanchenjunga, the world's third-highest peak at 8,586m/28,210ft), where access is controlled and photography forbidden. You can apply for a permit, which must be done at least four weeks in advance, to The Under Secretary, Ministry of Home Affairs, Foreigners Division, Lok Nayak Bhavan, Khan Market, New Delhi 110 003.**

BUREAUCRACY

If you thought French or Spanish bureaucracy was impenetrable, you need only take a look inside a typical Indian government office, where armies of civil servants plough their way through stack upon stack of papers,

files, folders and binders under the slowly churning blades of ceiling fans – any faster and the dusty papers would start flying about the musty room. Don't be surprised if you're asked to write out an application to obtain an application form – only to discover that the said form is in the personal custody of a clerk whose whereabouts are unknown.

Efforts at improving the system and expediting paperwork have been made, such as the introduction of one-stop offices called 'Single Windows'. Here all kinds of information and documentation are available and you can apply for anything and everything – whether it's for an employment or residence permit, a business or driving licence, tourist car registration plates, the import of funds or the payment of taxes. However, you'll still need to make regular visits to 'chase up' your applications if you don't want to wait for ever.

Computerisation of records and processes has also been successfully implemented in the cities and most large towns, but the apathy of civil servants (see below) is more difficult to overcome.

Here are some tips for dealing with Indian red tape:

- More important than finding out the opening hours of the relevant office or the time the official concerned 'signs in', is to discover what time he's actually in his office.

- Always make a duplicate of everything for your own records.

- Expect to spend days, weeks, even months, on 'follow-up' trips to government offices.

- Accept bureaucratic obstacles as part of life in India – just as the Indians themselves do.

- Remain calm and polite at all times.

India doesn't yet have a full-fledged system of personal identification for its citizens. Although a Multinational National Identity Card (MNIC) programme was launched in 2003, its target of providing 2mn adult citizens in 12 states with identity numbers and cards is still a long way off. In the meantime, the ration card issued by the Civil Supplies department is used for the purpose of identification, although Indians aren't obliged to carry their ration cards. Foreigners, on the other hand, should always carry their passport and visa or photocopies.

Civil Servants

India's bureaucrats are derisively called *babus* (a derogatory term for native Indian clerks coined during the era of British rule) by the press, who portray them as social parasites, serving only themselves.

With few exceptions, Indian civil servants are anything but civil and expect to be served rather than to serve. In fact, the term civil servant is no longer used, as they prefer to call themselves 'government officials'.

Besides job security (it's almost impossible to be dismissed even under a charge of corruption, as this seldom results in a conviction), short working hours with long lunch breaks and frequent tea breaks, numerous holidays, annual salary increases based on seniority rather than merit and an annual bonus, civil servants can also look forward to a generous pension on retirement.

Not surprisingly, 'government official' is a popular profession. Every year young men and women in their hundreds of thousands, many of them holding qualifications in engineering and even medicine, sit the civil service entrance examination, only a few hundred of whom are ultimately selected. Many candidates spend years studying for the exams and there are specialist academies and private tutors throughout India that provide the necessary training.

As a result, civil servants regard themselves as holding a privileged and prestigious position and expect you to be not only polite but deferent – although even deference isn't guaranteed to get you what you want. Apathy, inefficiency and corruption are rife in the Indian civil service, and there's little you can do other than grin and bear it.

Getting Round Bureaucracy

Even if you're conversant with the Indian rules and regulations that affect you, and you have the patience of a saint, it's still recommended that you use the following 'side doors' to the Indian administrative system.

'Tipping'

A 'tip' is almost always expected, even if all your papers are in order. The difficulty is not so much knowing whether to tip (the message will be conveyed to you more or less discreetly) but how much to tip. Some states are known to be more corrupt then others

– particularly the northern states of Bihar, Delhi, Madhya Pradesh and Uttar Pradesh. For routine matters, 10 per cent of the cost of the service may be sufficient; for 'under the table' dealings, the percentage may be as high as 300 per cent, e.g. Rs2,000 (US$40) for an illicit driving licence.

How much is expected may also depend on your perceived wealth. As a foreigner you'll be regarded as well off, but if you sport an expensive watch or thick gold rings, or travel in a luxury car, tipping expectations are likely to soar – so contrive to look as poor as possible!

At the lowest levels, tipping may take the form of merely ordering tea from an office boy – though you'll need to order for everyone in the office, which may be as many as ten people. This may gain you an 'audience' with the relevant official, who will expect a more substantial 'incentive' than a cup of tea, such as a wrapped gift of the appropriate value.

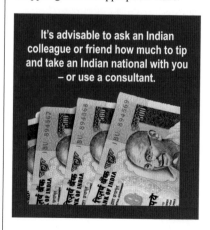

It's advisable to ask an Indian colleague or friend how much to tip and take an Indian national with you – or use a consultant.

Networking

Dealing with the 'right' people is another way of expediting an application. If you know someone who knows the relevant official, it might be advantageous to mention the fact – particularly if your acquaintance is influential or wealthy.

Consultants

It's common practice to engage the services of a consultant, also known as an agent, who's an expert in administrative and/or tax procedures. The consultant acts as a middleman between you and the civil service and is the easiest and most cost-effective way of getting around bureaucracy, although certain officials frown upon consultants while others have their 'favourites' and won't cooperate with anyone else.

Srinagar, Kashmir

Consultants can be contacted at their offices or at government offices, where they can often be found during visiting hours (around noon). Usually they introduce themselves when they spot a prospective client, i.e. a bewildered-looking foreigner, otherwise you can ask any junior official for a recommendation.

Consultants don't charge on an hourly or annual basis but per assignment – and they too expect tips, of at least 2 per cent of their official fee, which is often called a 'commission'.

ACCOMMODATION

Accommodation in India is generally good value, but luxurious Western-style housing in Delhi and Mumbai, particularly in areas popular with foreigners, can be as expensive as in any Western city.

Rented Property

In Delhi, there are beautiful bungalows to let while in Mumbai apartments are more common. Both furnished and unfurnished property can be found, although the latter is standard for long-term rentals. Properties to rent can be found through local newspaper advertisements or agencies.

Permission from the Reserve Bank of India is necessary for a foreigner to rent property for more than five years.

Landlords & Agencies

You can rent directly from a landlord or through an agency (letting company). There are many agencies, Magic Bricks (⌨ www.magicbricks.com) being one of the leading companies. Simply type 'letting companies' or 'renting companies' plus 'India' into a search engine (e.g. Google) to find a list.

There are advantages and disadvantages to renting direct or through an agency, as detailed below:

● Most landlords prefer renting property to foreigners because the type of foreigner who comes to live and work in India is generally honest, polite, well behaved and, most importantly, sure to leave before long (Indian law makes it difficult to evict long-term tenants). It can therefore be easier to secure a property when dealing directly with the landlord.

- Indian landlords can be extremely possessive of their properties and have the irritating habit of 'visiting' to check that you aren't making holes in the floor or painting the walls black, whereas agencies usually afford tenants greater privacy.

- Properties managed by an agency are usually better maintained, but you'll need to pay more, as agencies charge a commission of one or two months' rent.

Whether you rent through a letting company or directly from a landlord, it's essential to establish and maintain good relations. You should begin by abiding by the 'house' rules and regulations. In India, as elsewhere in Asia, if you need anything done, ask politely but firmly – as if you expect your wish to be granted.

Contracts & Payment

Most landlords let properties on eleven-month 'lease agreements'. These are renewable, but you can expect a 10 per cent rent increase each time the lease is renewed (inflation in India is running at around 11 per cent). The landlord also takes a 'damage' deposit equivalent to ten months' rent.

Make sure you obtain a receipt if you pay your rent in cash. Many landlords try to avoid issuing receipts in order to reduce their tax liability – leaving tenants without proof of payment.

Buying a Home

Foreign nationals (except citizens of Afghanistan, Bangladesh, Bhutan, China, Iran, Nepal, Pakistan and Sri Lanka) must be resident in India for at least 183 days in each financial year to be allowed to buy property and must obtain permission from the Reserve Bank of India. It's illegal to buy property on a tourist visa.

House buyers can get an idea of market values through the National Housing Bank's 'Residex' service, which is currently available in Bangalore, Bhopal, Delhi, Kolkata (Calcutta) and Mumbai; for example, Delhi's can be found on 🖥 http://

Jodhpur, 'the blue city', Rajasthan

nhb.org.in/whats_new/delhiresidex.htm.
In addition to average prices for each
area, the factors that most affect price,
such as orientation, age and type of tenure
(freehold or leasehold) are listed.

When buying a house, you should do
the following:

● Engage a registered valuer to verify
that the asking price is the true
market value.

● Hire a lawyer to draft the Sale Deed
(or Sale Agreement), obtain the 'nil-
encumbrance certificate' and register
the deed (which costs between 0.5
and 2 per cent of the property's
value).

● Have an independent expert (e.g.
architect) check that all necessary
building permits have been obtained.
Illegal buildings are common in
India, with demolition squads on call
year round in the major cities.

As well as the Sale Deed, you must sign
a purchase contract, when you must
pay a deposit (generally 10 per cent of
the price). If you don't complete the
purchase, you lose the deposit, but if the
seller doesn't complete you get it back.

**You may be asked to pay at least 40
per cent of the price in cash, so that
the seller can save on income tax,
which in India applies to 'income'
from the sale of private property.
You'll also save on the registration
fee, which is normally 6 per cent of
the declared value of the property.
This is, however, illegal and you
should use all your negotiating
skills to avoid doing so.**

BUYING OR HIRING A CAR

If you live anywhere except the
middle of a city and in the vicinity of a
supermarket and/or school (if you have
school-age children), you'll need a car.
In fact, even in a city, where the roads
are hopelessly congested, you might
prefer to crawl along in the comfort
of your own vehicle rather than crawl
along while crammed into a bus or auto-
rickshaw.

Below are some tips on hiring
(renting) and buying a car in India.

Hiring a Car

There are few self-drive hire companies in
India. When you hire (rent) a car in India
it usually comes with a chauffeur. You can
even hire a driver for your own car – for
around Rs300 (US$6) per day. You pay
around Rs8 (US 15¢) per km plus Rs100
(US$2) per day towards the driver's meals.

If you wish to drive yourself, you must
be aged over 18 and have an international
driver's permit. Payment is by cash and
includes a deposit which can be as high as
the value of the car!

When choosing a hire car, bear in mind
the heat and dust of India and make sure it
has air-conditioning. The high accident rate
on Indian roads makes hiring a robust car
a must – the heavy, trundling Ambassador
is preferred by most foreigners for its
protectiveness and suitability for Indian
road conditions, despite its almost obsolete
design and petrol-guzzling engine.
However, modern sport utility vehicles
(SUVs) can also be hired.

Buying a Car

Buying a car in India is better than
importing one as the hassles involved
in the procedure seem designed to act as
deterrents. If you insist on importing a

vehicle, make sure that it's a right-hand drive model, as traffic drives on the left in India. To buy a car you must own a property or have a rental contract (usually for at least 11 months). The paperwork and legwork involved in a car purchase is taxing and is best handled by an agent (see above) for a fee of around Rs2,000 (US$40).

New Cars

New cars are usually advertised at 'list price', but competing dealers offer discounts, extended guarantees, financing arrangements (interest rates are usually high) and other incentives such as gifts or gift vouchers, particularly during festive seasons such as *Dussehra* (see **Festivals & Fairs** in **Chapter 8**) and *Diwali* (see **Family Occasions** in **Chapter 8**).

> Car dealers tend to have a fat margin, leaving plenty of scope for bargaining.

Used Cars

There are around a million used cars for sale at any one time in India, private sales accounting for around 80 per cent of the market. Most of these take place at weekly 'fairs' (known as a *mela*) on the outskirts of cities. These are generally to be avoided, as there have been a number of cases of stolen cars being sold at *mela*. You're better off buying from a manufacturer that also sells used cars, which currently include Ford India Maruti Udyog and Hyundai Motor India, with General Motors India considering entering the market. International used-car

dealers Gulliver International of Japan and Manheim of the UK are also likely to set up in India in the near future.

While selecting a reputable dealer is critical, it's equally important to check not only the physical condition of the car you intend buying, but also the documents that are supposed to come with it. Other things to check include:

- Ask for the original registration certificate – don't accept 'certified true copies' – and obtain an undertaking from the seller that it will be transferred into your name by a mutually agreed date

- Check that the engine number, chassis number and colour of the car match those stated in the registration certificate.

- If a compressed natural gas (CNG) or liquid petroleum gas (LPG) fuel system is fitted in the car, this should be also be specified in the registration certificate.

- Check that there's no outstanding loan on the vehicle by contacting the Road Traffic Officer (RTO); most Indian cars are purchased with a bank loan.

- Ask to see the current insurance policy: if it doesn't have a no-claims bonus endorsement, the vehicle may have been involved in a recent accident and the case could still be under litigation. In which case you should avoid the vehicle and look elsewhere.

- If the car is registered in a state other than the one you're residing in, you'll need a No Objection Certificate (NOC) from the RTO of that state and must pay road tax at the time of transferring the registration into your name.

- Obtain a receipt.

EMERGENCY SERVICES

Emergency services in India are far from world-class and in remote rural areas the time between call-out and arrival is usually several hours. Also bear in mind that most telephone operators speak a little English, your 'foreign' accent may be incomprehensible. Concentrate on pronouncing the key words slowly and clearly, while briefly conveying the type of emergency and your exact location – try to give a landmark, if possible (see **Hindi Emergency Phrases** here). The main national emergency numbers are shown in the table below:

Emergency Numbers	
Number	**Service**
100	Police
101	Fire service
102	Ambulance service
103	Traffic police

Hindi Emergency Phrases

accident – *accident* (the Hindi word for 'accident' is *durghatna* but common usage is *accident*)

car accident – *gaadi ka accident*

allergic reaction – *reaction, allergy ka*

attack – *hamla*

armed attack – *hathiyar se hamla*

bleeding (a lot) – *khoon ni-kal raha hai* (*ziada*)

broken arm – *tooti baju*

broken leg – *tooti tang*

burglary – *chori/dacoity*

fire – *aag*

heart attack – *heart attack*

I need an ambulance – *ambulance chaiyeh muzeh*

I need a doctor – *doctor chaiyeh muzeh*

intruder – *ghuspaithia*

mugging – *loot paat*

not breathing – *saans nahin hai*

(I am) on the road to x – (*mein*) *x ko jaanne waalli saddak par hoonh*

overdose – *adhik maatra*

unconscious – *moorchhit*

wounded – *zakhmi/ghaayal*

HEALTH SERVICES

As in many areas of Indian society, there's a huge gulf (chasm) between rich and poor when it comes to health services. Some 80 per cent of healthcare provision in India is in the private sector, yet less than 10 per cent of the population can afford private care – which means that the vast majority of Indians must make do with the inadequate state system.

State Healthcare

The public health service is available to everyone, but not everyone wishes to make use of it, as standards are deplorable. It consists of a 'step-up referral' network of sub-centres, primary health centres, community health centres and district hospitals. In urban areas there are also family welfare centres (where contraceptives can be obtained).

There's no appointment system at most centres, where you must simply wait your turn – sometimes for several days.

Private Healthcare

Eighty per cent of healthcare facilities in India are private, with thousands of dispensaries, clinics,

laboratories, nursing homes and hospitals. Corporate hospitals are among the best in the world, with state-of-the-art facilities. Around 400 hospitals are linked to the international telemedicine network, which provides instant 'video' consultations with specialists worldwide.

Doctors

The Indian Medical Association is the world's largest non-government medical organisation with 178,000 doctors and over 1,700 branches spread over the 23 states and seven union territories. Yet this gives India a doctor-patient ratio of just 1:1,722 (compared with around 1:300 in Western Europe and 1:400 in the US) and still leaves some two-thirds of the population without a registered doctor.

Always check the qualifications and experience of a doctor in India, as cases of false certificates and degrees surface from time to time in the newspapers. Age is another important factor – too young and he'll most likely be inexperienced, too old and he may be out of touch with the latest developments. Good doctors have a sort of 'fan following' who are ever ready to give testimonials about their 'healing touch.'

Most Indian doctors speak English; they are best found through referrals from your colleagues or neighbours, who will also tell you which ones to steer clear of. However, you should also check out a doctor's qualifications, as even popular doctors have been found to have false certificates. Another point to consider is that in India, the older a doctor, the better he's perceived to be. However, elderly doctors, particularly in towns, often don't keep up with the latest medical advances.

You should 'try out' a couple of doctors before appointing one as your family physician, as this can be a long-term association. However, you don't need to go through your family physician to gain access to specialist medical treatment and you're free to go directly to the specialist of your choice.

Doctors don't make home visits except in cities and towns, where they charge a high fee.

> Alternative medicine is popular in India, where there are thousands of unregistered homeopaths and practitioners of Ayurveda, the Indian system of (alternative) medicine. Some homeopaths prescribe Ayurvedic medicines along with regular homeopathic treatments.

Appointments

You don't require an appointment (although it's obviously preferable) and can simply go along during surgery hours and wait your turn. You're unlikely to be turned away, even if you have to wait until the evening, as many doctors have no fixed surgery hours.

Doctors usually work Mondays to Saturdays, but specialists in large city hospitals are available only on weekday evenings, as the mornings are reserved for theatre work.

Consultations

If you have an appointment, ask the receptionist when you arrive what your number is and which number the doctor is up to, in order to get an idea

how long your wait is likely to be. Be prepared to wait up to an hour after your appointed time. India is filled with 'government officials' (see **Civil Servants** above), who arrive without appointments and expect to be seen immediately. Discipline is expected only from 'ordinary' citizens and if you arrive even a minute late your appointment may be cancelled – with an accompanying admonishment from the receptionist!

Emergency Treatment

Most public and private hospitals offer emergency treatment. After admittance, you're examined by a nurse, who refers you to a suitable doctor or specialist. If your case has legal implications, e.g. an injury resulting from a car accident, you may find yourself embroiled in medical bureaucracy.

It's worthwhile carrying a basic emergency sterile medical kit in case you meet with an accident and are admitted to a state hospital, where equipment and supplies are limited. If you have your own supply, you'll at least be assured that your own needles, syringes and dressings are sterile.

Despite notices requesting quiet, emergency waiting rooms are noisy places due to inconsiderate mobile phone users in particular and the garrulous nature of Indians in general.

Medicines

Medicines are sold by medical stores (chemists or pharmacies), which can be found on main streets as well as in and around hospitals. Most medicines are available over the counter without a doctor's prescription – even antibiotics, although theoretically they require a prescription. (Not only doctors but also practitioners of alternative medicine prescribe antibiotics at the slightest sign of a common cold.) And prescriptions aren't date-limited, so you can reuse them if similar symptoms re-appear, thus avoiding paying a doctor's consultation fee again.

Unless you're receiving treatment in a public hospital, in which case medicines will be provided free from the hospitals' in-house pharmacy, medicines must be paid for. Chemists supply only the number of tablets you need, so you normally won't have any left over; if you do, check their expiry date before reusing them.

> **A typical medicine cabinet in an urban Indian home will have a stock of antacids (heartburn prevalence is at over 70 per cent), cough syrups (to combat sore throats and colds caused by polluted air), painkillers (known as analgesics and a general 'first aid' before seeing a doctor) and pills to combat diarrhoea (common due to the general lack of sanitation and hygiene).**

Hospitals

Public hospitals (known as government hospitals) provide surgical and convalescent treatment free of charge. However, you may need someone to wash and feed you, as few nursing services are provided. Public hospitals have single rooms with en suite bathrooms as well as general wards, but the former are normally allocated to government officials and the doctors' own relatives.

Private hospitals include clinics with hospitalisation facilities, mission hospitals (run by Christian missionaries) and corporate hospitals with five-star, hotel-style accommodation and state-of-the-art medical facilities. Private hospitals usually require a (large) deposit on admission.

Many private hospitals require patients (even emergency cases) to buy medicines, plaster casts and vaccines, and to pay for X-rays before procedures are carried out. Towels and bed linen are provided, but patients are expected to take pyjamas, robes and toiletries.

In both public and private hospitals, patients are given a registration card and sent to see a suitable doctor or specialist. A list of doctors is displayed on a board near the registration desk. Food is usually reasonable in private hospitals but of poor quality in public establishments.

Nursing Care

Although Indian nurses are properly qualified and exhibit professionalism, what they often lack is a sense of vocation. Hence the cold, impersonal and apparently uncaring attitude you're likely to encounter. It often seems that their main aim is to serve the doctors and not the patients, and in public hospitals rudeness isn't uncommon. It's therefore in your interest to have relatives or friends visit you and help you with day-to-day activities such as eating, washing and even ensuring the timely administration of medication.

Medical Procedures

Until the information technology boom began to demystify the medical profession, doctors were held in awe in India and their advice followed to the letter with blind faith (many even had 'faith' in the healing touch of their favourite doctors). Nowadays, patients are not only better informed but also more aware of their rights. There's even a Consumers Protection Act that allows them to voice complaints against doctors.

Nevertheless, medical staff will still send patients for scans, blood tests and other medical tests without explaining the need for them. There have even been reports in the newspapers of hospitals and doctors receiving 'commissions' for referring patients to laboratories for expensive, and often unnecessary, tests. In a recent indictment, the Delhi high court described the Medical Council of India, the country's premier medical body, as a 'den of corruption'.

Childbirth

India's infant mortality rate is high at 68 per 1,000 (compared with around 5 per 1,000 in the West), but its maternal mortality ratio (MMR) is the highest in the world at 450 deaths per 100,000 live births – mainly due to haemorrhage, anaemia, eclampsia (pregnancy-related hypertension), infection (sometimes resulting from abortion) and obstructed

labour. Only 35 per cent of deliveries take place in health facilities and only just over 40 per cent of infants receive immunisation vaccines. In private hospitals, caesarean rates are high yet incubators aren't always available. Partners aren't generally allowed to be present at the birth.

Post-treatment Care

As in the West, public hospital patients are expected to convalesce at home, often being discharged earlier than they would be from a private hospital. In fact, if business is slack in private hospitals, the stay of patients ready for discharge may be extended and patients not requiring hospitalisation may be hospitalised to ensure that all beds are occupied – and paid for!

INSURANCE

There are only two compulsory insurances for individuals in India: third party insurance for vehicle owners, and building insurance (including cover for fire damage) for mortgagees. Optional (but highly recommended) insurance includes comprehensive vehicle insurance, personal accident, medical, life, household contents and travel.

Health Insurance

As has been explained above, there's no statutory health insurance scheme in India, and state healthcare is limited, so private health insurance is virtually essential. In particular, make sure you have full cover during the interval between leaving your last country of residence and obtaining medical insurance in India. Indian companies offer policies only for those living permanently in India and these don't include repatriation cover. It may be possible to extend an existing policy to cover your stay in India.

Car Insurance

All motor vehicles and trailers must be insured for third party risks. If you import a car which is insured in another country, it won't be normally covered for third party liability in India, although you may be able to extend the insurance to cover India, although you usually need to take out a new insurance policy with a company registered in India. Insurance documents must be carried in the car at all times and you can be fined for not having them.

> Car insurance policies cover anyone driving the vehicle, provided he/she holds a valid driving licence and has the owner's permission to use the car. Hire car insurance, however, only covers named drivers.

Household Insurance

Although only 5 per cent of Indians take out household insurance, insuring your home and its contents is highly recommended. If you buy a property with a mortgage, one of the conditions of the lender is that you take out building insurance covering fire damage.

Indian household contents insurance doesn't usually include high-value objects such as antiques (for which a separate policy is required). If you take out burglary insurance, the building must be made secure, with iron bars on windows and reinforced windows and doors. Most insurance companies offer a discount if you install a burglar alarm.

Insurance Claims

Claims can be made by telephone but should be followed by a written application on the prescribed claim form. You're given a claim reference number, which you should retain. If the claim is for theft, insurance companies require a copy of a police First Information Report (FIR) within 24 hours. If your car is stolen, the insurance company won't consider a claim until you submit a police's Final Investigation Report, which is usually issued after 90 days.

EDUCATION

Despite a widespread network of public schools and an ever-growing number of private schools in cities and towns, the Indian education system caters to less than a third of its school-age (5–14) children. However, there has been an increase in both the quantity and quality of schools in recent years, during which a number of private enterprises have established world-class institutions. The number of foreign students enrolled in Indian institutions of higher learning – particularly in fields such as technology, management and life sciences – has also increased rapidly, as India has become a more important player in the global economy.

When it comes to choosing between an Indian and an international school, various factors will influence your decision: the age of your children, the duration of your stay in India, your next place of residence, your plans for your children's further education, and, not least, your financial resources.

have lots of homework with huge blocks of text to memorise.

International Schools

India has a number of international schools, some of which were schools for children of Christian missionaries during the Raj, such as Kodaikanal International School in South India and Woodstock International School in North India. International schools have excellent facilities and curricula that allow graduation in the International Baccalaureate, English 'A' and 'O' levels, and American high school diploma. They also have good boarding facilities, particularly those in Dalhousie, in north-western India, and Mussoorie in North India, which teach to British GCSE exams and offer extra-curricular activities such as sports, music, gymnastics and theatre. Annual tuition fees range from Rs500,000 to 800,000 (US$10,000-16,000).

International schools are ideal if your stay is short term (say, up to five years), as your children won't have to readapt every time you move to another country. These schools generally have a good success rate in getting pupils into top European and North American colleges and universities.

If you plan to stay in India long term, an Indian school may be preferable. Your children will learn Hindi (although options for a second language will usually be limited to the regional language) and have easier access to national institutes of higher learning such as the Indian Institutes of Technology (IITs) and the Indian Institutes of Management (IIMs), not to mention employment. Education at Indian state schools (called 'government schools') is free and fees at private schools are considerably lower than those charged by international schools.

However, irrespective of the length of your stay, you may want to think twice before placing children over the age of ten in an Indian school, as learning the language(s) may be an insurmountable obstacle and they will

> **'British' schools in Dalhousie include Dalhousie Hill Top School, Dalhousie Public School and The Sacred Heart High School, while Mussoorie boasts the Convent of Jesus & Mary, Mussoorie International School, Mussoorie Modern School, Mussoorie Public School, Oak Grove School, Pine Wood School, Woodstock School and the Wynberg Allen School.**

Indian Schools

According to the Indian Constitution, education is compulsory up to the age of 14. The Indian education system is divided into pre-primary (junior kindergarten and senior kindergarten – from age three to four), primary (classes I to IV – from five to eight), middle (classes V to VII – 9 to 11), secondary (classes VIII to X – 12 to 14), and higher secondary (classes XI to XII – 14 to 16).

There are government, semi-government and private schools in almost every part of the country, most of them being affiliated either to the Central Board of Secondary Education (CBSE) or to local state boards. Higher education includes technical schools (such as the IITs), colleges and universities.

The Indian education system has a few peculiarities, a number of which are listed below.

- Learning is mostly by rote and students are expected to memorise large chunks of text, figures and facts. This is one of the reasons Indian students excel in general knowledge competitions.

- Learning is largely teacher-driven with hardly any project work.

- All subjects have textbooks and most Indian teachers follow them to the letter.

- Few Indian teachers in state schools speak English.

- The first external examinations are taken at around 15, when students sit the Secondary School Certificate (SSC) board exams.

- Students can be required to repeat a school year if they fail exams. The maximum number of years a child can repeat is two in primary and one in secondary.

- Most state schools and all private schools have uniforms, although there's no 'uniform' footwear in state schools, as many children go to school barefoot in rural areas.

- Some state primary schools provide lunch but secondary schools don't. Packed snacks are permitted during morning break.

The school day in primary state schools usually lasts from 9am to 2pm and at secondary level from 8.30am to 1.30pm or from noon to 5pm.

The school year begins in mid-June, after a two-month summer holiday, and is divided into three terms of unequal length, separated by the *Diwali* **holiday (two to three weeks in October/November) and a winter holiday (from the end of December to the end of January or, in Christian schools, 23rd December to the first Monday in January).**

- There are no mid-term breaks but local, regional and national holidays are observed.

- Classrooms in Indian state schools usually have a photograph of Mahatma Gandhi on a wall. The Indian flag is raised on special occasions, e.g. Independence Day, when the national anthem is sung.

- Homework is of at least half an hour a day in primary state schools. In private primary schools, one hour per day is usual. At secondary level, state school pupils have at least two hours homework per day and private pupils around three.

Subjects

● The general level of English is high.

● Maths and science lessons are more advanced than in most developed countries.

● The use of calculators in maths classes isn't allowed.

● PE, arts and music are given less importance than academic subjects.

University

● Higher education in India is taught in English.

● A number of grants and scholarships are available and banks have recently started offering student loans.

● Degree courses last at least three years after higher secondary education, and postgraduate degree courses at least two years.

● Many Indian universities and colleges have arrangements with foreign universities allowing students to undertake part of their courses abroad. Similarly, multinational corporations (such as Microsoft India) offer employees flexible higher education progammes at Indian universities.

COUNCIL SERVICES

Refuse Collection

Except in rural areas, refuse collections are made daily (at night in cities and early in the morning in towns) with the exception of Sundays and public holidays. You put your rubbish bags in a large communal container on the street or in a bin in the 'compound' behind your building. If you live in an apartment block the concierge may collect rubbish from your door. Refuse collectors take domestic rubbish only and anything else (e.g. broken household appliances, furniture or rubble) is usually left behind.

Recycling

Ninety-five per cent of India's domestic waste ends up in landfills, although much natural waste material is 'recycled' as compost. Official recycling systems are virtually non-existent, but various unofficial services are offered by transporters and re-processors as well as by 'rag pickers', who form the backbone of India's waste collection system.

Waste paper and cardboard is used as raw material in paper mills; glass bottles (especially beer bottles) are bought by scrap dealers and sold to recycling plants that wash them and sell them back to the beer producers for reuse; and tin cans and plastic bottles, crushed and pressed into bales, are similarly resold to keep the wheels of industry turning.

Other waste materials and products can be recycled as follows:

- **Computers & mobile phones** – Local junk depots will buy these for the re-usable parts.

- **Furniture, household goods & electrical appliances** – In rural areas, Christian missionaries collect these for charity; elsewhere, you may be able to sell them to scrap dealers and should keep an eye out for the occasional 'exchange schemes' offered by companies, e.g. 'Bring in your old TV in any condition; take away a brand new one and pay the difference in easy monthly instalments!'

- **Rubble** – Scrap dealers will buy discarded building materials for use in landfills.

UTILITIES

Telephone services and electricity and water supplies that are taken for granted in the developed world, cannot always be relied upon in India. While the Indian telephone service is good and the electricity supply is improving, a reliable, clean water supply cannot be assured, and arrangements for the connection and supply of these 'necessities' aren't yet standardised.

Electricity

Electricity is supplied by the state and the vast majority (over 80 per cent) is generated by fossil fuels, around 15 per cent by hydro-electricity, 3.5 per cent nuclear and less than half a per cent from 'clean' sources, e.g. solar and wind power. Power from the National Grid is distributed to the various State Electricity Boards (SEBs), which in turn provides power to consumers at 50Hz, 230 volts AC.

> A report published in *The Times of India* in April 2007 revealed that Mumbai's electricity is the world's most expensive.

Supply Problems

Power cuts are frequent in India – more so in the summer months, when more power is consumed (by air-conditioners and fans combating the heat) and low reservoir levels affect the hydro turbines. These may be planned (known as 'power shutdown days') and notified, when businesses in the affected area are closed, or accidental, resulting from malfunctioning electricity installations and bad weather – especially monsoons and cyclones – which play havoc with overhead supply lines.

Power cuts and power failures can last for hours or, in remote areas, days. When there's a power failure at night, the darkness is almost total as even the street lights go out and therefore candles, matches and torches should be kept where you can easily locate them in the dark.

There are several ways to combat power cuts. You can install rechargeable lamps, which have a built-in battery that's charged when there's power and takes over when there isn't; these are usually florescent tubes, which are mounted on walls and plugged in. An inverter works on the same principle but consists of several batteries and provides enough power to run a fridge or fan. A third option is to buy a fuel-powered generator.

Even when the power isn't interrupted, it's subject to surges and fluctuations that necessitate the installation of surge protectors and stabilisers for appliances such as TVs, refrigerators and computers, without which you risk having equipment damaged or destroyed. It's advisable to extend your household insurance to cover electronic equipment, as the electricity department doesn't pay compensation for such damage.

In towns the power may keep tripping off when you attempt to use a number of high-power appliances simultaneously, e.g. an electric iron and a water heater, due to a low power rating. This can be rectified if your apartment block applies for an upgrade of its power supply.

Gas

Except in some areas of a few cities, where piped gas is supplied to homes, bottled gas is standard for most of India and is often used for cooking. A number of gas companies supply standard gas bottles through a network of agencies that make weekly door-to-door deliveries, and there are seldom shortages.

Water

> **Even the Indian President wasn't spared the effects of a water shortage in June 2007, when officials at Rashtrapati Bhavan (his official residence) had to order tankers to deliver supplies from Delhi.**

When it comes to water, India is caught between the two extremes – droughts and floods – although even the latter don't alleviate the prevailing scarcity of this precious resource. Poor management and maintenance worsen the problem, and it's common to see water spouting out of malfunctioning municipal taps on street corners, although efforts at water conservation and 'water harvesting' (collecting rainwater) are being made.

In many areas, the municipality supplies water only at certain times of day. Houses and buildings have underground or overhead tanks for storing water, which is then pumped up

tea plantation, Kerala

or allowed to flow down as required. In some arid parts of the country, water is supplied door to door by tankers and may not be drinkable.

Quality

Untreated water in many parts of the country is hard, particularly in coastal areas, but this may be the least of your concerns. Wherever you live, tap water should always be filtered and kept at a rolling boil for ten minutes before being used for cooking or drinking. Alternatively, install a water purifier or use bottled water, which is increasingly widely available.

> If you eat or drink anything other than in an upmarket establishment, avoid iced drinks and anything that might have been washed in untreated water, such as salads or fruit.

Telephone

Telephone services have seen an amazing improvement in the last five years, most of the country now being covered by landline, local wireless loop and mobile phone infrastructure, making the Indian telecommunications network the fifth-largest in the world. WiMax networks were installed in five Indian cities in early 2008, and the government plans to make broadband internet connection available nationwide by 2009.

India's telephone services aren't , however, the cheapest in the world: local calls cost Rs2-4 (5-10 cents) a minute and calls to the UK and US over Rs7 (20 cents) per minute.

Installation

Bharat Sanchar Nigam Limited (BSNL) is currently the only company that can install a telephone line. BSNL offices can be found in district, town and city centres and installation takes up to a week in urban areas (longer in rural areas) and costs Rs500 (US$10). BSNL issues bills every two months and you can pay in cash or by cheque.

However, in some areas private companies install wireless local telephones – called the poor man's mobile, as they allow you to make calls only within a small area. As it's wireless, installation is quick and easy. Bills are sent out monthly.

Dealing with Telephone Companies

If you have a problem with your telephone service, report it to the nearest office of your telephone company. It will usually be resolved the same day unless   there's a fault with

the line itself, in which case it may take a day or two.

STAYING INFORMED

Given that India has the third-largest English-speaking population of any country, there's no dearth of English programmes on television and radio, as well as wide availability of English newspapers, magazines and books.

Television

Indian television is known more for its strict censorship than for its entertainment value. Programmes containing sexual scenes, excessive violence, abusive language and even innuendo are strictly censored by the Ministry of Information & Broadcasting, and the advertising of cigarettes and alcohol is banned.

Programmes are in Hindi as well as English and generally consist of soap operas, sports coverage (with cricket dominating), music and children's programmes. Watching TV is a family activity – soap operas are the favourite programmes. All channels carry advertisements, which are often louder than the programmes they interrupt.

Doordarshan is the state television company, which broadcasts on 21 channels, including its flagship DD1 channel, with some 400m viewers. It also has a free satellite service (called, confusingly, 'direct-to-home/DTH'). The four other DTH service providers are Airtel Digital TV (125 channels), BigTV (200 channels), DishTV (200 channels) and TataSky (160 channels). Most satellite packages include English-language programmes such as BBC News and CNN.

India's cable TV market is one of the world's largest, with over 60mn subscribers. The main broadcaster in English is Star TV network, which incorporates BBC World News.

Radio

Indians aren't avid radio listeners except when the Indian cricket team is playing. All India Radio (AIR) is the state radio company and broadcasts nationally and internationally. A few private stations operate in major cities, broadcasting mostly music and traffic information, as AIR has a monopoly on other types of news. However, the BBC World Service can be picked up on short wave. World Space satellite radio broadcasts music in many genres, 24 hours a day.

> **When the Indian cricket team is playing, Indians are seen walking the streets with small transistor radios pressed to their ears, listening to live commentary.**

The Press

The Indian press, the freest in Asia, is mainly aimed at the middle class and is lively, particularly on political topics and when engaged in the constant war of words with Pakistan. Comments about the government are common and aren't always favourable, but most newspapers are part of the political establishment.

Newspapers cost around Rs3.50 (7 cents) and many Sunday newspapers include supplements covering entertainment, IT, travel, art and literature. Most newspapers have free online editions.

India's main national newspapers, all of which are in English, include:

- **The Asian Age** – a conservative tabloid published simultaneously in India, London and New York;

- **Deccan Herald** – Bangalore, daily;

- **The Hindu** – Madras, daily;

- **The Hindustan Times** – New Delhi, daily;

- **The Indian Express** – New Delhi, daily, usually critical of the government;

- **The Pioneer** – New Delhi, daily;

- **The Statesman** – Kolkata, daily;

- **The Times of India** – Mumbai, daily.

Foreign publications such as the *International Herald Tribune*, *Time*, *Newsweek*, *The Economist* and the international editions of the British *Daily Express*, *Daily Telegraph* and *Guardian* are available in the main cities.

Some 4,700 daily newspapers in over 300 languages and another 39,000 journals and weeklies are published in India. It can take a while to open an account with an Indian bank, particularly if you don't have residency status (which can take some time). In the meantime it's advisable to have an overseas account from which you can withdraw cash. Two UK institutions – the Nationwide Building Society and the Post Office – don't charge a fee for overseas cash withdrawals.

BANKING

Banking in India has improved tremendously over the last three years and in some aspects, e.g. the facilities provided by cash machines, ranks among the most modern in the world. Opening a bank account is easy and can be done on the spot, Axis Bank and HDFC are reportedly among the easiest to deal with. Most banks in urban areas have English-speaking staff and cater for expatriate clients.

The following are some of the main characteristics of Indian banking.

- **Bank charges:** These are generally low and you aren't charged for paying money into your own account. If you carry out a lot of transactions other than cash deposits and withdrawals, ask your bank manager for a reduction on charges or a fixed monthly charge.

- **Bank managers:** Indian bank managers are generally personable, approachable and helpful –

most maintain cordial relations with their regular clients.

- **Cash machines:** Instructions are usually provided in English as well as Hindi. If you make a cash withdrawal from a machine that doesn't belong to your bank, there's a charge of between Rs5 and Rs20 (12-50 cents), on a per transaction basis rather than a percentage of the amount withdrawn. Cash withdrawals made by credit card always attract commission – usually 2.5 per cent of the amount withdrawn.

- **Cheques:** Payment by cheque is common in business transactions, but few shops accept personal cheques. You should be cautious when making out cheques to the bearer, as these can be cashed by anyone. You cannot stop payment by cheque once it has been made out.

- **Credit card payments:** Monthly credit card bills are usually paid by direct debit from your bank account. If you wish to make part payments you must arrange this with your bank, not the credit card company.

- **Internet banking:** Most Indian banks offer internet banking.

- **Opening hours:** Opening hours are generally 11am to 4pm. Few banks remain open after 4pm and not all banks open on Saturdays (those that do, open from around 11am to 1pm only).

- **Payment by debit & credit card:** India uses a chip and PIN system but it's more common in urban areas, and most outlets in rural areas are unable to accept debit or credit card payments at all.

- **Queues:** Although most banks now have single file queuing so that you wait for the first available desk or cashier, you should expect to queue for 20 minutes. In addition, you should allow up to 15 minutes for bank transactions, particularly if they involve cash (see below). To avoid queues and transaction delays, bank in the afternoons or use cash machines.

- **Standing orders:** These are easy to set up and highly recommended, but banks don't always pay them, therefore check your statements regularly.

- **Cash:** Cash transactions involve manual counting – not once, but twice. If you're depositing cash, the clerk will hold up a note now and then to check that it isn't a fake; if it is, the note will be torn into shreds, you'll have to explain where or who you got it from, and you may be detained for questioning or even jailed!

> Don't assume that notes you withdraw from a bank are genuine, but ask for small-denomination notes – Rs100 at most, as larger denominations are more likely to be counterfeit.

According to a recent report in the *Times of India*, forged banknotes in circulation in India have a total value of Rs1.7 trillion or US$40bn. India is a cash society and withdrawals of large amounts, i.e. between Rs100,000 and

Rs200,000 (US$2,000-4,000), are commonplace. However, if you need more than Rs50,000 (US$1,000) in cash it's advisable to order it at least a day in advance.

● The Indian currency is the rupee (abbreviated to Re in the singular and Rs in the plural, but often referred to by the letters INR), which is available in notes of Re1, Rs5, 10, 20, 50, 100, 500 and 1,000 and coins of Re0.50 (also called paisa), Re1, Rs2 and 5. In January 2009, there were around Rs50 to the US dollar and all conversions in this book are based on this exchange rate.

TAXES

Given its millions of bureaucrats and myriad inherited rules and regulations, India's tax system should be among the most complicated in the world, but the last decade has seen a concerted effort by the government to simplify the payment mechanism as well as filing of returns. Unfortunately, this doesn't make it any easier for the layman to calculate his income tax liability and it's best to employ a tax consultant unless your income is from employment only.

Take expert advice before moving to India, preferably from someone with knowledge of the tax systems of both India and your home country, so that you can benefit from the advantages of tax planning. It's essential to be aware of which taxes you should be paying and when – and those you can (legally) avoid paying.

Most expatriate workers in India are required to pay income tax, although there are exemptions for foreigners employed in embassies and foreign enterprises, subject to certain conditions.

The Indian tax year is from April to March and tax payments are usually made in arrears. The onus is on the taxpayer to file a return and make payments at the appropriate times, although employers must deduct their employees' tax at source and issue a certificate.

Tax Fraud

Nowadays, it isn't easy to avoid paying taxes in India and penalties are severe. Nevertheless, tax evasion is still widespread – for decades Indians have regarded avoiding taxes as an admirable feat rather than a crime. Paying in cash (therefore avoiding declaration of earnings and the payment of central sales tax, excise, service tax and VAT, to mention but a few of India's many and various impositions) and under-declaring property sale prices are common, although large cash withdrawals (e.g. over Rs50,000/ US$1,000) may be reported by a bank to the tax authorities if fraud is suspected.

Many Indians, particularly the self-employed and those in casual

Personal Income Tax Rates	
Income Range	**Tax Percentage**
Up to Rs100,000	Nil
Rs100,000 to1,50,000	10
Rs150,000 to 2,50,000	20
Over Rs250,000	30

employment, don't declare their income to the tax authorities. This is illegal and offenders are liable to heavy fines. The tax authorities are permitted to claim unpaid taxes up to five years in arrears (plus interest and penalty payments) and you should keep all tax-related documentation for at least six years.

COST OF LIVING

The cost of living in India is low by the standards of developed countries, although it varies from region to region and city to city, as well as between rural (low) and urban (high) areas, and from small towns (low) to major cities (high).

A survey by ECA International in May 2007 showed Mumbai (India's most expensive city) as the world's seventh most expensive city in terms of accommodation cost. However, in a survey by Mercer Consulting (💻 www.mercer.com/costofliving) in 2008, the city ranked 48th out of 143 of the world's major cities.

A simple but nutritious meal can cost as little as Rs40 (US80¢), a café meal Rs90 (US$2) and a restaurant meal Rs280 (US$5.50). Public transport is also inexpensive. Similarly, the cost of private healthcare is reasonable and medicines are cheap. While the price of food is reasonably stable, however, property prices and rents are rising steeply due to the country's expanding economy and double-digit inflation, especially in neighbourhoods that attract foreigners.

rickshaw – the workhorse of India

4.
BREAKING THE ICE

The best way of getting over culture shock and feeling part of life in India is meeting and getting acquainted with Indians on their own turf. Making new friends anywhere is never easy, but nowhere is it easier than in India. Indians thrive on social interaction and hospitality. Graciousness is their hallmark. If you're a Westerner, be prepared to acquire 'celebrity' status – and for the flood of invitations that accompany it. Your first encounter with an Indian is likely to earn you a drop-by-any-time welcome – and unlike many people, they mean it! Whatever the situation, the locals will usually take the initiative.

> 'If there's one thing nearly everyone who lives and works abroad has to get right, it is this: they must be able to get along with the local people.'
>
> Craig Storti, *The Art of Crossing Cultures*

This chapter provides information about aspects of Indian society that may be unfamiliar to you, advice on how to conduct yourself in social interactions and topics that are best avoided in conversation. It also gives information about the expatriate community and, should it be necessary, advice on dealing with confrontation.

COMMUNITY LIFE

As a foreigner in India, you're most likely to be living in a city, where the vast majority of accommodation is apartments. There are also bungalows, but they're prohibitively expensive. This also applies to the flood of villagers moving to the cities in search of work, although to them it doesn't come as a shock, as even in the country Indians have always lived three or four to a room, with 10 to 15 people under one roof. Indians not only prefer living huddled together in groups but even travel that way, so strong is their sense of community.

Blocks tend to have at least six apartments per floor and many are high-rise and built around a central patio overlooked by kitchen windows. Front windows invariably have a balcony, on which residents hang their washing. Thin walls and ceilings provide little in the way of soundproofing – vociferous conversations, altercations between neighbours, bawling children, blaring radios and televisions, and food processors that seem to run from early morning to late evening – all can be heard clearly by neighbours above, below and alongside. Children playing in the corridors, doorbells ringing and lift doors opening and closing, all add to the cacophony. Winters are a little quieter as people go to bed earlier than in summer.

Family Values

Indian society is family-centred, which means that social etiquette is usually based on family precepts, which include the following:

● A young person should touch the feet of his elders every time they meet.

● You should never raise your voice or be rude to your elders, but respect them and address them as *aap* (see **Chapter 5**).

● You should always take the advice of elders when faced with an important decision.

● Men should respect women.

● You should always speak the truth and avoid violent behaviour.

● You should maintain strong bonds with your relatives.

● You should be hospitable to everyone who comes to your home, irrespective of his caste, creed, financial position or status.

Atithi Devo Bhavah is an Indian Tourist Board slogan meaning 'our guest is God'. Statues of Hindu gods (there are thousands of Hindu gods) are bathed, revered and then offered milk and food including the choicest fruit and sweets. You should do likewise for your guests.

● You should remember and bow to God first thing in the morning.

● You should practise yoga and meditation.

Sometimes values vary from family to family. For instance, in some houses girls aren't allowed to wear skirts after they reach a certain age.

Neighbours

Although your neighbours will be curious and want to know everything about you the minute you move in, their first approach (which will be immediate) is prompted more by their sense of hospitality than curiosity. The family next door will introduce themselves to you, carrying with them a tray laden with cups of piping hot tea, biscuits and sweets. It's the Indian way of welcoming a new neighbour. If the block has a concierge (*chowkidar*), he will give you information about your neighbours without your even asking for it – and will be the first to give them an appraisal of you.

As soon as you move in, you should introduce yourself to your other neighbours. As for other inhabitants of your block, encounters in the lift will turn from formal *namaskars* (see

Chapter 5) to small talk in a matter of days. Using the communal facilities and shopping in local shops will expedite the process of integration. If you're a woman, other women in the block will usually offer to accompany you to the shops, which will give you the chance to practise your Hindi – and them their English.

> In India, the terms 'community' and 'communal' are normally used in the context of religious groups and 'society' is the term used to describe a group of people living together in a group or block.

Social Regulations

Societies (communities) draw up rules and regulations governing shared areas, e.g. patios, gardens, swimming pools, gyms, playgrounds, entrance halls, parking spaces, maintenance and security compounds, and private areas visible from outside, such as balconies and facades. When you move into your flat, obtain a copy of the society rules and regulations, and read them carefully.

Society rules are generally of the 'don't do this, don't touch that' kind, i.e. protecting the interests of the estate owners rather than those of the tenants/occupants – and usually cover the following topics:

- **Pets** – generally permitted, but not always;

- **Rubbish disposal** – where, when and how;

- **Safety** – with regard to the use of lifts, electrical installations, swimming pools and other recreational facilities;

- **Security** – the 'powers' as well as the duties of watchmen, e.g. if you buy a refrigerator, the watchman may have the authority to prevent the delivery men from using the lift to take the fridge up to your flat – they may have to carry it up the stairs!

Rules will also specify how maintenance costs are to be shared among tenants and the fines to be paid if rules are broken or property is damaged. If you wish to make a change to the exterior of your property, you'll need to file an application, requesting permission from the society.

Usually, the more upmarket the block, the more numerous the rules and regulations, most of which are self-imposed restrictions rather than national or local laws. Rules and regulations are ratified by majority vote at society meetings and therefore, even if you don't agree with some of them, you're obliged to follow them at least until the next meeting.

Generally, it's better to conform than to confront. Not only is it unpleasant having to live on bad terms with neighbours, but you may need to turn to them for help sooner than you think.

SEXUAL ATTITUDES

The seeming contradictions of Indian attitudes towards sex are best explained by India's history, the country having played an important role in the history of sex, from writing the first literature that treated sexual intercourse as a science, to (in modern times) being the origin of the philosophical focus of many new-age groups' attitudes to 'free' sex.

It may come as a surprise that in the land of the Kama Sutra and the explicitly erotic sculptures that fill the walls of temples such as Khajuraho and Konark in central and eastern India, that Indians are conservative and orthodox to the point of being prudish. Indians are traditional with clearly defined roles for men and women, which is particularly true in small towns and rural areas.

There's strict state control of sexual and violent content in the media – print, cinema and television. For example, nudity and even kissing still aren't permitted in Indian films. Any infringement of codes of decency by television channels results in them being banned.

Similarly, in 'real life', demonstrations of affection in public, even towards your own spouse, can get you into trouble, and public displays of affection and sex are largely taboo. The public are under the watchful eye of the 'moral police', a term coined by the media for police and other law enforcement officers who take it upon themselves to 'protect' Indian culture from harmful 'Western influences'; they don't have the power to issue court summonses, but can arrest people and file a case in court.

> A passionate public embrace and kiss bestowed on Bollywood star Shilpa Shetty (former winner of Celebrity Big Brother on British TV) by American actor Richard Gere at an anti-AIDS rally in Delhi in April 2007, led to official court complaints, demonstrations in Mumbai and the setting fire of effigies of the Hollywood star, while protesters in other cities shouted "death to Shilpa Shetty".

India has a significant HIV/AIDS problem, which is partly to do with its immense population, but also a product of poor sexual health education, stigmatisation and general ignorance. The first case of HIV in India was reported in 1986, since when around 2.5mn people have been infected, many of whom have no medical care and are often unaware that they are carrying the disease and infecting others.

Modern Attitudes

With increased exposure to world culture due to globalisation and the proliferation of progressive ideas thanks to better education, more travel and greater wealth, India is ironically beginning to go through a Western-style sexual revolution. However, it's still a long way from consuming the country, although attitudes to premarital sex and extramarital sex are slowly changing, particularly in the south. Most young people are against premarital sex but still indulge in it, although the vast majority believe that extramarital sex for either the man or woman is taboo. In rural areas, attitudes are far more traditional and unmarried Western couples need to be discreet and tactful about their relationship.

According to a survey by Outlook magazine (💻 www.outlookindia.com) in 2008, Indians today are having less sex, despite a far more open and liberal sexual environment. The frequency has reduced in the last decade or so and so has the time spent on foreplay; all work and no (fore)play, it would seem, has made Jack a duller boy. More couples in full-time jobs, longer working hours, battling traffic jams on the daily commute, worrying about pink slips, home loans and terrorism

– the typical pressures of life in the city today have no doubt taken their toll on the romantic life of urban couples. However, the outlook isn't entirely gloomy. Couples may be more pressed for time and energy, but they're trying hard to squeeze all the fun they can out of life, and they're more open to experimenting; there's more spontaneous sex, early morning sex and oral sex, and greater adventurousness in trying out new positions.

Men

Indian society is male-dominated and patriarchal, the senior male being the head of the family and defender of its honour. Most males are chauvinistic – and are indulged by their parents. Boys and young men aren't expected to help their mothers with household chores such as cleaning, washing the dishes and cooking, and they preserve this 'privilege' throughout their married life.

When it comes to sexual relationships, for Indian men it's all about 'taking' pleasure and not about giving it, as women are expected to play the passive and subordinate role. (Surveys by condom manufacturers claim that most Indian women don't achieve orgasm – and many fake one.) Women who break out of this traditional role are perceived as being 'loose'.

Despite employment legislation in recent years giving women equal status with men, in reality women are still treated as second-class citizens at work, some organisations paying only lip service to equal opportunities and rights.

Although Indian women may see foreign men as a means of escape from a world bound by tradition into one of equality and freedom, most are willing to pay the price of loss of freedom for prosperity and leisure, as the status of a family is determined by the extent to which it can keep its women in comfort in the confines of the home.

Women

Despite their subordination to men, Indian women occupy a special position in the home and in society.

All important decisions pertaining to the home are taken by the senior woman of a household (usually the wife's mother or mother-in-law), although some decisions may still be made by the patriarch, who may call a meeting or initiate a debate before arriving at a decision. However, as it's considered the woman's role to look after the home, the matriarch's advice and opinions are respected and given considerable weight.

Outside the home, women have always commanded a position of respect and are treated with dignity by Indian men. There have been prominent women throughout Indian history, such Rani Laxmi Bai of Jhansi (a leading figure in the Indian mutiny of 1857), Indira Gandhi (former prime minister) and Pratibha Patil (the current president of India). Women are also making their mark in other fields, such as tennis player Sania Mirza, actress Aishwarya Rai and film director Meera Nair, who are among the many Indian women who have achieved international recognition. Middle-class women are increasingly breaking down the barriers to sexual equality and today there are many noteworthy women in Indian politics and business, while women professionals are commonplace.

With increasing financial freedom and independence, Indian women have become more aware of their needs and desires in the sexual arena, although they need to be discreet. Foreign women in general, and scantily clad Western women in particular, are perceived by Indian men as having dubious morals. The portrayal of women as 'sex objects' in Hollywood movies and in the pornographic videos and DVDs that have swamped the country (despite strict censorship laws) in recent decades has had a detrimental effect on the morals of some Indian men. As a result, foreign women often find themselves the victims of 'eve teasing' – harassment, lewd remarks, insolent looks and even molestation in public places.

> British Actress Liz Hurley married Indian businessman Arun Nayar in a traditional Indian wedding in Jodhpur in March 2007.

A foreign woman in a relationship with an Indian man will find herself in the unenviable position of being a daughter-in-law in a household that's ruled by the oldest female – the mother-in-law, who will treat her new daughter-in-law in the same way that she herself was treated by her mother-in-law – although probably even worse for being a 'loose' Westerner.

Abuse of Women

While sexual harassment in the workplace isn't common in India, violence at home is. Machismo is an intrinsic part of Indian society and, according to UN figures, over two-thirds of married women between 15 and 50 are victims of beating, rape or forced sex. A dowry-related death (see Taboos below) occurs every hundred minutes. The dowry system, which although illegal still persists, means that many couples want a male rather than a female child, which in turn leads to female foeticide. Despite a law declaring prenatal sex determination illegal, some unscrupulous doctors not only conduct the tests clandestinely, but may even report a male foetus as female, to earn from the abortion that follows.

Prostitution is common among the poor of India and – as in many countries – sex workers are exploited and exposed to rampant infection, including HIV. It has also created a huge people-trafficking industry, with many poor young women being trafficked from villages and sold into sex slavery.

Homosexuality

Although homosexuality is a criminal offence under Section 377 of the Indian Penal Code, attracting punishment of up to ten years' imprisonment, there hasn't been a single conviction in the past 20 years. In recent years, due both to increasingly liberal attitudes and the need to control HIV/AIDS, several non-governmental organisations (NGOs) and leading citizens have demanded the decriminalisation of homosexuality (though as yet no political party has included gay rights in its party manifesto).

Though frowned upon by Indian society – in which people are expected to procreate – homosexuals aren't persecuted, and the Hindu religion is silent on the subject. If gay clubs, discotheques and other nocturnal haunts are occasionally 'raided' by the police, it's to extract bribes from 'offenders', not to arrest them.

Marriage

Around 95 per cent of Indian marriages are arranged by the parents. In some cases the bride- and groom-to-be have the right of veto after seeing a photograph of the intended partner, and in progressive families the decision may only be made after the couple have met. Today, families and individuals are increasingly turning to the internet to find marriage partners, which has led to a proliferation of matrimonial 'detective agencies' to check the background of prospective spouses.

In the past, most weddings consisted only of Hindu rites performed by a priest in a temple. However, the legal registration of a marriage isn't carried out during the religious ceremony but afterwards – except in the case of Catholics in Goa, Daman and Diu, which still follow Portuguese law, whereby a civil marriage must take place before a church ceremony.

Nevertheless, many people still don't register their marriages, and those in remote villages are often unaware of the legal requirement to do so.

The legal age for marriage is 18 for women and 21 for men, although marriages often take place between younger partners, as many people in rural India don't know their date of birth (despite the fact that registration of births is mandatory) and no documentation is required for a Hindu marriage.

MEETING PEOPLE

Making the transition from acquaintance to friend isn't only easy but is also spontaneous with Indians, whose predisposition to hospitality bridges any cultural gaps. Besides, having foreigners among one's friends is seen as prestigious.

Below are some of the many ways of meeting Indians (and expatriates) as a first step towards making friends:

- **At work:** Meeting people isn't a problem if you're an employee, and your colleagues will usually take the initiative and ask you to join them for lunch or coffee. Pub culture is catching on in the major cities, particularly those with large expatriate populations. Partying with office colleagues is encouraged by corporate India, as it's believed that this improves relationships at work. In the cities, companies organise *Diwali*, Christmas and New Year's Eve parties, and some celebrate their own 'Annual Day' in a big way. Indians like to invite new office colleagues to their homes and introduce them to their family.

- **At play:** Find out about clubs and associations in your area (local newspapers, town halls and telephone directories are good sources of information) and join one or two as soon as possible. If you play a sport, consider joining a local club – cricket and tennis are the most popular; these are ideal for meeting people while staying fit. The gym is another good place to meet people, as more and more Indians are becoming fitness conscious.

> Despite the fact that most Indian marriages are arranged, internet dating and matchmaking websites are popular; but the best opportunity for the sexes to meet is at *Dandya Ras* (devotional community dance) venues during the annual nine-day *Navratri* festival in October (see Festivals & Fairs in Chapter 8).

- **Expatriate networks:** Most large cities – especially Bangalore, Delhi, Hyderabad and Mumbai, which have large expatriate populations – have expat networks whose activities encompass a range of pastimes and social events. Look in the local expat press (see **Appendix B**) for details of organisations or contact your local embassy or consulate.

- **Language institutes:** These are attended not only by expats wanting to learn Hindi but also by Indians learning a foreign language. Institutes regularly organise social events for students and teachers. If there are no institutes in your area, you can set up a language exchange programme yourself, which will inevitably lead to friendships in a country where teachers are revered.

- **School or childcare facilities:** If you have children at school, you have a ready-made source of acquaintances and friends. Arriving a few minutes early to drop and/or collect your children will give you time to get acquainted with other parents. Keep abreast of school activities by checking the notice board at least once a week. Most schools have a parent–teacher association (PTA), which has regular meetings and organises social events and activities.

- **Social work:** Many foreigners volunteer to do social service, such as working in orphanages or shelters or teaching in classes for street children. Doing so will not only gain you friends but also respect within the local community.

Where & When to Meet

Most Indians like to meet at home, and you'll be perceived as doing your

INVITATIONS
Receiving Invitations

Indians are family oriented and their home is the first place they like to take their friends. Even chance acquaintances will give you an 'open' invitation (any date, any time, for any meal) to their home, which foreigners can find overwhelming.

A lunch invitation will normally be for around 1pm, dinner around 9pm, but arriving 15 to 30 minutes late is not only excusable but also often appreciated by the host. Arriving before the appointed time isn't.

Invitations automatically extend not only to your partner or spouse and children, but even to a visiting relative, although it's polite to let your hosts know who you'll be bringing with you.

Dress Code

Indians are conservative in their dress. Age, social status and the occasion largely dictate what you wear. The young, for example, tend to sport Western casuals, T-shirts, jeans and trainers. Mature women wear *saris* or the traditional *salwar-kameez-duppatta* (baggy trousers, knee-length tunic and scarf) ensemble. Men wear trousers with shirts tucked in or a safari suit. Jackets and ties are reserved for weddings in winter. Patent shoes are standard wear for men and sandals for women in Indian attire.

In India as elsewhere, it's always best to err on the side of formality. If you're a woman, modesty is expected of you. Western women may wear knee-length skirts in large cities or long trousers but plunging necklines and strapless tops should be av•ided. Although adopting the customs of the host country is

hosts an honour by going to their home. Early evening is the best time to visit. Although you'll never be turned away even if you arrive unannounced, it's polite to telephone before dropping in. Note, however, that if you've arranged a time, it's normal (and preferred) to arrive between a quarter and half an hour late.

Paying the Bill

Indians always treat foreigners as guests and more often than not will pay for drinks in a pub or bar if you meet there. If you reciprocate, however, they will accept. Once you become part of a group at work, the custom is to take turns to pay for a round, as in the UK or US. If you're given a pay rise or a promotion or have anything else to celebrate, such as your birthday, you're expected to pay for the drinks.

generally recommended, adopting the Indian dress may not always be a good idea in urban India as many Indians feel that Western women don't look their best in Indian clothes; you may even be the target of some ridicule. In fact, good quality Western dress commands respect in India.

A plain sari can be a good compromise: Italian Sonia Gandhi wears one and is the top role model for Indian women. In contrast, in more rural parts of the country, adopting the local style, particularly salwar kameez, will be greeted with enthusiasm and appreciation by your neighbours and colleagues.

Gifts

It isn't traditional to take a gift when visiting an Indian family, even if you've been invited to dinner, but the continental European trend of offering flowers and imported delicacies (such as chocolate for the children, cosmetics

for the lady of the house and good Scotch whisky for the man) is catching on fast in urban areas. In semi-urban and rural areas taking alcohol as a gift is likely to cause offence. Frangipanis (small white, fragrant flowers) are a no-no as they're strictly for funerals. Black or white wrapping paper is also to be avoided; red or green are lucky colours for Indians. Don't give pigskin or lizard-skin items or alcohol to Muslims or anything made from cowhide to Hindus.

The Meal

Drinks and nibbles are normally offered on arrival. Men usually start with beer, although good Scotch whisky is popular; women usually opt for a soft drink.

> **No country in the world is as strongly associated with vegetarianism as India, where the majority of the population rarely or never eats meat – 20 per cent by choice, the rest through economic necessity. Yet recent surveys show a marked increase in the consumption of meat, chicken being the favourite.**

Food may be served Western style in courses, starting with soup, followed by the main course, and ending with dessert. Portions are always generous and your hosts will insist on serving you extra – it's considered rude to decline, as this indicates that you don't like the food. The main course will incorporate rice, dhal (lentil stew), vegetables, meat (usually chicken or mutton, never pork if your host is Muslim or beef if Hindu), fish, yogurt, salads and a variety of pickles and chutneys. Dessert is either fruit in custard, *kulfi* (Indian ice cream) or *kheer* (rice pudding). Usually the food is laid out buffet style.

A traditional Indian dinner comprises some of the same food, but served in a different way. It's usually a *thali* meal, which is almost always vegetarian. A *thali* is a large, round, rimmed stainless steel plate on which rice is piled in the centre and six stainless steel bowls arranged around it. The bowls hold a vegetable in gravy, a vegetable without gravy, a raw vegetable salad, a *dhal* (lentil stew), a yogurt and a sweet. Unleavened bread (*chapati*) is served piping hot as the need arises. You should break small pieces with the fingers of your right hand and fold them around the vegetables or yoghurt. Most Indians eat with their fingers. You may ask for cutlery, but if you don't specify a fork, a spoon will be provided. If laid out, cutlery will consist only of a spoon for eating rice.

At the table, don't help yourself unless it's a buffet. Stay seated while the meal and drinks are served, usually by the hostess or servants. (Most middle- and upper-class families have at least one servant.)

Alcohol is rarely served with the meal, although wine consumption is on the increase in India. Meals are normally accompanied by *lassi* (a yogurt drink) and water. At the end of the meal, a tray of spices and the quintessential sugar-coated fennel seeds and crystallised candy (called 'rock sugar') is served to freshen the mouth. Men sometimes smoke after a meal, but never during one.

> Indians (both Hindus and Muslims) always wash their hands before and after meals at a washbasin provided for this purpose in the dining room itself. You should use only your right hand for taking and eating food. The left hand should never be used and is usually left on the lap rather than on the table.

Making Invitations

When you invite Indians to your home for a meal (lunch around 1pm and dinner around 9pm), you must do so personally over the telephone even if a printed invitation has been sent. Invitations should be sent early, but a reminder call should be made a few days before the date. Be prepared for three things to happen: some invitees who have confirmed they would be attending won't turn up; most people will arrive between 15 and 30 minutes late; and some guests will bring along their own guests.

What to Serve

Serve drinks and nibbles (cashew nuts are a favourite) when guests arrive. Chivas Regal whisky and Kingfisher beer are the most popular drinks for men (but exercise caution and try to ascertain if your guests drink alcohol before the event). Keep a good stock of soft drinks in the refrigerator for the women and children. A three-course meal is normal (see The Meal above). Make sure you prepare more than enough, to allow for unexpected guests and the fact that Indians often ask for second helpings. To run out of food for guests is to 'lose face'.

Indians are used to rich, spicy food and find most European food bland. If you aren't experienced in this sort of cuisine, it's best to engage a local caterer. Remember that Indians eat rice as well as bread for lunch as well as dinner. As the majority of Indians are vegetarian, make sure that there are a good number of vegetarian dishes and preferably label the food at a buffet table – to indicate not only which are the vegetarian and non-vegetarian dishes, but also what meat is contained in the latter.

By all means offer wine with the meal, but also serve *lassi* and water. Most Indians don't drink tea or coffee after a meal, although they drink tea at all other times. South Indians, however, like strong, sweet coffee with milk.

> **Tea and coffee are served with milk and sugar already added.**

RESPECTING PRIVACY

There's no privacy in Indian life and no word for it in Indian languages.

Bedrooms are shared, inquisitive neighbours and relatives regularly 'pop in', and door-to-door vendors are a part of daily life. The Western concept of 'needing one's own space' isn't understood. When an Indian invites you to his home, the invitation isn't restricted to the sitting or dining room; you're given access to the entire house – except, perhaps, the head of the family's bedroom.

Similarly, the moment a person strikes up a conversation with you, be prepared for an interview-cum-interrogation. You'll be asked questions about your country, home town, age, qualifications, marital status, religion, diet, even your salary – and ultimately your opinion about India. And Indians will volunteer as much information about themselves.

TABOOS

Indians are relaxed and understanding when it comes to foreigners' *faux pas*, but an awareness of what is and isn't acceptable behaviour will help you avoid making them. Social taboos include the following:

- not taking your shoes off at the front door, unless your host tells you it isn't necessary or the host and his family themselves are wearing shoes. If you see a collection of shoes and sandals just outside the door, take yours off also.

- smoking near a Sikh place of worship (gurdwara);

- eating meat or fish (referred to as 'non veg') in the grounds of a Hindu temple;

- serving beef to a Hindu or pork to a Muslim;

- if you're male, touching a woman. Don't proffer your hand to a woman but if she proffers hers (very rare), do reciprocate.

Conversation

Ideal topics for conversation are hobbies and interests (particularly art and the cinema), family and children, especially the academic progress of the latter. When men are left to themselves, they usually talk shop and women discuss shopping and recipes. In general, politics and religion are best avoided and the following topics should never be discussed.

The Dowry System

Although illegal, the dowry system – whereby the bride's parents 'provide for' their daughter – persists. A dowry can include a large sum of money (depending on the groom's social standing and education), besides gold jewellery, a car or a motorcycle, household appliances, furniture and sometimes an apartment or a bungalow. Demands from the groom or his parents often continue even after the marriage. Even when a dowry isn't demanded,

the bride's parents often feel that their prestige is at stake if they don't provide for their daughter.

The dowry system can lead not only to female foeticide (see above) but also to bride killing or suicide, sometimes referred to as 'dowry-related death'. This may result from the bride's parents being unable to meet the continued demands of the bridegroom's family after the marriage, or from the bride's failure to inform her parents of the demands until it's too late. In most of the former cases, young brides are killed by their in-laws, usually with the connivance of the husband, so that their son can find a more 'suitable' partner.

Kerosene is a fuel commonly used in Indian kitchens and is commonly used to disguise a murder as an accidental death by dousing the bride with it and setting her on fire – hence the term 'kitchen death'. In some cases the bride sets herself on fire, unable to bear the torture inflicted by her parents or in-laws.

> **King Charles II of England received the 'estate' of Bombay as a dowry when he married Princess Catherine de Braganza of Portugal in 1661.**

Sati

The Hindu attitude towards a widow is that she's a bringer of bad luck and therefore shouldn't be allowed near young and newly married couples or to attend auspicious occasions. Besides crushing her glass bangles and wiping off the *bindi* on her forehead (originally a sign that a woman was married) on the death of her husband, many women shave their heads.

Some widows go to Vrindavan (one of the seven sacred cities of the Hindus, in Uttar Pradesh in northern India) and live there in utter poverty for the rest of their lives, while a few choose *sati*, which reverses their status from that of castaway to that of goddess. Outlawed in the 19th century, *sati* (or *suttee*), the self-immolation of a woman on her husband's funeral pyre (as described by Jules Verne in *Around the World in 80 Days*), is still practised in remote areas of the country.

Religion

Religion is a personal issue and is best left that way. Whether you're an orthodox Hindu, a staunch Muslim, a devout Christian or a non-believer, religion isn't generally a suitable topic for discussion even among believers of the same faith. In India, this is particularly true because of the diversity of its religions. Even a seemingly casual conversation can erupt into an argument and foster serious animosity.

Although India is officially a secular state, over 80 per cent of the population practise Hinduism and conversion to other religions is regarded by some as 'un-Indian'.

Politics

Like religious beliefs, political leanings and opinions are best not aired in social circles. Indians are touchy about their political preferences, which isn't surprising as religion is at the core of such preferences. Even when your Indian friends are discussing controversial political issues, it's advisable to keep out of it by merely being a listener, and

when asked for an opinion, make a non-committal comment, such as "I don't know much about Indian politics."

India & Indian Customs

Indians are proud of their country and its heritage and will not take kindly to criticism from foreigners – particularly Westerners, whom they regard as imperialists. Always avoid negative comments about India and Indian customs in the presence of Indians even if they themselves are engaged in such a conversation. It's best to keep these thoughts and observations to yourself or share them only with other expats.

Dress

Upper-middle-class Indians are fashion-conscious and have huge wardrobes of expensive clothes. They particularly like to sport international labels. At home, many wear casual clothes (such as the *kurta*-pyjama – a loose, long-sleeved shirt with two or three buttons) or 'working' clothes (a housecoat or tracksuit), but most change before leaving the house.

Bare body parts are frowned upon and women in bikinis are a rare sight even at swimming pools. While Indian women do wear swimsuits at the pool, on the beach they wear casual clothes and venture out into the sea in them. Men don't walk the streets bare-chested even in resort towns and sitting down to a meal in swimwear, even at the poolside, simply isn't done.

> **Hoardings displaying male models in revealing briefs are often objected to and are occasionally pelted with stones.**

EXPATRIATE COMMUNITY

India is a popular destination, not only for tourists and pilgrims but also for business people, who have been arriving in ever-increasing numbers in recent years. The opportunities in the information technology sector in cities such as Bangalore, Hyderabad and Pune have resulted in a concentration of expats there, while expats in Mumbai and particularly Delhi, where there are embassies from over 160 countries, are mostly engaged in consular services.

If you move to an area with a concentration of people from your home country, your shared culture and language are your gateways to effortless socialising. Bangalore, Delhi, Hyderabad and Mumbai have well established expat networks, and fitting into these is temptingly easy – and can be beneficial in 'breaking you in' to your new environment.

However, becoming dependent on expatriate society has its pitfalls. It's a small world, in which everyone knows everything about everyone else and the 'real world' outside is more or less excluded, with the result that you may be perceived as elitist by the locals. Expats tend to come and go, sometimes rudely interrupting friendships.

It's therefore wise to begin 'networking' among Indians as soon as possible, extending your contacts within the community and getting to know your hosts. This will not only open doors to you which would otherwise remain closed, but also add spice to your social life.

The advantages and disadvantages of mixing with the expatriate community are summarised below.

Advantages

- It's a home from home – like pressing the 'Restart' button on your computer.

- It lets you unwind and speak your own language.

- It's a platform for venting your views and opinions of your host country without reservations.

- There are expats who love the culture they've embraced – they're always fun to talk to.

Disadvantages

- Spending most of your time with expats could mean that you aren't sure of your move.

- Time spent with other expats could be put to cultivating better relationships with locals.

- Some expatriate groups are nothing but 'grouse mills', contributing only to making newcomers negative about India.

● You may find yourself socialising with people you wouldn't mix with in your own country (although not necessarily a bad thing).

> The fast growing and challenging Indian market is quickly becoming a training ground for ambitious managers in multinational companies. Most expatriate managers who initially plan to stay in India for a couple of years end up staying longer for the rich experience.

CONFRONTATION

Indians, in India, are known for their uncouth, almost hostile behaviour among themselves and are perpetually scowling. While the reverse is generally true when they interact with foreigners, especially Westerners, whom they go out of their way to please, disagreements can and do happen – particularly in the workplace. Another possible cause of confrontation is an argument between your children and those of Indians, when the latter join in the vocal duel, in defence of their children.

Such incidents are rare and aren't a cause for concern, as Indians like to come to a compromise whenever there's a problem – and the process only strengthens a friendship.

DEALING WITH OFFICIALS

Given the hierarchical nature of Indian society and the legacy of the 'Permit Raj' (also known as the 'Licence Raj' and referring to the tightly controlled state allocation of industrial and commercial permits that operated from 1947, when India became independent, and 1990, when the government adopted liberalisation policies), encounters with officials, e.g. civil servants, the police and notaries, cannot be avoided. Officials in India consider themselves superior to the average Indian, the main historical reason for this being the years of subjugation to British rule: the new administrators consider themselves to be the new rulers!

The following are the golden rules for dealing with Indian officials:

● Learn some Hindi, which will give you greater confidence in your dealings if nothing else.

● Speak in English, which will give you the upper hand.

● Dress conservatively, which will earn you respect.

● Don't lose your temper even if you're made to wait for hours in a government office – it's standard practice and you aren't being victimised.

● Lower ranking officials pretend to be busy and seldom look up even when you stand by their desks – interrupt their reveries with a polite 'Excuse me.'

● Officials seldom smile. Instead, they maintain a poker face because it makes them feel important. Mimic them – you'll be perceived as important too.

● Tips and bribes are words in your dictionary, not theirs – such payments are their due.

Police

The Indian police have earned themselves a poor reputation not only in India but also internationally, thanks to a high number of custodial deaths and 'fake encounters' (the term used by the media for set-ups by rival criminal gangs, whereby the victim is shot dead 'in self-defence'), not to mention rampant corruption.

> If you're stopped by the police for any reason – usually for checking your driving licence – be polite and present the requested documents. If you think you've been stopped or fined illegally, make a formal complaint at a police station afterwards; arguing with a policeman will only make things worse for you.

Civil Servants

You will need the services of Indian civil servants as soon as you set foot on Indian soil. All essential permits and permissions such as your residence (and work) permit, driving licence, etc., are issued by them – after you've completed the requisite forms and complied with the myriad requirements. Your interaction with them will therefore be frequent and prolonged. In your dealings with civil servants you should always be as polite and calm as possible. Thanking them for their help will not always suffice – tips (in cash) are always expected.

Most middle level civil servants speak English, and those who don't will have colleagues who act as self-appointed interpreters. However, always speak slowly and carefully and be prepared to repeat things several times. Remember that your 'version'

of English is as foreign to Indians as Indian English is to you.

Teachers

Few teachers in government-run schools, especially in rural areas, arrive early or leave late, and all school business, with the exception of staff meetings, takes place within school hours. Therefore, don't expect a teacher to stay behind after school to see you or help your child with his work – some teachers will do so if asked, but most will see parents and children only during school hours. If you wish to see the head teacher, phone for an appointment.

All classes are conducted in Hindi or the regional language and all correspondence from schools will be in Hindi or the regional language. Few state school teachers speak English, although most private school teachers do.

Hindi and English are used everywhere

5.
THE LANGUAGE BARRIER

Many Indians are multi-lingual and, given that the country has 15 official languages, 300 minor languages and 874 regional dialects, multi-lingualism is considered natural. Hindi is the national language and the primary tongue of 30 per cent of the people. However, whereas most of the people in the northern states of India speak Hindi, most of those in the southern states don't understand the language and rely on English to communicate with their countrymen in the north. Similarly, English functions as a neutral link-language among Indians from different regions of the country.

> 'The most important thing in communication is to hear what isn't being said.'
>
> Peter F. Drucker (Austrian writer)

In terms of the number of English speakers and the quantity of books published in English, India ranks third in the world after the US and the UK. English enjoys associate official status with Hindi and is the language of political and commercial communication; it can therefore be said to be the lingua franca of India, and it's possible to travel as well as live in India speaking only English.

However, Indian English has a unique identity, distinct from British English, American English and other recognised varieties of the language, so that even native English-speakers can have difficulty understanding Indians and making themselves understood by them.

INDIAN ENGLISH

The fact that English is spoken in India is a legacy of the British, but though closer to British English than American English, Indian English is more formal than British English – at least in its written form. To foreigners (particularly English-speakers), written Indian English seems archaic or literary – ornate, flowery and excessively polite. Terms such as 'Respected Sir', 'I beg to submit', and 'kindly do the needful' are used in everyday correspondence.

In contrast, Indians can appear rude in their use of spoken English. The words 'please' and 'thank you' are notably absent from Indian conversation, and 'excuse me' is commonly used to mean 'may I take your place', e.g. in a queue – you're expected to oblige, but don't expect a 'thank you'!

Indian English is also highly 'coloured' with what might seem to other English-speakers to be misuses. 'I like it very much' becomes 'I am liking it very much'; 'It was I who helped' becomes 'I only helped'. Decisions in India aren't made but 'taken', and soup isn't eaten but 'drunk'; medicine is 'eaten' and food 'taken'.

Such usages aren't confined to speech. *The Times of India*, for example, recently ran the following headline: "Concerns of global liquidity crunch sent the stocks world over on a tailspin."

Differences in the meaning of common words can make Indian English confusing to other English-speakers. For example, a 'homely girl' means a girl who is good at running a home and not merely plain-looking.

Idioms and figures of speech may also be 'distorted', e.g. 'Don't cry over *split* milk', 'split' being unwittingly used instead of 'spilt' because split is the Indian word for 'curdled'. And while many Britons begin almost every sentence with 'well', Indians tend to start with 'basically' or 'actually'.

Indian English, of course, has a characteristic pronunciation. For example canal is pronounced 'kennel', worker 'wurr-curr' (the Rs heavily accented), immediately 'immijiately' and pronunciation 'pronounciation'.

To further confuse native English speakers, Indian English comes in a variety of styles, flavours, accents and cadences, which are influenced by local languages. For example, the American word pal is pronounced '*paal*' in the north and '*paul*' in the south, egg is pronounced 'yug' in the south, van is 'vaahn' in the west (Gujarat), curds sounds like 'cards' in the east (Bengal) and miracle is pronounced as 'mireckle' in the north.

In Gujarat, initial Hs are generally silent but Hs are added to words that don't have them. So, for example, shoot is pronounced 'suit' and suit 'shoot'. This has given rise to a local joke involving rival clothing manufacturers Gwalior Suitings and Bombay Dyeing:

Q: "Why Bombay dying?"

A: "Because Gwalior shooting!"

> **It's generally accepted that the easiest English accent for foreigners to understand is that used around Mumbai.**

The most popular variety of Indian English is 'Hinglish', a combination of Hindi and English that is virtually a dialect in its own right. As its name suggests, Hinglish is English interspersed with Hindi words – or vice versa, e.g. 'Folks, *khaana* [lunch] is served' and 'Time *kya hua hai*?' ('What is the time?'). Its use is most common in urban and semi-urban parts of northern and central India, but it's now spreading to rural areas via television and Bollywood films.

This sort of linguistic mixture isn't limited to Hindi – English words have even entered the colloquial Portuguese of Daman, and Portuguese words have infiltrated the English spoken in this former Portuguese enclave on the west coast of India.

Consequently, although English is the language an expat will encounter most often, it isn't necessarily the best language in which to communicate with the locals, and learning Hindi and/or one of the major regional languages (depending on where you'll be staying and for how long) will make your stay more enjoyable.

LEARNING HINDI

Nothing is more pleasing to a native than hearing his language from the lips of a foreigner. This holds true for

India. All you need is a vocabulary of 500 words and a grasp of simple grammatical structures to ensure a warm welcome when you arrive, and you needn't fear ridicule. Indians love to hear their language spoken with a 'Western' accent. Add to this that Hindi isn't too difficult to learn – it's a phonetic language, meaning that the way a word is spelled corresponds to the way it's pronounced, and vice versa – and you'll see that the benefits of doing so are considerable.

Hindi is written in the *Devanagari* script (which derives from Sanskrit), from left to right and has no capital letters. The alphabet has seven vowels, 33 consonants and three conjunct consonants (combinations or two consonants). However, notices are often written in the Hindi script but with messages in English!

Why Hindi is Essential

- Locals will appreciate your effort and this will help you integrate.

- You'll have a deeper understanding of Indian culture.

- It will give you access to lower prices when shopping.

- It will get you more accurate information.

- Your circle of Indian friends will widen beyond the younger generation.

- It will give you a new perspective of rural India.

- Joining a language class is an excellent way of gaining contacts.

- You'll be perceived as being streetwise by the locals, decreasing your chances of being 'taken for a ride'.

Know Before You Go

Although you can learn the 'street' version of Hindi (significantly different from the written language, as it's used by illiterate people) in India itself, there's nothing like giving yourself a head start by learning the basic elements of the language before your trip – say six to eight months in advance. This can easily be done by enrolling on an online course, buying an audio course on CD, or finding a local tutor or even an India-based tutor via the internet. This will make learning less stressful and build your confidence in advance of your move.

A list of words and phrases you might need during your first few days in India can be found in **Appendix E**.

Once in India

North India is the best place for learning Hindi as it's the main language. In fact, the northern states, along with neighbouring Uttar Pradesh,

Utaranchal, Bihar and Madhya Pradesh, are collectively known as the 'Hindi belt', where standard Hindi is used in conversation, on radio and TV, and in Bollywood films, newspapers and literature. The Hindi spoken in most other parts of India is a dialect.

When you arrive in India, there are various courses you can enrol on. Many American and European universities, including the School of Oriental and African Studies of the University of London, send their students to the Landour Language School (LLS, Landour Cantt., Mussoorie, Uttaranchal 248179, ☎ 135-263 1487, ✉ lls@nde.vsnl.net. in), which teaches Hindi to embassy staff, non-governmental organisations (NGOs), volunteers and missionaries. Classes at the LLS are normally one-to-one, so students can progress at their own pace. Students can follow LLS textbooks or a programme of their own. The fee for a 50-minute class is Rs150 (US$3).

Bhasha Bharati (19/8 Thatheri Bazaar, Varanasi 221001, ☎ 542-420447, 🖳 www.bhashabharati.com) is an institute running Hindi courses ranging from one-week crash courses to six-month advanced courses. Bhasha Bharati also runs classes in Delhi but these are exclusively for VIPs and foreign diplomats.

The International Language Institute (31-A, Stanley Road, Allahabad 211 002, Uttar Pradesh, ☎ 532-2600 388, ✉ wrldvwbib@yahoo.com) runs a three-year programme (ten months a year) and students are expected to sign on for at least half an academic year and pay in advance (Rs35,000/US$700 for half a year). Classes are for three hours a day.

Private Hindi tutors are available in every town in India. Most private tutors specialising in Hindi for foreigners have websites, and an internet search will bring up a number, but word of mouth is the best way to find a good tutor. Local schools can also be contacted, as many schoolteachers also teach Hindi in their spare time. Fees range from Rs150 to Rs300 (US$3-6) an hour, depending on the tutor's qualifications, skill and popularity and whether he's based in a metropolitan city or a small town.

> **Hindi is the world's second most widely spoken language (after Mandarin Chinese).**

Tips for Learning Hindi

- **Stay motivated** – Take every opportunity to practise, even if it's 'only' small talk with the maid.

- **Persevere** – Practice makes perfect and Indians love to hear foreigners speak Hindi with an 'English' accent.

- **Daily drill** – Practise the four different 'd' sounds and four different 't' sounds.

- **Read out loud to yourself** – Fortunately, Hindi is a phonetic language.

- **Write out sentences** – You must practise writing the script as well as get used to writing on different 'levels'.

- **Watch Bollywood movies** – They can be the ultimate 'university' when it comes to Hindi – and Hinglish for that matter.

- **Learn at least ten words a week** – Start with food and grocery items.

- **Keep sex on your mind** – Objects have a gender too. Assign 'male/female' tags to your furniture.

- **You'll always be rewarded for your progress** – 'Even' the maid will show admiration every time you use a new word.

Children

If you're relocating as a family to India, your children will have to take up Hindi as a second language in an English-medium school. There's hardly any reason for a foreign child to go to a Hindi-medium school, as higher education in India is imparted in English and most middle-class parents send their children to English-medium schools.

For most children aged under ten, learning Hindi – or any other foreign language – isn't difficult. However, children over ten, particularly those who are monolingual, may find it difficult, particularly in the first few months, although Indian children are always friendly towards foreign children and eager to help.

Arranging Hindi classes for your children before you leave isn't essential but is desirable, as it will give them a head start when they arrive in India. There are thousands of India-based tutors teaching via the internet. Once in India, your children will need to attend extra classes to learn Hindi – as do Indian children whose mother tongue isn't Hindi. Finding tutors in India is easy.

> It's helpful for children to be able to say their telephone number and address in Hindi but not essential, as most Indians also understand English numbers and addresses.

OTHER LANGUAGES

India has 14 regional languages (described below): Assamese, Bengali, Gujarati, Kannada, Kashmiri, Malayalam, Marathi, Oriya, Punjabi, Sanskrit, Sindhi, Tamil, Telugu and Urdu, which have equal status with Hindi in the regions where they're spoken. (English has 'associate' status.) Road signs and street and building names are usually in the regional language as well as in Hindi and often in English as well. However, notices and official documents are usually only in the regional language, causing a lot of inconvenience even to Indians who don't know the language of the region.

This is an important consideration if you plan to relocate to an area where there's a strong regional language, e.g. Gujarat, where many officials are reluctant to speak any other language. In such areas, bilingual Indians will often lapse into their regional language in mid-conversation, giving you the feeling of being left out. Although this is never the intention – it's just force of habit – always bear in mind that for most bilingual Indians, their regional language is more highly esteemed than the national language, patriotism notwithstanding.

Assamese

Assamese is the official language of Assam, in the northeast of India, spoken by 13mn people. It's also spoken in parts of Arunachal Pradesh and other bordering states. It has its own script.

Bengali

Bengali, spoken by 189mn people, is the second most widely spoken language in India, after Hindi. It's the native language of West Bengal. If you're planning to relocate to Kolkata (Calcutta), an elementary knowledge of Bengali is essential.

Gujarati

Gujarati is one of the most 'Western' of Indo-Aryan languages and is the native language of Gujarat and of the Gujaratis

living in Mumbai (Bombay) and other parts of the country, totalling around 41mn people. It isn't a very difficult language to learn and is good to know if you intend to live in Gujarat for an extended period, as Gujarat is one of the states where English isn't prevalent.

Kannada

Kannada is the state language of Karnataka, one of the four southern states in India, with 44m people speaking it. It has its own script.

Kashmiri

Around 60,000 people in the valley of Kashmir speak Kashmiri, which is only a spoken language. The number of speakers is decreasing, and the primary official language of the state of Jammu & Kashmir is Urdu.

Malayalam

Although closely related to Tamil, Malayalam is a Dravidian language with a script of its own and is spoken in Kerala, by around 30m people. It's also spoken in Lakshadweep and areas of Tamil Nadu.

Marathi

This 1,500-year-old language spoken by 70m people is the official language of Maharashtra. It's also spoken in the neighbouring states of Andhra Pradesh, Goa, Gujarat, Karnataka, Madhya Pradesh and Tamil Nadu. It's extensively spoken in Mumbai (Bombay), the capital city of Maharashtra along with Hindi and Gujarati.

Two European languages (other than English) are spoken by around 85,000 Indians in India:

- Portuguese – spoken by 70,000 people in the former Portuguese enclaves of Goa, Daman and Diu;

- French – spoken by 15,000 people in the former French colony of Pondicherry (now Puducherry).

Oriya

Mainly spoken in Orissa, this language of 28m people is Eastern Indo-Aryan. It strongly resembles Bengali but is written in its own, Oriya, script.

Punjabi

Punjabi is the official language of Punjab. It's also spoken in the neighbouring states of Himachal Pradesh and Kashmir. A total of 23m Indians speak it.

Sanskrit

Sanskrit is the principal 'root' language of India; it's to South and Southeast Asia what Latin and Ancient Greek are to Europe and the Mediterranean. Unlike those languages, however, Sanskrit is still spoken, by around 50,000 people in traditional institutions in India, as well as being widely used in Hindu, Buddhist and Jainist religious rituals.

Sindhi

Sindhi is an Indo-Aryan language with signs of Dravidian influence. It's the language of the Sindh region in Pakistan but is spoken by over 2m Indians of Sindh origin, scattered across all states. Sindhi can be written in *Devanagari* or Arabic script.

Tamil

Tamil is a Dravidian language spoken by around 66m people in southern India. It's more difficult to learn than Hindi to learn because of its nasal 'overtones'. It has two 'i' sounds, three 'r' sounds and five 'n' sounds. Even the script looks indecipherable with its elaborate curves and squiggles. However, English is spoken or understood in most of southern India.

Telugu

Over 100m people speak Telugu, a Dravidian language, in Andhra Pradesh. It's one of the most used languages in Carnatic music, the classical music of South India.

Urdu

Urdu, an Indo-Aryan language, is spoken by around 43m people in India. Although it sounds similar to Hindi, and in fact uses many of the same words, Urdu is written in *Nastaliq* calligraphy style of the Perso-Arabic script, deriving from Persian, while standard Hindi is written in the *Devanagari* script, drawn from Sanskrit.

Education in Bilingual Regions

Most government-run schools in the states teach in the regional language, e.g. in Gujarat all subjects (except Hindi and English) are taught in Gujarati. Most private schools, however, teach in English, with the regional language as an optional second language.

> If your move to a bilingual area is for less than two years, you need only learn some basic phrases in the regional language (as well as in Hindi) to help you fit into local society. If your move is longer term, it's advisable to learn the regional language as well as Hindi.

Accents & Dialects

Like most languages (including Indian English), Hindi is spoken with a number of accents in different parts of the country. Hindi has two main dialects, western and eastern, but these are affected by regional accents so that there are four recognised dialects: Bihari, Bombaiya, Pahari and Rajasthani Hindi. It's generally accepted that the clearest Hindi is spoken around Mumbai.

SLANG & SWEARING

Hindi is more interspersed with English words than slang, which makes it easier for the foreigner to comprehend as well as to learn the language. Although many Indians swear spiritedly, it's best to avoid it completely. All too often, foreigners make terrible *faux pas* by swearing inappropriately or using slang in the wrong context. However, even in Hindi it's fashionable to use English swear words, Bollywood style!

BODY & SIGN LANGUAGE

Besides gesticulations such as the flailing of arms, stamping of feet, shaking of heads and other movements, Indians use vivid facial expressions, sometimes contorted, while recounting an incident and a scowl when listening intently. To a Westerner, this may appear aggressive, but to an Indian it's part and parcel of normal communication.

Gestures

You may come across the following Indian gestures:

- **Palms of both hands together as if praying, fingertips just under chin** – *Namaste*, the Indian greeting gesture (see **Greetings** below);

- **'Rotating' the head from side to side** – a definite 'no'*;*

- **Nodding** – a definite 'yes';

- **Lightly slapping forehead with one hand** – someone has a cheek;

- **Touching the fingertips to another's feet** – a gesture of respect, usually reserved for the elderly.

> A V-sign with the palm folded shut but facing outwards means 'two'. As in many other countries, it's offensive to raise your middle finger.

Personal Space

Most Indians have never had a room of their own, not so much on account of the affordability of accommodation but because Indians love to huddle together, sleeping in the same room as other family members. Indians cannot comprehend the Western preference for privacy, which is equated with loneliness.

Indians tend to move in close to their conversation partners, keep tight up to the person in front of them in a queue and push through crowds without bothering to excuse themselves.

Indians also stare curiously at foreigners and will ask personal questions such as your name, nationality, marital status and even your salary. Indians feel they're only being polite to a lonely stranger – if you feel 'threatened' by such behaviour, discreetly take a step backwards, with a non-committal smile.

FALSE FRIENDS

Some Hindi words sound similar to English words but have a

different meaning, which can lead to misunderstandings and, in a few cases, embarrassment. These words are often known as 'false friends'. The following is a brief guide to the false friends you're most likely to come across in everyday situations, with examples of the correct use of the Hindi words.

- *bath*: rice, e.g. *dakshin bharat mein log jyada bath kha-te hai* (in the south of India, people mostly eat rice)

  bath: *snaan*

- *bait*: to sit, e.g. *aaram se bait jayo* (sit down and relax)

  bait: *gult*

- *bill*: hole, e.g. *saap aap-ne bill mein chala gaya* (the snake went into the hole)

  bill: *raseed*

- *bus*: enough, e.g. *aab bus karo* (now, that's enough!)

  bus: *motor-gaadi*

- *come*: insufficient, e.g. *paisa gee-na to come thaa* (on counting, the money was found to be short)

  come: *aana*

- *cone*: who, e.g. *cone hai?* (who is it?)

  cone: *samnku*

- *cub*: when, e.g. *aap cub tak ayen-ge* (when will you be back?)

  cub: *vanya pashu ka bacha* (literally 'young of a wild animal')

- *day*: to give, e.g. *yai paise bheka-re ko day do* (give this money to the poor)

  day: *din*

- *dine*: witch, e.g. *iss ki harka-te dine jaise hain* (she behaves like a witch)

  dine: *samub bhojan*

- *fake*: to throw, e.g. *kach-de ko kuda daan mein fake dho* (throw the rubbish in the dustbin)

  fake: *nak-li*

- *gum*: sorrows, e.g. *zindagi ka gum* (life's sorrows)

  gum: *gond*

- *hut*: clear off, e.g. *chalo, sub hut jaon* (come on, everybody clear off!)

  hut: *jhopdi*

- *keel*: nail, e.g. *deewar par jo keel hai, oos-pe yeh frame laga do* (hang the frame by the nail on the wall)

  keel: *buddy shutter*

- *key*: of, e.g. *Sanjay key betti* (the daughter of Sanjay or Sanjay's daughter)
  key: *chaabi*

- *late*: to lie down, e.g. *ho bistar pe late gaya* (he lay down on the bed)
  late: *dher*

- *lay*: take, e.g. *iss paise ko lay lo* (take this money)
  lay: *sona*

- *rose*: every day, e.g. *rose hum-me bhagwan ko dhanyawad kah-ne chahiyeh* (we should thank God every day)
  rose: *gulab*

- *soon*: to listen, e.g. *aap soon rahe hai ya nahinh?* (are you listening, or not?)
  soon: *jaldi*

- *teak*: okay, e.g. *sab teak hai* (everything's fine)
  teak: *seesam*

Watch Those Vowels

There are several words in Hindi where a change in a vowel sound can cause red faces, e.g.:

Jaban means 'tongue', but *joban* means 'breast'. (If you're a woman, make sure you don't misunderstand the doctor when he asks you to stick your tongue out!)

Bhajan is a session of devotional hymns, but *bhojan* is a meal. (If you accept an invitation to a *bhajan*, you'll find yourself singing all evening, with no supper in sight!)

Indian English also contains a few false friends. For example, 'gram' are chickpeas (sold at the roadside and in bus and railway stations). Watch out in particular for the letters 'MC', which don't stand for Master of Ceremonies, but for menstrual cycle. And if someone tells you that your post office is open, it means you've forgotten to zip your fly.

FORMS OF ADDRESS

Tu, Tum or Aap?

Some European languages make a clear distinction between the formal or polite and informal or familiar modes of address, e.g. *vous* and *tu* in French and *Sie* and *du* in German. Hindi has three levels of formality, *tu*, *tum* or *aap*, the choice of which to use being determined by the degree of respect due to the person being addressed.

Tu is used for servants or by elders when addressing small children; *tum* is used between friends and relatives; *aap* is for everyone else, particularly the elderly, those of high caste and those in positions of authority.

As a general rule, *aap* should be used whenever you address adults you don't know well, particularly older people, and *tum* should be used for friends and young people. *Tu* is best avoided.

If you relocate to India with children, make sure they practise the *aap* form of address, which they must use in most situations in which they're addressing adults. Note, however, that Indian children often address elders, even those who aren't relatives, as 'uncle' or 'aunty'.

Names & Titles

Indians have different naming systems, although they generally have a single surname or family name. Parsees (the singular is usually spelled parsi) often derive their surname from their occupation or profession, e.g. Doctor or mistry (carpenter).

In some regions, there are conventions for the creation of personal names. In Gujarat, for example, the father's first name becomes the children's second name. For example, the son of Mr Babubhai Naranbhai Desai might be called Mahesh Babubhai Desai and the daughter of Mr Bharat Raju Naik may be Geeta Bharat Desai. However, if Mahesh and Geeta were married, Geeta would not only take her husband's surname but also replace her middle name with his first name, becoming Geeta Maheshbhai Desai.

In the south, two initials precede the personal name, e.g. P V Rao, where P stands for the name of the ancestral village and V for the father's name.

You should address older people by prefixing their surname with *shri* (male) or *srimati* (female); alternatively, you can suffix a man's name with *saab* (male) and address women simply as *memsaab*. If you don't know a person's name, say simply *bhai* (male) or *ben* (female). If you're on familiar terms with someone, address him or her by their first name followed by *ji*, which indicates respect.

If a man has Singh as his middle name, he's an orthodox Sikh, but if Singh is his last name, he isn't. The equivalent for women is Kaur.

GREETINGS

On being introduced, most Indians greet you with a *namaste* ('I recognise the self in you') or *namaskar* ('I pay my respects to you'), whether you're a man or a woman. This is the equivalent of 'hello', 'good morning', 'good evening' and other such Western greetings. It also means 'goodbye'. A namaskar shows greater respect, e.g. to elders. As with names (see above) *ji*, suffixed to either greeting, conveys additional deference, e.g. *namaskarji*. You should respond with the same, although under normal circumstances you'll be expected only to perform a *namaste*.

A *namaste* is executed by bringing the palms together with the fingertips just under chin level in the classic praying posture, followed by a slight nod and the word '*namaste*' itself. For a *namaskar*, begin with the namaste position and then hold it while bending at the hip and finally touching or grazing the feet of the other person with your fingers, saying the word namaskar as you do so. (Practise this one at home!)

If you're a man, kissing a woman – even a peck on the cheek – is taboo. Neither do female acquaintances kiss each other or shake hands with each other. In urban areas, men shake hands with each other but not with women. Male relatives and close friends shake hands and pat each other's backs with the left palms.

With children aged under around 12, the usual form of greeting is just a pat on the cheek. Older boys expect a handshake and girls a *namaste*.

Muslims will greet you with *assalam alaikum* (peace be upon you), to which you should respond *vaalaikum salaam* (and peace be upon you also). Sikhs say *sat sri akal*, to which your response should be the same.

These greetings are usually followed by *kya hal hai?* (how is your health?) to which you may respond *teak taak* (the Indian equivalent of 'fit as a fiddle').
Western greetings such as 'hello' and 'hi' are used informally, and can be said to children or people you know well. Don't kiss anyone in public, in India – even your wife!

TELEPHONE, LETTERS & EMAIL

The use of email is becoming increasingly common in India but the telephone is still the preferred means of communication for the vast majority of people, in both business and private communication.

Telephone

Indians are becoming as addicted to the mobile phone as Westerners. It isn't only the 'upwardly mobile' that must have them – many taxi and rickshaw drivers, fishmongers, maids, hawkers and labourers cannot do without them. But Indian telephone manners will shock you. When you answer the telephone, more often than not the caller will ask, 'Who's speaking?' Rarely do callers identify themselves.

Businesses are an exception. The telephone operator will greet you and say the name of the company, followed by 'How can I help you?'

As a general rule, if speaking Hindi on the phone, use the *aap* form of address unless speaking to children.

Letters

Letters are often used, particularly in businesses, although many are sent by fax rather than post, on account of the slowness and unreliability of the Indian postal service.

Starting

Half of the personal and most of the business letters written in India are in English. Letters to government officials start with 'Sir' (most government officials are men), but other formal letters start with 'Dear Sir', 'Dear Madam' or 'Dear Sir/Madam'. If you know the name of the person you're writing to, the opening should include it, e.g. 'Dear Mr/Ms Doctor'. Informal letters start with

Addresses

Addresses are usually written as follows:

Name of recipient	Mr G S Sauhta
House/Building name and number	Eldora, 2802/A
Landmark, if any	Near Hiranandani Hospital
Street number (if available) & name	24, Hiranandani
Suburb	Powai
Town or City and Postcode	Mumbai – 400 076

'Dear' plus the addressee's name, e.g. 'Dear Sanjay'.

Date

Dates are usually written at the top right of personal and business letters, as well as cheques, and in the British format (Indian computers are preset to this style). On greeting cards, the date is written directly below the signature and is usually preceded by the name of the place where the card is signed, e.g. *Daman, 30/07/2007*.

Signing off

Sign-offs in business letters and job applications are standard and similar to those used in British English, though sometimes with an Indian flavour, e.g. 'Yours respectfully' or 'Yours obediently' when writing to a superior or an elder.

Popular sign-offs are:

- 'Yours sincerely' (in response to a letter from a customer);

- 'Yours faithfully' (used extensively in business letters);

- 'Best regards' (in informal business letters);

- 'With kind regards' (in personal letters to an authority or elder);

- 'See you' or 'Bye' (in casualpersonal letters).

Email

Email is extensively used in personal as well as professional and business communication. While personal and professional emails are usually written in the format of a formal letter with 'Dear Mr/Ms' as the standard greeting, the younger generation tend to use 'Hi'.

However, if you're sending an email to someone you don't know, use formal address and language, and for business communications begin with 'Dear Sir/Madam' and end with 'Yours faithfully'.

Most official organisations and companies have email addresses, but although they usually respond to email enquiries, the telephone is still preferred by most.

6.
THE INDIANS AT WORK

Despite the cultural gulf between them, Indian business culture is a compromise between traditional practices and Western influences, with a tendency towards the latter due to Western-style management education (acquired from prestigious institutes in the West), the English language being the binding force. Nevertheless, although corporate 'orientation' and 'induction' programmes ease and accelerate the adaptation process, foreign employees are likely to face many challenges during their first few weeks in India – as are foreign entrepreneurs when they come face to face with Indian company board members or government officials.

> In a 2007 survey by Pricewaterhouse Coopers, almost 40 per cent of over 5,000 company representatives polled said that they had to pay bribes to obtain licences or secure orders in India.

This chapter provides an insight into the work- and business-related idiosyncrasies of Indians, information on setting up a business in India, and tips regarding business etiquette.

WORK ETHIC

That Indians are hardworking is a known fact. However, the nature of that work may be very different from what you're used to. In India, 'division of labour' is the guiding principle, and once roles have been assigned, Indians won't budge from them. The classic example of this practice is the office assistant calling the peon (general dog's body) to fetch him a folder from a cabinet immediately behind his desk.

The motto 'Do only what you're told to do (by your superior)' is so deeply ingrained that incorrect instructions are never challenged and in a crisis situation there's a total lack of initiative, as everyone is waiting for instructions from 'above', wherever that may be. While this can be frustrating, it's important to remember that many Indian-owned and Indian-run companies are hierarchical and you should avoid openly challenging or questioning your manager in public as this can easily cause offence.

WORKING HOURS

Although the official Indian working week is 40 hours from Monday to Friday, following the universal 'nine-to-five' routine, the working day is generally long, often going beyond ten hours and sometimes even over 12 – mostly due to poor time management. The Factories Act stipulates that no worker is permitted to work more than 48 hours a week and nine hours on any given day, but this rule is often disregarded.

Many businesses, especially software and Business Process Outsourcing (BPO – call centres) sectors, have adapted to the working hours of their clients in Europe and North America with far-reaching consequences on the health, family and social life of their employees due to the time difference.

Some companies allow employees only the second and fourth Saturdays of the month off. Sunday is the only official day off in most of India, but in industrial areas, where the electricity supply is inadequate to power every factory simultaneously, each company has a weekly 'power shutdown' (or 'staggering') day, when no work is done – but employees must make up the time lost during the rest of the week.

Coffee Breaks

Few companies have scheduled coffee breaks, but coffee or tea is served at least twice a day in most companies – and brought to your desk. If you're lucky enough to work for the government, you'll have a peon to bring you tea to order throughout the day.

WORKING WOMEN

Women are flying high in India. During the last 25 years, the government has amended several laws that discriminated against women, and ratified international conventions such as the Convention on the Elimination of Discrimination against Women. A policy for the Empowerment of Women, drafted in 1996 but still awaiting enactment, proposes that women should occupy 118 seats in the Indian parliament.

Globalisation has provided opportunities for the educated middle-class woman in fields earlier perceived as male domains, e.g. flying. More and more women pilots are being inducted into airlines and, according to the National Association of Software and Services Companies (NASSCOM), some 40 per cent of programmers in the information technology (IT) sector are women. In the corporate sector, women managers and entrepreneurs are on the rise, although there are few women at the top. Nevertheless, women constitute a mere 4 per cent of registered workers, while almost 80 per cent of women in regular work are (unregistered) agricultural workers.

Sexual discrimination is prohibited, and a woman doing similar work to a man and employed by the same employer is legally entitled to the same salary and other terms of employment. However, while the law is upheld in the professional and highly skilled sectors, unskilled women, particularly in agriculture and other 'unorganised' fields, are usually paid 35 per cent and sometimes 50 per cent less than men for the same work.

Nevertheless, women are accorded respect in most organisations. Foreign women aren't discriminated against and foreign women in senior positions have no problems with their subordinates as it's the hierarchy that counts – a boss is a boss, whether male or female, Indian or foreign. You should always dress modestly with the least possible exposure of skin, and avoid anything that may be interpreted as flirting or showing interest in male colleagues.

> It's reckoned that almost half of Indian women (over 18) – at least 200mn – are illiterate.

PERMITS & PAPERWORK

The 2008 Global Relocation Trends Survey, conducted by GMAC Global Relocation Services (🖳 www.gmac globalrelocation.com), revealed that India is one of the most challenging locations for foreign workers. Among the obstacles cited were 'administrative formalities during immigration, unclear tax and employment laws, a lack of acceptable services and accommodations, inadequate education facilities, security concerns, timing difficulties and cultural challenges.'

To begin with, foreigners require a work permit to take up any job in India. Under normal circumstances, this doesn't present a particular challenge, but Indian civil servants have a tendency to make their 'customers' go round in circles – largely because they themselves aren't too familiar with the rules. There are two ways to apply for a work permit: either you apply to the Indian Embassy or High Commission in your own country, or the employer who is offering you a job initiates the application process in India.

Whichever route you choose, you'll inevitably become embroiled in Indian administrative paperwork, which comprises a seemingly never-ending series of forms to be completed (usually in triplicate), the attestation of documents, and the submission of photographs and specimen signatures.

Complex money export laws complicate matters for expats. In theory, an expat on the payroll of a foreign company can receive up to 75 per cent of his salary outside of India, but the process entails obtaining the approval of the Reserve Bank of India (RBI) and the Income Tax Department, which require copies of your passport, income tax card, etc. and takes weeks or even months for clearance.

There are qualified and experienced professionals who will (for a fee) do the form filling and running around from office to office on your behalf, but even then your presence will be required at most meetings.

FINDING A JOB

If you have the right qualifications and experience, finding a job is relatively easy in the Indian job market, where demand for skilled, semi-skilled and, of late, even unskilled personnel far exceeds supply. India has fared better than many countries in the global economic downturn and the potential for employment in a skilled occupation remains good.

The first thing to do is post your CV on the top job portals, such as TimesJobs (🖥 www.timesjob.com –150m page views a month) and Naukri (🖥 www.naukri.com – 120m), although this isn't a targeted approach.

Although most large and many medium-size companies use all-in-one Enterprise Resource Planning (ERP) software systems – such as those marketed by BaaN, JD Edwards, Oracle and SAP – to manage their human resource recruitment, networking is still effective in securing a job in India.

Demand in some sectors is so urgent that formal letters inviting candidates for interview are almost defunct, a mobile phone call being common practice. For semi-skilled personnel, 'walk-in' interviews are often conducted in unlikely places such as churches and car parks.

> Most expatriates working in India, other than those working in consulates, are in the IT field, which is concentrated in Bangalore, spreading out to Hyderabad and Pune.

Strategic Links India (🖥 www.strategiclinksindia.org) is a non-governmental organisation (NGO) that helps find employment for the spouses of workers posted to India.

Language

Most business communications are in English – particularly written communications. In fact, a knowledge of English is a big advantage when looking for a job and a prerequisite for any management position. (Even scripts for Hindi films are written in English!) Indian English may not be easy for you to understand, however, as it differs significantly even from British English, on which it's largely based (see **Indian English** in **Chapter 5**).

While speaking Hindi isn't essential, it's desirable, as Indians unconsciously lapse into Hindi as often as they lapse into English. The omnipresent office peons are good people to practise your Hindi on – and they will want to practise their English on you.

Qualifications

Most qualifications – particularly those in medicine and law – acquired in Western countries aren't just accepted but are highly valued in India, especially in the private sector. A university degree is a big advantage when it comes to choosing candidates for an intra-company transfer to India.

Indian consulates can provide information on the recognition and validation of foreign qualifications.

India is becoming the preferred destination for Master of Business Administration (MBA) students from Massachusetts Institute of Technology (MIT) to do their internships, and quite a few return to start their careers with Indian firms.

Discrimination

Under Indian law, discrimination on the basis of caste, creed or sex is prohibited, meaning that theoretically anyone who meets the criteria for a job has an equal chance of being hired. In practice – and despite a recent rule requiring companies to allocate a certain proportion of jobs to minority groups and those of low caste – 'traditional' employers are still sometimes reluctant to take on young married women (for fear they will fall pregnant and take maternity leave) and people from certain communities – and even certain regions – in India. More often than not, traditional family-managed companies have regional preferences for top positions.

If you think a job wasn't awarded to you due to discrimination, you've the right to appeal, but your case won't just be difficult to prove, it will also be time-consuming – time which would be better spent in moving on.

Employment Agencies
Government

The Employment Exchanges Act provides for compulsory notification of vacancies to local employment exchanges by all establishments employing 25 or more people in the private as well as the public sector (excluding agriculture). When a vacancy arises in a government organisation,

registered candidates who are suitably qualified are called for interview. In the case of a vacancy in the private sector, lists of suitable candidates are sent to the company, which chooses those it wishes to interview.

Private

India's recent economic boom means that headhunting and recruiting agencies have proliferated in all cities and large towns, and even in many small towns. There are agencies specialising in certain sectors, such as IT, hospitality, call centre staff or blue-collar personnel. There are also large numbers of web-based job portals, with millions of registered members. Periodically, job fairs are held in the metropolitan cities where candidates can appear for interviews on the spot and, if selected, can walk away with appointment letters. Interviews are held at most universities and institutes of higher learning every year before final exams, when representatives of companies 'camp' with students for a few days in order to recruit promising candidates.

Writing a CV

Most CVs are written in English, Microsoft Word templates being the favoured format. Besides following the conventions of putting your contact details (including email address) at the top and tailoring the contents to the job opening, you should highlight your mobile telephone number, as you may be called for interview on your mobile at short notice.

List your experience in reverse chronological order, and qualifications with the highest first, e.g., postgraduate degree followed by bachelor's degree. Although you may list all your qualifications, make sure that you highlight those that are most relevant to the job for which you're applying.

Include your date of birth, nationality, and a recent passport-size photograph, limiting the CV to no more than two A4 pages (one side only). Unless you're applying via email, enclose photocopies of the relevant certificates.

Selection Process

The job selection process in India usually involves a written test (often followed by psychometric tests) taken at the company premises or online, followed by at least two interviews, particularly if you're applying for employment in a large company. At the first interview, your job-specific skills are evaluated, and at the final interview you negotiate your remuneration package and terms of employment.

For senior positions, the interview process takes the form of a series of long discussions. In the case of blue-collar jobs, tests are conducted on the relevant machines and, for successful applicants, followed by the final interview.

While references from previous employers will be asked for in due course, copies of your academic qualifications are at the top of the list of 'essentials' for your prospective employer.

> If you apply by letter, it's always wise to follow up with a telephone call, as Indian companies almost never acknowledge receipt of CVs, and therefore there's no way of knowing whether yours has reached its destination. If you apply by email, the same rule applies, as Indian companies don't acknowledge such emails.

Salary

Most Indian salaries are well below those in the West – for example, senior financial, marketing and HR executives earn less than a fifth of their US counterparts – although executives in the IT sector are on a par with their Western counterparts.

However, Indian salaries are rising fast. According to Global HR, the average salary increase in 2007-08 was 15 per cent and, despite the global slowdown, Hong Kong-based HR Business Solutions (HRBS) forecast an average 16 per cent pay increase for 2008-09, one of the highest in the world, and the latest Mercer report stated that India will likely see a double-digit increase in salaries until 2011

In any case, expats are often paid more than Indians: airline pilots, for instance, earn at least 10 per cent more, with monthly salaries ranging from Rs450,000 to Rs550,000 (US$9,000-11,000).

The legal minimum wage is between Rs50 and Rs86 (US$1-1.70) per day (**yes, day!**) according to the industry and the location, e.g. it's higher in urban than rural areas. There's also a quaintly named Variable Dearness Allowance (VDA), which is reviewed and if necessary revised by the state governments every six months.

Salary Payments

Salaries are generally paid directly into your bank account at the beginning of the month. You're issued with a computer-generated salary slip – a complex document stating your attendance, details of the various components of your salary, tax deductions and social security deductions (see below). Extra payments such as overtime and incentives are also listed. When you receive your first salary slip, ask someone in HR to explain it to you.

> When an expatriate retires, he can repatriate in full all his assets, including dividends, pension fund, savings and the proceeds of the sale of personal effects, simply by filing an application with the Reserve Bank of India.

CONTRACTS

As in many Western countries, once a worker has signed an employment contract by way of a letter of appointment, it's difficult and time-consuming for an employer to fire him. This means that employers tend to favour temporary or short-term contracts, but even these are heavily biased in favour of the worker.

Employment contracts are highly specific, sometimes running to four or five pages. They contain the terms and conditions of employment as well as a brief job description, hours, pay and leave entitlement. Contracts are binding from the day you start work. Keep a copy of your contract in a safe place in case of any disputes.

Collective Agreements

Employment conditions for most non-supervisory positions are determined by collective agreements negotiated and approved on an annual basis by management and unions. Collective agreements cover working conditions and salary scales.

STARTING OR BUYING A BUSINESS

In recent years, foreign companies have been moving into India in a big way – Microsoft has over 4,000 staff there, and all six of its global divisions are represented in India; Yahoo! has over 1,000 employees in its two divisions; General Motors (GM) is building a technology base with the only research and development (R&D) lab outside the US; and Cisco set up its globalisation centre and is also establishing a centre of excellence. The rules that have enabled these major companies to set up in India have also facilitated small business start-ups, particularly in the construction industry.

Loans

Obtaining a loan from an Indian bank is easy, as there are a number of banks vying for business and they complete all the necessary paperwork for you. Nevertheless, most banks require a guarantor and there are loan sanctioning limits at each level, e.g., branch and regional. The repayment period is between 5 and 15 years and interest rates are competitive.

Grants

Grants are available at national, state, regional, district and local levels. The application process takes a few months, however, therefore it's worth requesting as many grants as you're eligible for without factoring the grant money into your financing.

Premises

Most business premises are leased or rented, as buying a commercial property is an expensive proposition and involves a long and complicated procedure.

Leasing

Buying a lease is the fastest way of acquiring business premises. You make a one-off payment which includes fixtures and fittings, and then pay the property owner an annual rent. Usually there's a clause in a lease agreement permitting the tenant to sublease. When you sell the lease, you must give the landlord first refusal; if he chooses not to take over the lease himself, he'll usually take a commission on its sale of between 10 and 20 per cent (as stated in the lease agreement).

When buying a lease, negotiate the longest possible term – five years is standard, although some government land is leased for up to 99 years. During the term of a lease, your landlord cannot raise the rent unless there's a clause to this effect, in which case an annual percentage is usually stated. However, when a lease is renewed, the landlord is free to increase the rent by any amount.

Renting

By renting, you avoid the cost of purchasing a lease, and tenants with watertight contracts enjoy considerable rights, so it's difficult for a landlord to evict them. On the other hand, rental contracts are usually for 11 months at a time and at the end of the period the rent can be increased – usually by at least 10 per cent.

Working from Home

Under Indian law, you cannot set up certain businesses in your home – there are extensive regulations concerning what you're permitted to do (which vary according to the local council) and, not surprisingly, lots of paperwork to be completed in order to obtain permission. In some cities commercial activity of any kind is prohibited in certain residential areas. If you're considering working from home, visit your council and find out the local regulations.

Self-employment

While being self-employed in India is as financially challenging as in any other country – particularly in the early years – loans are easy to come by and there are no social security payments to be made. On the other hand, the self-employed must save for their retirement and take out insurance against loss of earnings. Income tax (starting at 10 per cent on all earnings above Rs110,000/US$2,200 after deduction of allowed expenses) must be paid annually, although many self-employed people don't declare their actual income in order to evade tax.

Marketing

In India, business thrives on relationships and it's word of mouth that gives a company the edge, as most Indians tend to ask around for recommendations. Contacts are therefore the key to success. Most professionals and businesses spend time networking and nurturing their contacts by telephoning regularly, making courtesy visits, attending industry conferences and dinners, and presenting corporate mementos such as diaries and desk sets on appropriate occasions, such as the New Year or on launching a new product.

BLACK ECONOMY

The black economy (also called the 'parallel' or 'informal' economy in India) is estimated at over US$50bn or 20 per cent of gross domestic product. This is made up of legal transactions on which only a percentage of the income is declared as well as illegal transactions, financial scams and the smuggling of gold (in particular).

Black money is laundered through 'investments' in paintings, property, jewellery, luxury cars, gold and the stock market, and transferred abroad by 'dealers' known as *hawaladar*.

> **Despite the droughts, the floods, the red tape and the corruption, India became a trillion-dollar economy in April 2007, a few weeks after ousting Japan from the no.1 spot in Asia's billionaires list.**

Corruption is an unpleasant fact of life in India, where businessmen regularly pay huge sums of money to politicians and bureaucrats for expediting applications or endorsing files. Transparency International's Global Corruption Report 2007 alleged that bribes amounting to Rs26.3bn (US$526m) are paid every year to court officials, particularly in the lower tiers of the judiciary.

But the black economy operates at all levels, not only at the top – among employers, employees, workers, doctors, lawyers and shopkeepers, who accept payment in cash or invoice for half a job, declaring only part of their income. It's impossible to live and work in India without encountering some aspects of the black economy and without becoming part of it, even if unwittingly. However, it's in your own interest to avoid it as much as possible, as the authorities are clamping down heavily on tax evasion.

BUSINESS ETIQUETTE

In business circles and at the workplace, there are certain standards, customs and conventions that should be followed – small investments that can have large returns!

Appointments

Make appointments at least two days in advance, although longer than a week isn't necessary unless the person you want to meet is away when you make the appointment. However, you need to be prepared to have the appointment postponed at short notice. Appointments are usually made by telephone, and it's a good idea to phone just before you leave your office to make sure the person that you're planning to see is 'in'. In the case of appointments with government officials, it's usual to be kept waiting at least 30 minutes. If you're late, the other party will usually be accommodating.

Business Cards

Indians cannot do without business cards – even after retirement. The first thing they do on meeting new people, whether socially or in the course of business, is to proffer their business card with courtesy and wait expectantly for yours. So make sure you take a few with you every time you go to a meeting or business lunch.

Business cards are elegant, well designed and in English – the *lingua franca* of business in India. A typical Indian business card is a miniature CV with not only the person's name, title and contact details on it but also all his degrees and honorary positions, and a list of the professional associations, trade bodies and clubs he belongs to. This is why most business cards are printed on both sides.

> Have plenty of business cards and hand these out at every opportunity; most businessmen maintain voluminous albums of business cards collected from their associates.

Business Gifts

Business gifts, called 'corporate gifts' in India, are highly popular and are often bribes in disguise. They're usually offered after some business success, e.g. the signing of a contract or agreement, or in advance of such an agreement, in particular to 'entice' government officials. Corporate gifts range from the sophisticated to the ostentatious. Silver or gold coins are common and statuettes of *Ganesha*, the elephant God (a boy with the head of an elephant) the most popular.

Diwali (see **Chapter 8**) is a time when corporate India doles out hampers en masse to business associates and government officials. Corporate gifts are usually wrapped in silver or gold paper. A foreigner may present items from his country, such as a bottle of scotch, perfume or an elegant pen or desk set.

Indians don't open a gift as soon as they receive it. It's customary to thank the giver and keep it aside, unopened.

Business Lunches

Business lunches in India are short, lasting around an hour, typically from 2 to 3pm. Business isn't usually discussed during the meal, which is seen as an opportunity to get to know business associates better for building an all-important personal relationship. Meals are usually vegetarian, although not always, and alcohol is rarely served.

Beef is never ordered in the company of Hindus, nor pork in the company of Muslims. Cutlery is minimal as most Indians aren't adept at using it, preferring to use their fingers instead – hence the hand-washing ritual before and after meals.

Dress

Most Indians dress smartly for work in Western trousers and shirts. In many organisations, especially in corporate and marketing offices, ties are worn and, in winter, jackets. However, the traditionally conservative Indian office dress code is seeing a metamorphosis, as more and more workers don 'business casuals'. Some 40 per cent of workers, both men and women, in IT and media businesses and what is known as the 'business process outsourcing' sector, wear dark jeans and casual shirts, and an increasing number of such companies are allowing 'Friday dressing' (casual) every day of the week. Some progressive companies have introduced a common 'uniform' for all their employees from shop-floor worker to Chief Executive Officer (CEO). Otherwise, top male executives generally stick to their 'power suits', and middle level executives wear dark trousers and powder blue or white shirts, with ties to match.

Women are expected to dress smartly and modestly. Low necklines and high hemlines aren't in keeping with India's conservative, male-dominated workforce.

Meetings

Business in India is based on relationships. Indians seldom do business with someone they've met briefly or know little about. Therefore

first meetings are an opportunity to get to know a business counterpart and are often taken up entirely with a personal 'question-and-answer' session, rather than actual business. Trying to force a business agenda may be perceived as being blunt or, worse, rude. Take the initiative from your meeting partner and don't hesitate to ask about his family – especially his children and their academic pursuits in particular.

Internal meetings are generally seen as an opportunity to discuss or review issues, over endless cups of tea. Few decisions are reached at meetings, as most organisations are pyramidal and decisions are often made at the next level in the structure, based on the recommendations of those participating in the meeting. Not surprisingly, seating is also hierarchical. The boss sits at the head of the table, to his right the next in command and to his left the third in command; others sit in pairs facing each other across the table, with the most junior employees at the foot of the table.

Important meetings are often scheduled for a day that's

astrologically auspicious rather than merely convenient.

> Although Microsoft PowerPoint presentations are common in meetings, Indians tend to accompany them with long-winded explanations.

Agenda

Most meetings are rigid and authoritarian, consisting largely of instructions rather than discussion – and there's little room for camaraderie or levity. You'll usually receive a copy of the official agenda in advance, but although this will probably have been revised a number of times, it will rarely be adhered to.

Language

Corporate communication in India is generally in English, both written and spoken. Meetings are usually in English; even if they aren't, the minutes will be written in English. Indians are comfortable using Western idioms such as 'the ball's in your court' (though not slang) when speaking, although they tend to use archaic English in minutes.

Negotiating

When negotiating a business deal with Indians, bear in mind the following:

- Negotiation, at least in the initial stages, is seldom one-to-one. You'll be negotiating with a group of Indians, who will use the term 'we' rather than 'I' while making a point.

- Indians have respect for age, irrespective of a person's position in the hierarchy.

- Never criticise or patronise an Indian in front of others.

- An Indian may not disagree with you outright, in order not to appear rude.

- Don't expect a decision to be reached at a meeting, as Indians tend to consult with their superiors before making a commitment.

- Be patient at all stages of negotiation as Indians hate being rushed.

- Always obtain written confirmation of an oral agreement.

- In the case of disagreements, Indians tend to compromise in the interest of long-term relations.

India uses the metric system for everything (except TV screen-sizes, which are stated in inches) so you should quote in kilos/metres/litres/centigrade/etc.

Regional Differences

The huge cultural differences between the regions of India have an impact on business practices, as many companies are family owned and run, e.g. the Marwari Group is run by the Marwari family, which is based in the Rajasthan region, and each have their trademark business styles and ethics. They also prefer to recruit people from their own region or community, particularly for senior positions and positions requiring trust.

Timekeeping

Timekeeping and punctuality are concepts that are generally confined to school. When Indian businessmen decide to meet, it's common for them to suffix the time with an -ish, e.g. 'tenish', which can mean any time between 9.45 and 10.15. Rarely do meetings, business conferences, or seminars begin at the appointed time. The time on invitations to business functions is usually followed by the word 'sharp', but it has little noticeable effect.

Nevertheless, Indians repeatedly praise the Western sense of punctuality – so don't disappoint them by arriving late yourself!

EMPLOYING PEOPLE

Indian labour legislation is designed to protect employees from exploitation to the extent that employers have virtually no rights. Nevertheless, employing staff in India is generally not a risky proposition for two reasons: the industrial climate is healthy and the law enforcement agencies are either not particularly vigilant or turn a blind eye when pacified with gifts or outright bribes.

Workers are entitled to a minimum wage, a provident fund, 15 days' paid holiday and seven public holidays, and an annual bonus. As the number of employees grows and the longevity of an establishment increases, so more statutes become applicable.

Contracts

Entering into a permanent contract with an employee is a risky proposition, given that the law makes it difficult to terminate his employment if he isn't found suitable – unless he has committed a heinous crime. The one safeguard is that employees must generally serve six or nine months'

probation, during which time they can be dismissed (or quit) without notice. Outside this period, if a court rules that the dismissal of an employee is unfair, the employer is liable not only to reinstate the employee but must also pay lost wages.

> Oral agreements are valid under Indian law, and if you pay someone for work, you're deemed to have entered into a contractual relationship, even if there's no written contract.

Domestic Staff

Engaging domestic staff, such as housemaids, nannies, gardeners and even chauffeurs, is common in India, where such labour is cheap. It doesn't require a contract, but you're expected to care of their daily needs (e.g. meals, toilet facilities and, in the case of live-in servants, a bed or mattress) as well as pay them. If they fall sick, you're expected to take them to your doctor or to a public health centre.

In case of an accident incurred in the course of their duties, you're liable to

pay compensation in accordance with the Workmen's Compensation Act, and although few Indian employers take out insurance against compensation claims, as a foreigner you're recommended to do so, as you'll be perceived as 'rich' and therefore well worth suing!

Social Security

Social security contributions are minimal in India, as there's no state health insurance scheme. You must contribute 12 per cent of your salary to the Provident Fund (PF) from the first day of your employment and your employer contributes the same amount. This provides for a pension, payable from the age of 58. You must also pay 2.25 per cent of salary towards the Employees' State Insurance scheme (employers must pay 5 per cent), which covers you for hospital treatment in the event of an accident at work – although state hospital treatment is so poor that many workers take out private insurance. These benefits, and maternity benefit, are available to all workers, irrespective of their nationality, with the exception of high earners.

Tax

You're responsible for making monthly deductions for income tax – and in some states professional tax – from an employee's salary. Additionally, you're required to issue a monthly payslip and an annual 'certificate of deducted tax'.

TRADE UNIONS

Industrial relations, which were at their worst in the '70s, have been steadily improving since then – particularly since the '90s, with the liberalisation of the economy. The number of strikes (always a good indicator of industrial relations) fell annually between 2000 and 2006 from 426 to 154.

Employees aren't obliged to join a union, but all businesses with 100 or more employees are required to have some sort of employee representation. Out of around 60,000 registered workers' unions in India, only ten are national organisations. The Indian National Trade Union Congress (INTUC) is the most dominant, with around 35 per cent of total union membership, and is affiliated to the International Confederation of Free Trade Unions in Brussels. With the average membership per union at around 600 and subscriptions as low as Rs1 per month, it's impossible for unions to provide any compensation for members during strikes. However, although bereft of funds, India's top trade unions are powerful due to their political alliances.

> *Bandh* in Hindi means 'closed' and is a form of protest used by political activists to close factories and other businesses, which risk damage and aggression if they remain open, usually for a day. Sometimes, whole cities close down – a *bandh* is a regular occurrence in Mumbai.

HOLIDAYS

Although the statutory minimum number of paid leave days is 15, most companies grant 30 days, but you cannot divide your holiday into more than three periods. The vast majority of workers take the whole of a month off, usually May, to coincide with school summer holidays, which run from mid-April to mid-June. Those who can afford to go on holiday twice a year take a fortnight (two weeks) during this period and a fortnight in October, which coincides with the *Diwali* holiday in schools and colleges. However, the allocation of holidays is decided by strict hierarchy, those at the top getting the first choice of dates. If you're a new recruit, you're unlikely to be allowed to take any holiday in your first year of service.

Palolem beach, Goa

Although Indians love to take holidays, some can afford to do so only once every two years – and some companies pay a biennial holiday travel allowance. By law employees are entitled to receive pay in lieu of holiday, and the majority of blue-collar workers 'cash in' at least part of their leave. However, most employees who work away from home make a point of visiting their home town at least once a year.

There are certain times of the year in India when it's best to avoid doing business (see below); if you have to work during these periods, you should expect things to take longer than usual.

July & August

During the wettest weeks of the monsoon period, many businesses come to a standstill, as the incessant rain floods roads and railways. To make matters worse, the rice crop has to be transplanted during spells of heavy rain, resulting in an exodus of unskilled workers to their native villages. Companies don't usually close down completely, however, but continue operating on a skeleton staff, working overtime.

Holi & Diwali

Out of literally hundreds of festivals in India, *Holi* (mostly celebrated in the northern states around February or March) and *Diwali* (celebrated in October or November, almost everywhere except in the south where it's low-key) are the most popular for holidays, as they involve partying as well as religious rituals. However, while many employees officially take leave during *Diwali*, *Holi* sees a lot of absenteeism, particularly among semi-skilled and unskilled workers. When this happens in March, it can be more disruptive than the monsoon period, as sales personnel sometimes have to work round the clock to meet annual targets by 31st March, the end of the financial year.

Public Holidays

There are an average of 17 public holidays in each state, although the dates vary as holidays celebrate different occasions in different parts of the country. Besides these, there are around 30 'restricted holidays', which apply to one or other of India's religions (there are at least seven major religions). However, only the three public holidays listed below are national holidays throughout India:

National Public Holidays	
Date	**Holiday**
26th January	Republic Day
15th August	Independence Day
2nd October	Mahatma Gandhi's Birth Anniversary

Labour Day on 1st May is a public holiday in many states, although not a national public holiday.

All public offices, banks, post offices and industrial establishments are closed on public holidays and only essential work is performed. Banks are closed on two other days, 1st April (for the annual closing of accounts) and 30th of September (for half-year accounting). Foreign embassies and consulates in India usually observe all Indian public holidays, **as well as** their own country's national holidays.

When a holiday falls on a Saturday or a Sunday, another day isn't granted in lieu. Sundays and public holidays are shown in red on calendars.

Local Holidays

Many localities have annual celebrations that last a week or more, but only one of the days is usually a public holiday. During the rest of the week local businesses, banks and public offices remain open, although trying to do business during such festivals is generally a waste of time as few people are in the mood for work.

Leave

Most companies allow up to seven days' 'sick leave' and seven days' 'casual leave' a year. As the name implies, casual leave may be taken without prior approval, but in case of sickness you're expected to phone to report that you're unable to work. If you're absent for more than two days in a row, you must submit a medical certificate on your return. Maternity leave and leave in case of miscarriage are also provided for by law. Paternity leave isn't mandatory but a few progressive companies have introduced it.

Ganges, Varanasi (Benares)

auto rickshaw

7.
ON THE MOVE

Public transport in India – both city and intercity – is inexpensive, but it may not be the fastest or the most comfortable way to get around. As well as planes, trains, buses and taxis, Indian public transport includes boats and the famous rickshaws. This chapter also contains information on motoring in India, including road rules, driving etiquette and the vagaries of parking in India.

> 'Lunar craters' is a popular description of the potholes on Indian roads.

SAFETY

India isn't a safe country in which to travel. Accidents are an ever-present danger, and thieves and diseases frequent travel companions. Not only are safety standards low, but those standards are routinely disregarded and rules flouted. The following precautions will go a long way to cushion you from the potential perils of travelling in India:

- **Bus & train stations** – These are generally safe, even at night, when many people travel. However, leaving a station in the middle of the night may not be so safe. If you're due to arrive at night, either ask someone to meet you or be prepared to wait until dawn before you venture out.

- **Food & drink** – Eat only factory-packed food and check to see that bottles of water are properly sealed before you open them. Unscrupulous vendors often refill used water bottles with tap water and sell them in train stations, where people are in a hurry and don't usually check the seals – a safer bet is to buy your water at a shop in the city.

- **Footboard riding** – Suburban trains don't have doors and the footboards are always crowded with passengers hanging on to handrails even on speeding trains. Never attempt this and keep well away from the doorways.

- **Hitchhiking** – This isn't popular with Indians, except labourers, who hitch rides on trucks on the highways. Motorists rarely stop to pick up hitchhikers and women should never attempt it.

- **Jay walking** – Although this is a common sight on railway tracks, you should never do it, as the fatality rate is high and it's illegal.

- **Petty thieves** – Long-distance trains are their haunts and they will make off with your suitcase in the middle of the night. Suitcases should be chained to your seat and secured with a padlock, both of which are sold at most railway stations.

- **Pickpockets** – These are endemic on public transport, particularly on suburban trains in large cities (Mumbai in particular). Hold your belongings in front of you, and keep your money and passport in an inside pocket or money belt.

- **Single women** – Local and suburban trains (sometimes appropriately called 'slow trains') have 'ladies' compartments', prominently labelled, with an image of the head of an Indian woman (hair styled into a bun and a dot on the forehead) painted on them. However, it's better for women to travel in a general compartment than a ladies' compartment if the latter is empty or there are only a few women in it. Cases of women being molested and robbed at knifepoint aren't uncommon, particularly in the major cities.

- **Terrorism** – Avoid travelling during the days immediately before a national holiday, as this is when the potential of a terrorist attack is at its highest, as is evident from the security alerts during these periods. Also, avoid public places when large events are being held.

- **Travelling late** – Travelling by train late in the evening or at night is best avoided as cases of assault and robbery and even rape, despite the presence of fellow passengers, have been reported. If you must do so, ride in a carriage where there are several other passengers.

- **Window seats** – You should avoid sitting at an open train window when passing through slum areas of large cities, where miscreants often throw rocks at passing trains. Mumbai is notorious for this, where a number of passengers have been hit in the face, causing grievous injuries and loss of vision.

Travel Insurance

Travel insurance is essential for three reasons: the high rate of accidents and thefts and the health risks. A typical travel insurance policy provides cover for the loss of luggage and tickets as well as cash and cheques, subject to a certain limit. In the event of theft, you must file an FIR (first information report) with the police and later obtain an official statement from them. In the case of hospitalisation and medical treatment, keep the receipts, as these are required when filing your claim.

DRIVING

India has the highest rate of road accident fatalities in the world, with some 130,000 people killed in traffic accidents annually – more than one in 10,000 people, which is roughly twice as many as in the UK. Aggressive and reckless driving, untrained drivers and poorly maintained roads are the main reasons for this carnage.

> "Speed thrills but kills." Message on highway signboards.
>
> "Drive to care! Not to dare!" Theme of National Road Safety Week, 2008

The traffic authorities frequently run campaigns to sensitise the public to road safety, besides frequent checks on highways and other roads, in a somewhat desperate attempt to reduce the accident rate.

Drivers

Even normally patient and polite people tend to turn hostile once behind the wheel of a car. Men dominate the roads in India and the few women who drive seem to be the only ones who drive defensively and follow the traffic rules. Tailgating (i.e. driving too close for comfort to the car in front) is standard practice, as is honking and flashing headlights from behind to overtake and from the front to claim right of way – the unwritten rule being 'he who flashes first gets the right of way'. Horns and lights aren't used to warn or alert but to 'clear the way'.

Overtaking is carried out not only on blind bends but even on the wrong side (i.e. to the left instead of the right). Indicators are rarely used when changing lanes, red lights are meant for jumping and brake lights often don't work. Driving the wrong way – even on highways – isn't uncommon, and the sight of motorbikes weaving through dense traffic, with hazard lights flashing, is unremarkable.

Indian Roads

India has the world's third-largest road network at 3mn km (1.9mn miles), although only half are surfaced. Many have crater-like potholes, which fill up with muddy water during the monsoon season. Add the unmarked 'speed breakers' (humps or 'sleeping policemen'), which are prevalent on all roads except major highways, and you may feel as though you're in a boat on a choppy sea rather than in a car. Only 4 per cent of Indian roads conform to international structural norms, but recent improvements, particularly on the national highways, are impressive.

India has several toll roads (though tolls tend to be levied only on certain parts of a road), which are better maintained than most other roads and therefore provide a quicker and more comfortable means of travelling long-distance – although if anything they are even more dangerous, as drivers tend to speed recklessly and flout the most basic traffic rules. 'Toll taxes', however, are insignificant by American or European standards; for example you can drive the 180km from Mumbai to Vapi for a mere Rs70 (less than US$1.50). Tolls are payable at booths on joining a toll road, where there's a notice saying 'Please tender exact change.'

Toll roads aren't necessarily 'expressways', but most expressways

are toll roads. The latter are dual-carriageways with at least two lanes in each direction, on which no motorbikes or scooters are permitted.

> Avoid driving close to the shoulder of the road during the monsoons, as these tend to give way and you'll find yourself stuck in slush.

Roundabouts

Few cities have roundabouts, which are a recent introduction, and most Indian drivers aren't familiar with them. They're unlikely to indicate or give way before entering a roundabout, and some treat roundabouts as if they weren't a junction at all, driving straight across them. Be on your guard!

Road Rules

Buy a copy of the *Indian Motor Vehicles Act*, available from newsagents and bookshops, and familiarise yourself with the road signs and rules. Among the most important points are:

● Indians drive on the left-hand side of the road.

● Speed limits in India vary according to the state and vehicle type, although a nationwide speed limit of 100kph (62mph) for cars and 65kph (40mph) for motorcycles has been proposed. Generally, cars are limited to 80kph (50mph) and motorbikes to 60kph (37mph) on main highways, while on most expressways the limit for cars is 100kph. The Pune-Mumbai expressway has a speed limit of just 80kph but is reckoned to have one of the highest accident rates of any major road in the world.

● Front-seat occupants must wear seatbelts.

● Motorcycle riders must wear helmets conforming to the Indian Standards Institution (ISI) specifications and bearing the ISI mark.

● Only one pillion rider is allowed on bikes.

● The use of a mobile phone while driving is prohibited unless it's a hands-free model with earphones.

- White lines are used for traffic lanes. A solid single line means no overtaking – you can overtake only when there's a single broken line or double lines with a broken line on your side of the road.

- Use of horns is prohibited in silence zones (such as in the vicinity of hospitals), identified by a 'Silence Please' sign and an image of a black horn crossed with a red X.

- As in other countries, hazard warning lights are commonly used by motorists to say 'I won't be long' when parking illegally, instead of to warn vehicles of a hazard.

- The following documents (originals not copies) must be carried in your car: registration and road tax booklet, insurance certificate and PUC certificate (see box). You should have a spare wheel and tools for changing a wheel. It's also recommended that you carry a first-aid kit. And never forget your driving licence – the police will ask for it on any pretext.

PUC Check

All motor vehicles must undergo a 'Pollution Under Control' (PUC) check and you must obtain a certificate, valid for six months, and a sticker, which should be stuck in the top left corner of your windscreen (windshield).

Penalties & Fines

As in other countries, contravention of the road rules makes you liable for fines (though these are almost derisory) and more serious penalties, although there's no licence endorsement (penalty point) system in India.

- **Driving without a licence or PUC certificate** – Driving without a valid driving licence can result in imprisonment for up to three months or a fine of up to Rs500 (US$10) or both. Driving without a valid PUC certificate also attracts a fine of Rs500.

- **Driving without registration** – Driving a motor vehicle without valid registration papers can result in a minimum fine of Rs2,000 (US$40). However, vehicles used in an emergency, such as taking sick or injured people to a hospital or transporting food and medical supplies to relieve distress, are exempt.

- **Driving without insurance** – Driving an uninsured vehicle can result in a fine of Rs1,000 (US$20) or imprisonment for up to three months, or both.

- **Exceeding speed limits** – Exceeding the prescribed speed limit attracts a fine of up to Rs400 (US$8) for the first offence and Rs500 (US$10) for subsequent offences.

- **Drunken driving** – Punishment for drunken driving is imprisonment for up to two years or a fine of up to Rs3,000 (US$60) or both, and the offender can be arrested on the spot. In Mumbai alone, 3,106 cases of drunken driving were registered during the first six months of 2007.

In a bid to put the brakes on undisciplined driving, the Motor Vehicles (Amendment) Bill 2007 was tabled, proposing increased fines and jail terms. Speeding may result in a fine of up to Rs1,000 (US$20) for the first offence, doubling on the second. Drunken driving could lead to a three-month suspension of your driving licence, six months in jail and a fine of Rs2,000 (US$40); a second violation can result in a two-year jail term and a fine. Underage drivers can be jailed for up to three months and fined Rs1,000 for the first offence and Rs2,000 for subsequent offences. Fines for vehicles without registration papers were increased to Rs10,000 (US$200) for the first offence and Rs20,000 (US$400) for a repeat offence.

Finding Your Way

Maps may not be comprehensive or up to date and road signs often aren't visible. Trying to change lane in order to turn off or slowing down to read a street name prompts a tirade of horn sounding, shouting and rude gestures from drivers behind you, but if you ask for directions, Indian drivers are happy to oblige.

> There are many hotels along the highway as well as places advertising 'Boarding & Lodging', the Indian equivalent of 'Bed & Breakfast'. In the interior regions of India, little colonial cottages called '*dak bungalows*' give the impression that the British have only just left. Expect to be served only Indian food in these places – and don't forget to carry a few rolls of toilet paper.

Motorcyclists & Pedestrians

Watch out for motorcyclists, who often overtake on the left, particularly in towns. Also look out for pedestrians who cross the road without looking or suddenly step out in front of you. Pedestrian crossings, called 'zebra crossings' in India as in the UK, are black and white stripes across the road and sometimes have traffic lights. You aren't obliged to stop at a crossing unless the light is red or there's a pedestrian already on it but if you want to stop, make sure you look in your mirror first, as the driver behind won't be expecting it and could run into you.

Traffic Jams

Traffic jams are the order of the day in Indian cities, not so much due to accidents – as is the case on national highways – but simply due to the fact that roads are too narrow and too few to cope with the volume of traffic. Other causes are roadworks – whether for repairs to the road itself or for the maintenance of electrical and telephone cables, water-pipes or drains – plus roadblocks to allow VIPs to pass. While people wait patiently on highways for jams to clear, city drivers honk as enthusiastically as on New Year's Eve.

To minimise the risk of being stuck in a traffic jam, try to avoid rush hours (8 to 10am and 5 to 8.30pm), as there are usually no alternative routes. The quietest period is 1 to 3pm, when most people are having their lunch.

Parking

India's low car density of 10 cars per 1,000 people is misleading. The parking problem in Indian cities and towns is as big as the traffic congestion problem. The large number of cars and the narrow streets in most Indian towns and cities make parking daunting and time-consuming. The problem is compounded by the many signs prohibiting parking near the entrances of private as well as commercial buildings.

Official parking spaces include underground car parks in the major cities and open yards in smaller cities. In smaller towns, people tend to park almost anywhere, even in no-parking areas as these aren't monitored. A practical alternative is to park on the outskirts and walk or take a rickshaw into the centre.

Double Parking

Don't be surprised to find someone else's car parked beside yours, leaving you trapped. When this happens, it's common practice to honk away until the owner of the other car appears – although even if he can hear you, he may take no notice, and if he cannot be found you may be left fuming for an hour or more. You've the option of calling the local police and asking that the offending vehicle be towed away, but this may take even longer.

Parking Illegally

You cannot be fined more than Rs100 (US$2) for parking illegally, but you risk having your car towed away: instead of your car, you'll find a message scribbled in white chalk on the road telling you which police station to contact. The fine and towing charge will amount to around Rs500 (US$10), but the inconvenience may be more costly.

Petrol Stations

Petrol stations are plentiful throughout India except in some rural areas. None are self-service, however. You don't need to tip an attendant unless he washes your windscreen or checks your tyre pressure, in which case Rs10 or Rs20 (US20-40¢) should suffice. Most petrol stations in cities are open 24 hours, while in towns they're open from 6am to 10pm. When filling up with petrol, you're supposed to turn off

the engine, lights and electrical equipment (including the radio) and your mobile phone, but this rule often isn't followed, especially in towns.

Petrol stations have tyre pressure pumps and water supplies, and some have vacuum cleaners and car washes. Many stations sell snacks, soft drinks, mineral water, newspapers, confectionery, suitcases, toiletries and car 'accessories', including oil. Toilets are available but usually deplorably unhygienic. You need to take your own toilet paper.

PUBLIC TRANSPORT

A few general points apply to most kinds of public transport in India:

- Online and telephone bookings can be made with most large transport companies, but not all.

- For journeys at peak holiday times – *Diwali*, *Holi* and national holidays – you should book a seat at least a month in advance.

- Food and drink on trains and planes, although not expensive, is mediocre.

- Alcoholic drinks are prohibited on public transport.

- Smoking is prohibited at airports, bus and train stations and on public transport.

Planes

Flying is by far the quickest way to travel long distances, but air fares are among the most expensive in the world. However, India's principal domestic carrier, Indian, offers 25 per cent discounts for under 30s and students, 50 per cent for over 65s and under 12s (90 per cent for those aged under two), and there are a number of 'no frills' airlines, including Air Deccan and SpiceJet. You can book your ticket on the internet and take advantage of an assortment of bargains and even ticket auctions.

Other domestic carriers are the innovative Kingfisher 'funliners' with their all-female cabin crew called 'flying models', Air Sahara, GoAir Airlines, IndiGo Airlines, Jet Airways and Paramount Airways.

Indian airports are busy and the terrorist threat omnipresent, which results in prolonged and tedious security checks, requiring a check-in time of up to two hours. Flight and general information at large airports is given in Hindi and English.

Air India has a good safety record that's the equal of most Western carriers and although Indian Airlines – the state-owned domestic airline – isn't quite as safe, India in general is given the highest safety rating (category 1) by the Federal Aviation Administration. The Airline Quality website (💻 www.airlinequality.com) gives Air India three stars (out of five) and Indian Airlines two stars.

> Always padlock your suitcase to the chain provided underneath the seat of the lower berth and never leave your passport or wallet unattended, even when visiting the toilet.

Trains

With a rail track length of 64,000km (40,000mi – the world's second-largest network) and 7,000 stations, Indian

Railways transports 1.7m passengers every day. Its financial turnaround in recent years has become a case study for top business schools, including Harvard. Nevertheless, trains are often late, sometimes by hours, and there are no refunds for late arrival.

There are just two classes of compartment: first and second. All first-class and some second-class compartments (labelled 'Reserved') have numbered seats, therefore it's possible to reserve a particular seat. Second-class compartments without numbered seats are called 'general' compartments and can be extremely crowded, uncomfortable and, on some routes, unsafe.

Not all trains have air-conditioned compartments, although most long-distance 'Express' trains do. A few trains, including the Rajdhani Express from Mumbai to Delhi, are totally air-conditioned.

All long-distance trains have 'sleeper' compartments containing 'berths'. There are two types: three-tier (cheaper) and two-tier (more expensive). On air-conditioned trains, berths are padded and a pillow, a blanket, two bed sheets and a towel are issued to you once you've settled in. On other trains, berths consist of bare wooden strips, each around two feet wide and six feet long, which are latched to the back of your seat when not in use. There's a handrail to help those on the top tier climb into bed.

Berths may be used between 9pm and 6am, which means that if the person with the bottom berth decides he wants to turn in at 9pm, the other(s) must also make up their berths and lie down. Similarly, if one person wants to rise and shine at 6am, so must his fellow traveller(s).

The various types of compartment are listed below in order from the most expensive to the least expensive:

Types of Compartments

First-class, air-conditioned

Second-class, air-conditioned, two-tier

*Second-class, air-conditioned, three-tier and 'Chair Cars'

First-class, not air-conditioned

Second-class, not air-conditioned, sleeper

Second-class, not air-conditioned, reserved

Second-class, not air-conditioned, general

* with aircraft-style seats that can be tilted back

It's advisable to plan your journey and book your ticket as far in advance as possible in order to secure a ticket. If you book well in advance, you're likely to get a 'ticket to ride', i.e. a confirmed seat. However, when all the bookable

seats in a train or class have been sold, the railway company starts selling reservations against cancellation (RAC) tickets, which are converted to bookings in the event of a cancellation. When all the RAC tickets have been sold, you can pay for a 'waitlist' (WL) ticket – or take a bus.

There's a foreign quota on long distance trains and it's worth enquiring about availability under the foreign quota if you're told that all seats have been booked. You'll be asked to produce your passport when booking and the ticket inspector is also likely to ask to see your passport during the journey.

> **Waiting rooms at train stations are mediocre and toilets unusable – use a local café if you arrive early.**

Only Delhi and Kolkata (Calcutta) currently have underground (metro) networks, while Mumbai's is scheduled for completion in 2010. On underground trains, doors open and close automatically at stations. Most (overground) suburban trains don't have doors.

Buses

Some parts of the country aren't accessible by train – including most of the Himalayan valleys – but buses serve even the most remote areas. Besides the government-run state transport bus service, there are a number of private bus companies with vehicles ranging in comfort level from 'ordinary', with thinly padded seats and upright backs, to 'deluxe' or 'luxury' with cushioned recliners, tinted windows, air-conditioning and, in some, films.

Note the following when travelling by bus in India:

- Bus stations are usually poorly maintained and lack hygiene.

- There's usually a separate queue for women at bus station ticket counters.

- When you buy a ticket, it will have your seat number on it as well as the registration number of the bus you'll be travelling on. Avoid the back seats – they're pulverising on bumpy roads.

- Luggage is stored in the hatch of 'luxury' buses and on the roof of 'ordinary' buses.

Taxis & Rickshaws

Taxis are common in most towns and cities and are usually black with a yellow roof, although 'Cool Cabs' – Mumbai's air-conditioned taxis – are sky blue.

You can order a taxi by phone, go to a taxi rank (called a 'stand'), and take the one first in the queue or hail one in the street by signalling with an outstretched arm; a taxi showing the words 'For Hire' is available. At airports and larger railway stations there's a pre-pay taxi service, which it's advisable to use.

Although taxis are cheap in India, there's a cheaper and more popular mode of transport: the auto-rickshaw – a three-wheeled contraption whose front half is a motor scooter but whose back seat has been widened to accommodate two or three people side by side. It has the same colour scheme and meter as a taxi. In some parts of India, cycle-rickshaws are still used – like an auto-rickshaw but environmentally friendly – and you may even encounter a traditional rickshaw, powered by running legs.

While auto-rickshaws are fitted with meters to calculate tariffs within urban areas these are seldom used, particularly in Delhi. Journeys outside urban areas usually have fixed rates and you should **always** agree the fare with the driver before starting a journey. Ask friends and colleagues what you would expect to pay on a popular route to avoid being overcharged. Tipping the driver isn't necessary.

Ferries

Most rivers have ferries – even those that have bridges across them. There are also boat services connecting the Andaman Islands with Kolkata and Chennai (Madras).

OTHER MODES OF TRANSPORT

Cycling

Surprisingly few people use bicycles for day-to-day transportation, Indians generally preferring to take buses for short journeys, although an increasing number are switching to mopeds and mini-scooters, called 'scooties'.

Surprisingly, bringing a bike from abroad is one of the few procedures that requires no paperwork, but compatible spare parts may be difficult to find. Buying a bike in India is a better proposition (most towns have cycle shops), although Indian bikes are heavy and not suitable for mountainous terrain. Several adventure tour operators offer bicycle tours.

Pedestrians

Indians walk a lot and walk almost everywhere – out of necessity rather than choice – even on flyovers and other fast roads, where walking is prohibited. Many footpaths or pavements are obstacle courses, strewn with bins, rubbish, litter and wares from shops. You also need to keep an eye out for broken paving stones (loose and full of dirty water ready to soak your shoes and legs), dung, cows and, most dangerous of all, particularly on waterlogged roads during the monsoons, open manholes.

As motorists aren't obliged to stop at a pedestrian crossing unless the light is red or there's a pedestrian already on it, don't start crossing unless there's no traffic or oncoming vehicles have plenty of time to stop. Even if the light for cars is red and the green man is showing, check that traffic has actually stopped before crossing, as drivers routinely jump red lights. If the traffic light is flashing amber, take extra care as drivers don't have to stop and most don't, particularly in Delhi and Mumbai.

8.
THE INDIANS AT PLAY

India is such a vast and diverse country that even Indians themselves must adapt socially when moving from place to place; for a foreigner, social gaffes are almost inevitable. Thankfully, allowances are usually made for foreigners, whose faux pas are perceived as making fools of them rather than offending others. However, this chapter should help you pick your way through the Indian social minefield, including information about how to dress; dining out (and in); attending family occasions, festivals and sporting events; and participating in other leisure activities. If you're at a loss, just do as the locals do.

> The myriad Indian social codes and etiquette result in a sense of casualness in formal settings and of formality in casual situations.

DRESS CODE

Indians dress conservatively and 'casual' wear tends to be smart and trendy. International labels are *de rigueur*, in both casual and formal wear, but Indian fashion is a blend of materials and styles, both regional and Western. Urban Indian men and women are invariably well groomed and fashionable, particularly in Bangalore, Delhi and Mumbai. Men wear Western dress – trousers and shirts year round except in winter, when jackets are brought out of the attic, particularly in North India.

Women dress traditionally, in saris that can cost many thousands of rupees or the fashionable *salwar-kameez* (salwar are baggy pants, kameez a sort of shirt-cum-tunic), which is also worn by some men, though they prefer the kurta-pyjama: 'drainpipe' trousers and a shirt with long, loose-fitting sleeves, no cuffs and no collar. Inevitably, jeans are popular among college students and young women working in the IT sector and call centres.

Home

At home, many Indians wear tracksuits, the *kurta-pyjama* or 'working' clothes (e.g. a housecoat), leaving their feet bare, and they change and put on footwear before leaving the house. However, increasingly young people wear jeans and T-shirts, needing no change of clothes for going out.

Places of Worship

Modesty is expected of both men and women at all places of worship. When entering a temple, women cover their heads with a fold of their saris or a scarf and footwear is removed by all.

Social Occasions

Social occasions, weddings in particular, often look like fashion parades. Women wear the finest silk saris, bravely smiling under the weight of gold jewellery and layers of foundation. Most visit the hairdresser's before such events, some even going directly from beauty parlour to party. Not to be outdone, men dress flamboyantly in expensive imported suits and patent shoes, with gold bracelets and chunky Swiss watches.

> Traditional costumes are still worn in rural India and everywhere on special occasions, such as fairs and religious and cultural festivals. Indian traditional costumes are colourful outfits which include headgear as well as ornaments, those of Rajasthani women being among the most eye-catching with fragments of mirror embedded in the embroidery.

EATING

When it comes to food, it's quantity that comes first, variety next and quality last. Most Indians aren't overly concerned about the amount of sodium or salt in their food or its cholesterol content. Eating in fast food joints – local as well as international (such as McDonald's) – is gaining in popularity, and on Sundays and public holidays, restaurants are overflowing with large family groups.

Indians spend a long time over appetisers (which they call 'bitings'), talking as much as they eat, but once they get to the meal proper they munch away rapidly, looking serious and smacking their lips regularly. Portions are large and meals normally include two main courses and a dessert. Meals tend to be lighter in the south and heavier in the north, particularly in the Punjab, where the food is so rich that you may find it necessary to skip the next meal.

Vegetarian and non-vegetarian dishes are laid out on separate buffet counters or tables, and are labelled as such.

Leaving food uneaten on your plate can be considered impolite, particularly in rural areas where there's more poverty and malnutrition. The most practical approach is not to load your plate too heavily and start with modest portions, returning for more if necessary. In restaurants asking for the uneaten portions to be packed to take with you is standard practise. These will always be welcomed by street dwellers if you don't want to take the food home with you.

Eat only with your right hand and receive or pass food or implements only with the right hand.

During your stay in India, you're sure to receive a number of invitations to both formal and informal meals. Knowing the local customs in advance will make not only you but also your host and other guests feel more at ease.

Breakfast

Indian breakfasts vary from region to region. In the north the standard fare is the *chana puri* (a lentil stew and deep-fried small, round, flat pieces of dough made of unleavened wheat flour) or *alu paratha* (pan-fried, flat, unleavened wheat bread stuffed with potato) with *dhal* (lentil stew) followed by tea. In the south it's *iddli sambar* (steamed rice cakes and a lentil and vegetable stew) or *masala dosa* (huge, crispy rice pancakes stuffed with spicy vegetables) followed by coffee. Many office workers in metropolitan cities have breakfast in cafés at around 10am, en route to the office. Children take a snack to school for their mid-morning break.

Lunch

This is the main meal of the day and is eaten between 1 and 2pm. Lunch is usually vegetarian and consists of two main courses and dessert (usually a sweet). A glass of buttermilk or *lassi* (a yogurt drink) is often served, as Indians don't drink alcohol at lunchtime.

Indians who work close to their homes may eat lunch at home and return to work at 2 or 3pm, while others take a packed lunch, have food delivered to the workplace or go to a restaurant serving a set menu. Indians seldom eat sandwiches for lunch and outside urban areas the tin *tiffin* canisters are a common sight (delivered by *dabbawallas*).

Dinner

In the evening, Indians eat any time between 7 and 10pm and, like lunch, dinner is usually vegetarian and consists of two main courses. Dessert may be *kheer* (a rice pudding) or *kulfi* (ice cream). If alcoholic drinks are served at dinner, it's always before the meal.

Seating

On formal occasions and in conservative homes, women sit together on one side of the table and men on the other, with the head of the family at the 'head' of the table. However, in more modern households, couples sit side by side. The hostess usually doesn't eat with the guests as she either serves them herself or oversees the service.

It's polite to wait for the host to tell you where to sit and not to sit down until you're invited to do so. On major social occasions such as weddings and banquets, cards with guests' names may be placed on the tables. It's considered impolite to change places before or during a meal but, after dessert, guests are free to mingle and sit elsewhere.

Buffets are popular at weddings as well as on informal occasions. Chairs are often laid out around the buffet counters, as most Indians prefer to sit while eating.

Cutlery
Formal Dining

Cutlery is minimal in India. The usual arrangement is a fork on the left and a knife on the right of the plate. A spoon for eating rice is sometimes placed at the top. Dessert is normally served in little bowls after the meal with a dessertspoon thrust into it or laid next to the bowl, on the right. Most Indians make little use of cutlery, frequently using the fingers of their right hand. Fruits such as apples and pears

are usually served cut into pieces and eaten with the fingers. Fruits that need to be peeled, such as bananas and oranges, aren't served.

When you've finished eating you should place your knife and fork side by side in the middle of the plate.

Informal Dining

In informal settings most Indians eat with their fingers. A piece of flat, unleavened bread is used for wrapping around food or mopping up gravy and conveying it to the mouth. Rice is eaten by mixing it with curry, thus enabling it to be moulded into little balls with the fingertips.

> The 'rule of thumb' for getting a rice ball into your mouth without making a mess is to hold it lightly with the first four fingers of your right hand, bring it to your mouth and push it in with your free thumb. Some people eat rice with a spoon.

Grace

Hindus say '*anapurna stuthi*' before meals. *Ana* means 'food', *purna* 'all' and *stuthi* 'praise'; *Anapurna* is the goddess of food. Christians say grace before they eat, and Muslims call to God ('*Du'aa*') after as well as before meals. If you don't belong to any of these religions, you should sit with your head bowed until the prayer is finished.

When to Start

It's polite to wait for everyone to be served (irrespective of the occasion) before starting a meal. At formal meals, you should wait for the host to start – unless he asks you to start first.

Bread

An essential part of an Indian meal, bread is usually home made. It comes in various forms but is essentially made from unleavened flour; *roti* or *chappati* are flat and baked on griddles; *paratha* and *naan* are baked in a deep oven called a *tandoor*; while *puri* is deep-fried dough.

In informal settings, bread is usually served hot off the stove; in formal settings, it may be served on small plates or little baskets placed to the left of each person. Unless you leave a portion of your bread uneaten or signal that you don't need more, the plate or basket will be replenished.

You should break off a small piece using only the fingers of your right hand by pinning it with your little finger and tearing off a piece with your thumb and forefinger. Wrap the piece round a morsel of food on your plate and put it into your mouth, or use it to mop up curry.

Bread is eaten as an accompaniment to other food and not on its own, except at breakfast, when it's stuffed with vegetables.

Conversation

Your host will usually do most of the talking – telling you about himself and his family and asking personal questions about you and yours. You're expected to be equally inquisitive; otherwise you'll be perceived as indifferent or cold. So don't hesitate in reciprocating with a similar barrage of questions.

> 'So, how do you find India?' is typically the first question an Indian will ask of a foreigner. He expects the answer to be 'Wonderful!'

Noises

Foreigners coughing and wiping their noses at the table aren't uncommon sights at an Indian table given that they aren't accustomed to hot, spicy Indian food, and such behaviour will be tolerated; in fact, your host is likely to offer you water to ease the burning on your tongue and the irritation in your throat.

Burping is difficult to control, as some additives in food are specifically meant to induce it and in some communities burping is tantamount to saying, 'That was a really good meal!' However, if in doubt, just say 'excuse me' quietly and carry on.

Table Manners

You should eat with your right hand only if there's no cutlery or only one implement is provided. Keep your left hand either on the table or on your lap. If a full set of cutlery is provided, go ahead and use both hands but only use the right to bring food (or drink) to your mouth.

Toasts

Toasts aren't common in India, although speeches are. If the host proposes a

toast, guests applaud or stand and then raise their glasses. On informal occasions, guests raise their glasses and say 'cheers!'

DRINKING

Alcoholism and drunkenness, though not a problem in India, are on the rise among low-income workers in the industrial sector, teenagers in urban areas and among marginalised communities in rural areas. Most Indians who drink, do so on special occasions. Although most Indians aren't regular drinkers, when they do drink they expect to become intoxicated. Drunks, however, have little credibility in Indian society.

For Indians, alcohol is expensive, as taxes are high, although the prices are unlikely to deter foreigners. For example, a can of beer costs between US$1.25 and $2, a bottle of wine

ranges from US$2.50 to $15 and a bottle of scotch ranges from US$15 to $30. Few Indians can afford scotch and not many can afford Indian-made spirits. Nevertheless, bar culture is growing in the major cities, and in the former Portuguese enclaves of Daman, Diu and Goa there are bars on almost every street. Some states, including Gujarat, are 'dry', which has given rise to an illicit trade in alcohol, although foreigners can obtain a permit to drink.

Bars and restaurants with a liquor licence can serve alcohol at certain times only, and there's an age limit of 21 in most cities – except Delhi, where it's 25.

CAFES, BARS & RESTAURANTS

India offers a variety of eateries, from luxury restaurants in five-star hotels serving gourmet meals to humble *dhabas* (shacks with string 'cots' to sit on) serving homely fare for a few rupees.

Smoking

Smoking in public places was banned in India on 1st October 2008. Cafés, restaurants, bars, public transport, offices and all public buildings are now smoke free and smoking in a public building can result in an on-the-spot fine.

Cafés & Bars

There has recently been an upsurge in the demand for coffee bars in India. Indian café chains such as Barista, Coffee Day and India Coffee House have a growing number of outlets in the cities, offering not only good coffee and snacks but also a 'taste' of the Western lifestyle, which appeals to upwardly-mobile Indians. Instant coffee is most commonly sold in India – and is sometimes sold as '*expresso*'; for a real espresso (and cappuccino) you must go to a good city coffee bar. Coffee is more popular than tea in South India.

Similarly, bar culture is growing fast, particularly in Bangalore and Mumbai among people from the IT and business process outsourcing (BPO – call centres) sector, many of whom are expats.

The following are some characteristics of cafés and bars:

- **Alcohol:** Cafés don't serve alcohol, only bars. Bottled beer, wine and spirits are available in bars, but the choice of wine, which isn't popular, is usually limited.

- **Noise:** Noisy customers and blaring music accost you when you enter an Indian bar. Cafés are appreciably quieter.

- **Opening hours:** Cafés usually open early in the morning and close late at night; 7am to midnight are typical hours. Those near public transport facilities such as mainline stations, highways and airports are usually open round the clock.

- **Ordering & paying:** Unless you're sitting at the bar (in which case you order directly from the bar staff) you must wait for a waiter to come

on public holidays, which are their busiest days.

- **Booking:** It isn't necessary to book a table unless you want a particular view or seating arrangement. Even on Sundays or public holidays you'll rarely need to wait more than 20 minutes or so. If you book and cannot make it, you're expected to call to cancel.

- **Seating:** When you enter a restaurant you're usually left to find a table by yourself. If you cannot, ask the *maître d'hôtel* to find one for you.

- **Table settings:** Depending on the type of restaurant, you may need to ask for a fork or there may be a full silver service with linen napkins. Water, salad dressing and pickles are usually brought to the table shortly after you sit down.

- **Menu:** Most restaurants offer three-course meals, including dessert, but Indians often do without a 'starter'. If you choose to have only two courses while other people are having three, the waiter will bring your meal with their second course.

to your table to place your order. When you've finished, ask the waiter for the bill and pay him. Often the bill includes VAT (typically 12.5 per cent), which may not be included in the price on the menu.

- **Service:** Waiter service is available at most cafés, although the number of self-service establishments has recently increased, particularly in more upmarket areas.

- **Tips:** There's no standard tip and in a café or bar most people leave small change unless part of a large group, in which case between 5 and 10 percent of the bill is usual.

Restaurants

When eating out in India, bear in mind the following:

- **Opening hours:** Restaurants generally open from around 11am or noon to 3pm for lunch and from 7 to 11pm for dinner. Most are open every day of the week and don't close

> Many eateries offer a 'menu of the day' consisting of two main courses (with a limited choice of dishes for each course) and dessert or coffee plus bread and a drink (usually non-alcoholic). Food is generally home cooked and of average quality and average value – expect to pay from Rs150 to Rs250 (US$3–5) per person. To find the best food, look for crowded bars and restaurants at around 1pm.

- **Service:** Waiting isn't a profession in India where, except in high class restaurants, most waiters are casual and standards of service vary from passable to poor. Waiters often pass plates across the table and at times over your head. The sound of trays crashing to the floor and breaking glass isn't uncommon, particularly on busy days. Wine isn't offered for tasting before serving and plates are often cleared before everyone has finished eating, except in up market restaurants.

- If service is slow, it's acceptable to mention this to the waiter and ask politely for quicker service, but if the restaurant is busy this may be beyond his control. In restaurants where food is cooked to order, you'll have to wait at least 15 minutes for your first course, but some dishes (such as 'sizzlers') take 30 minutes to prepare, so it's a good idea to ask the waiter how long the main dishes will take to cook before confirming your order.

- If a waiter is rude it's best not to take this up with him directly, but to ask to see the head waiter or manager. If your complaint isn't resolved satisfactorily, ask for the complaints book and make it in writing. The written word is taken seriously in India and merely asking for the complaints book invariably improves service.

- **Water:** Usually the waiter asks whether you want mineral water or tap water – the latter is always called 'plain water' and you won't be understood if you ask for 'tap water'. It's best to opt for mineral water, which some good restaurants provide free of charge.

- **The bill:** When you're ready for the bill, you should attract the waiter's attention. Indians usually snap their fingers at waiters and/or call out 'waiter!' Few waiters bring the bill unprompted but they usually come to the table and enquire, 'Anything else, Sir/Madam?' which may be responded to with a "No thanks. The bill, please."

- **Tipping:** There's no statutory amount that should be left as a tip. If you've enjoyed your meal and received good service, leave between 5 and 10 per cent of the bill. The tip may be added to your credit card payment or left as cash (which waiters prefer).

In most Indian restaurants, a little stainless steel bowl containing warm water with a thin slice of lemon floating in it is placed before you after a meal. It isn't for drinking! Dip the fingers of your right hand into it and squeeze the lemon to remove the grease from your fingertips and wash them at the same time, then dry them on your napkin.

NIGHTLIFE

Indians are now making the transition from bar culture to nightclub culture, particularly in cities, large towns and resort areas. Nightspots range from trendy jazz clubs and hi-tech discotheques to lounge bars, pubs and beach shacks. Goa is known for its beach parties, Mumbai for its cocktail clubs and hard rock discos, and Delhi for its lounge bars. However, Bangalore is the pub capital of India and has been host to Western rock concerts, recent performers including Bryan Adams and the Rolling Stones.

The following should help you tune in to the club scene in India:

● **Opening hours:** Nightclubs open between 9 and 10pm and close between 1 and 4am; city discotheques close around 1am. Beach parties in Goa last until the small hours. There's a law prohibiting the serving of alcohol after a certain time (usually 11pm), but this is often flouted.

● **Age:** You must usually be aged at least 18 to be admitted to nightclub, although whether or not you appear 'old enough' is largely a matter of the doorman's opinion! Students can show their identity card, although even this may not sway things your way. If you're aged over 18 and under 21, you aren't supposed to drink alcohol even if you're allowed in.

● **Dress code:** Casual wear is normal for most nightclubs, jeans being the preferred outfit, although many Indian women dress up.

● **Sex:** Unlike in some Western countries, single males and groups of males are normally allowed into nightclubs, although this is at the discretion of the doorman.

> ### Drinks
> **Clubs serve all kinds of alcoholic and non-alcoholic drinks. Entrance fees (usually from Rs100/US$2) sometimes include a drink; some clubs have no entrance fee and drinks cost from Rs100 to over Rs300 (US$2-6), depending on the establishment. Cocktails cost at least Rs150 (US$3).**

● **Buying rounds & paying:** In most clubs, you order at the bar and pay when your drinks are served. In venues where there's waiter service, you pay when the waiter brings a round of drinks rather than asking for the bill later, as in a restaurant.

FAMILY OCCASIONS

Family gatherings form an integral part of the Indian social calendar and are large, lavish and loud, giving the host(s) an ideal opportunity to showcase his achievements in general and his wealth in particular. The most important family occasions are as follows:

Birthdays

While birthdays are usually low-key occasions for adults ('landmark' birthdays being 21, 60 and 80), they tend to be elaborate affairs for children, the first birthday usually being the most elaborate of all. Schoolchildren distribute sweets to their classmates and teachers, sometimes to the entire school, and are treated to a party in the evening – either at home or, more usually, at a fancy restaurant or an amusement park.

In cities, themed parties are offered, with costumes, live music, performances and a birthday cake with the photographic imprint of the birthday boy/girl on top. Fancy invitation cards are usually sent and parents are also invited. Gifts, party masks and balloons are given to every child attending the party, and presents (toys or cash) to the child whose birthday it is.

Most bakeries in urban India make birthday cakes to order at reasonable prices. Designs are varied and can be customised. Cakes usually consist of several layers of sponge with a creamy filling and butter icing.

Christenings

> The vast majority of Indian children are born into Hindu families and are welcomed into the world by their father, who places a spot of ghee (clarified butter made from the milk of a buffalo or cow) and honey on the newborn's tongue as he whispers God's name in the infant's ear.

The Hindu counterpart of christening is called *namakarana* and is celebrated on the 11th day after birth. The baby is dressed in new clothes and the family astrologer announces the child's horoscope. The child's name is chosen according to the position of the moon in relation to the signs of the zodiac. For example, if the moon was in Sagittarius (*Kumbha*), the name would include one of the auspicious letters of this sign,

which (in Hindi) sound like 'go', 'saa', 'see' and 'su', e.g. thus probably Gopal or Saagar for a boy, Seeta or Sunita for a girl.

Hymns and sometimes a *havan* accompany these rites. A havan is a fire which is kept burning by the addition of rice bran and dried cow dung (which is also used as fuel for cooking in rural India) soaked in butter (ghee). This is done in order to appease the gods and to request a favour, e.g. good health or, in other contexts, rain, a good harvest or a male child. Sometimes, the havan is kept alight for several days or until the favour is considered to have been granted.

The naming ceremony is followed by a vegetarian meal at home, usually in the evening, attended by family and close friends. Gifts such as gold spoons, baby clothes, toiletry sets and cash are presented. Dress is traditional or smart-casual.

Engagement Parties

Although most marriages in India are arranged, engagement parties are gaining in popularity. The engagement is essentially a ceremony at which rings are exchanged. The party is held in the future bride's home and the only guests are the prospective groom's family and close friends. The groom presents the bride with an engagement ring, which she wears on her right ring finger, and the bride reciprocates. The date for the wedding is tentatively set, subject to approval from an astrologer.

This is a reasonably formal occasion, and dress is conservative. It provides an opportunity for the two families to go into the details of the wedding, as well as the often crucial topic of the dowry (see **Chapter 4**).

Initiation Ceremony

The initiation ceremony is exclusively for Hindu *brahmin* boys on reaching the age of seven, when they receive the *jenoi* (sacred thread) – hence the ceremony is also known as the thread ceremony. The boy has his head shaved and is bathed and dressed in new clothes. He may also beg alms from his mother and from other relatives.

> The initiation ceremony is a symbolic 'copy' of an ancient royal custom of sending the king's son to study with a *guru*. The boy, a *brahmin*, identified by a 'sacred thread' worn diagonally across his torso, must renounce all comforts and beg his teacher for food and lodging. Serving food to brahmins was and still is perceived to be an act of utmost kindness, which cleanses the sins of the donor.

There's a *havan* (see **Christenings** above) and the investiture of the sacred thread, which hangs over the boy's left shoulder. It's usually worn for life, although it may be replaced at intervals, in which case care must be taken not to remove it until a new one has been put on.

The ceremony is followed by a grand meal, usually lunch (strictly vegetarian with no alcoholic drinks), for which invitation cards are normally sent a fortnight before the event to upwards of 500 guests. Family members wear traditional attire and guests either traditional or smart-casual. Gifts are gold ornaments or cash.

In certain rural areas, a coming-of-age ceremony is performed for girls on reaching puberty, to make it known to the community that they're available for marriage.

Raksha Bandhan

This festival celebrates the bonding of siblings of the opposite sex, with the brother as the protector of the sister (*raksha bandhan* means protective bond). Held in late August, it consists of a simple ceremony in which a sister ties a band (known as a *rakhi* – ranging in style from a coloured thread to a trendy bracelet) to her brother's wrist and then puts a sweet into his mouth. He usually reciprocates by offering her a small gift, generally cash (Rs51, 101, 251 or 501).

This ritual is often extended to male cousins who don't have sisters and even to men who aren't related but whom a woman takes for a brother.

Diwali

Diwali is India's main festival (see below), in October (17th in 2009), when it's traditional for the whole family to gather for lunch. The meal starts around noon and lasts around an hour. Food is strictly vegetarian but sinfully rich – typical fare includes a variety of rice dishes and flat, unleavened breads, vegetables, curries, pickles, chutneys and salads – and there are several courses. Buttermilk is drunk and dessert is usually *kheer* (rice pudding), although a huge platter of traditional Indian sweetmeats such as *halwa* (halva), *peda* and *burfi* (the last two made from milk and sugar) is always provided. Family and friends exchange boxes of traditional sweetmeats, dried fruit, nuts and (lately) chocolates, which are now marketed in '*Diwali*' assortments.

The second or sometimes the third day of *Diwali* is celebrated as the Hindu 'New Year', when family and friends visit each other and exchange greetings. The festive season lasts a week.

Bhai Duj

Bhai Duj, which usually falls on the third day of *Diwali*, is the celebration of the affection between brothers and sisters. Brothers present gifts to their sisters and sisters in turn apply a vermilion mark (*tilak*) to their brothers' foreheads. On *Bhai Duj* morning, the streets are busy with brothers going to or returning from a visit to their sisters if they live separately.

New Year's Eve

The last day of the calendar year, 31st December, is also celebrated throughout India. Although it isn't a traditional family festival, the whole family usually dines at a restaurant late in the evening, and at the stroke of midnight whistles, horns and firecrackers go off non-stop for at least half an hour before the young take to the streets in cars and motorcycles, horns blaring.

Weddings

Weddings are the most important social event in India, and Indians sometimes spend their life savings on a wedding, often going into debt. The bride's parents traditionally foot the bill, which can be as much as Rs1m (US$20,000). There are usually at least 500 guests at the marriage itself and as many as 2,000 for the reception afterwards, and the festivities often begin two or three days before the wedding. Themed weddings are in vogue with the affluent in urban areas, and may include underwater weddings and palace weddings.

> **February to May is the most popular season for weddings, followed by October-November.**

Invitations

Formal invitations are personally handed out to close relatives and friends by the parents of the couple and others are sent by post a couple of weeks before the event. Invitation cards are expensive, fancy affairs. Hindus use red fonts on the cards and write the names of the invitees in gold or silver – black is never used, even on the envelope. Both sets of parents invite guests but costs are usually borne by the bride's.

Invitations usually include your entire household as well as your friends; if you invite only an individual or couple, they're likely to refuse to attend. A reply is seldom expected.

Gifts

Cash is most popular and is given in Rs100 or Rs500 notes with a one-rupee coin added to symbolise growing prosperity. Special envelopes are available with a pocket for the coin. Household items such as crockery, clocks and lamps are next in popularity and should be in the same price-range as cash gifts. Gold is usually given to the bride by her side of the family

Dress

Indians dress in their very best clothes for weddings; key players (see below) often dress in traditional costume or morning suits (but never black), while other men wear formal Western attire, although usually no jacket. Women usually wear saris, which can range in price from a mere Rs1,000 (US$20) to Rs100,000 (US$2,000) for a fine silk sari embroidered with gold thread. Men in the family wear morning suits (never black) but no hats. A visit to a beauty parlour is a must for female guests, all of whom will be highly made up and laden with gold ornaments – chains, bangles, bracelets, rings, earrings, hairclips and brooches.

Dressing smartly will not only get you a place of honour at the wedding, but will also increase the number of photos the photographer and videographer take of you. People who dress well are sometimes invited to a wedding expressly to feature in the video of the event, which is thought to reflect well on the married couple.

Key Players

Apart from the bride and groom, the following are the most important people at an Indian wedding, in order of importance:

- **Bridegroom's father** – accompanies the groom to the dais;

- **Bridegroom's mother** – also accompanies the groom to the dais;

- **Bride's father** – proclaims that he's giving his daughter in marriage to the groom;

- **Bride's mother** – with her husband, welcomes the groom and his parents;

- **Bride's maternal uncle** – accompanies the bride to the dais;

- **Witnesses** – In a Hindu marriage, all present are witnesses and no register needs to be signed, although the priest is often invited a few days later to sign as a witness during the civil registration at a registrar's office.

Procedure

The vast majority of weddings are held in the late afternoon and evening, although the time is determined by the priest in Hindu marriages. The actual marriage usually takes place at the bride's family's home, guests often spilling into the garden and the street.

The groom leaves for the bride's home at the head of a large procession astride a white horse, or is driven in a car bedecked with flowers. The procession is accompanied by a brass band and sporadic explosions of firecrackers, disrupting traffic as it meanders through the main streets of towns and cities.

At the bride's house, her parents welcome the groom and his parents and lead them to the dais, where a priest will perform the marriage ritual. Then, a maternal uncle of the bride leads the bride to the dais and seats her next to the groom. The bride's parents and close relatives follow them to the dais. When all are seated, the father 'delivers' his daughter to the groom.

The ceremony itself can last from half an hour to over two hours. It begins with the chanting of hymns called (mantras), followed by the lighting of a havan (see above). The groom then puts a *mangal sutra* (string of black beads) around his bride's neck and either holds her right hand in his or ties the hanging end of her sari to his upper cloth (a kind of scarf). Finally, he leads her round the open fire in the centre of the dais seven times, each round representing a blessing – food, strength, wealth, happiness, children, cattle and devotion. Mantras are chanted before each round, further prolonging the ceremony.

Afterwards, there's a reception, which is usually held in a hall. Everyone queues up to congratulate the couple and present their gifts while the cameras get busy recording every moment. The couple remain present throughout and leave for their honeymoon a few days after the wedding.

Food is generally vegetarian and alcoholic drinks are seldom served at Hindu weddings. Soft drinks and soups are served when guests arrive, followed by a buffet meal. Dessert is usually *kulfi* (ice cream). There are no formal speeches or toasts. Once people have finished their meal, they bid goodbye to the couple's parents and leave straight away.

> There's usually live music throughout the proceedings; men dominate the dance floor and women seldom dance with men.

FUNERALS

Cremation is common in India, where over 80 per cent of the population are

Hindus and the Hindu religion insists that the deceased are cremated in order to attain moksha (literally 'release' – in this context, from the cycle of death and rebirth). Other communities, such as Muslims and Christians, bury their dead within 24 hours and the Parsees expose the dead to vultures in specially constructed wells known as 'towers of silence.'

Despite the fact that cremations are performed within a few hours of a death, Hindu funerals are often attended by multitudinous processions, as news of a death travels fast and most acquaintances honour the dead by their presence at their funeral, when they can pay their respects to the family.

Women don't go to funerals in India, except in minority communities such as Christians, but gather at the house of the deceased to express their grief – which is done openly and loudly, the wailing being thought to appease the departed soul. On the other hand, 'strangers' may attend, merely in order to be seen, particularly if the deceased was an important person.

According to Hindu custom, the bodies of men and widows are bathed, draped in white shrouds (a woman leaving behind her husband is draped in an orange shroud) and laid on bamboo stretchers flat on the floor. The eldest son or, if there are no sons, the eldest male family member lights the pyre. In rural areas, bodies are cremated on open pyres while in major cities the ceremony takes place in crematoriums. Where possible, the ashes are scattered in a holy river such as the Ganges.

After the cremation, people disperse and go home to bathe and change into fresh clothes.

If you cannot make it to a funeral, condolences are accepted at the home of the bereaved during the ensuing week but usually not beyond the 11th day. To pay your respects you should approach the family (widow or widower first), join your hands in the *namaste* posture and bow slightly, in silence. Close family and friends place flowers at the feet of the deceased, but these aren't carried to the place of cremation.

Dress

Although it isn't obligatory, the wearing of white by family and friends is usual, particularly at a Hindu funeral, while others wear sombre colours. Hindu widows stop using the *bindi* (dot on the forehead) and *tikah* (vermilion along the parting of the hair), while male family members shave the hair off their head and often wear a cap until the hair grows back.

The Hindu equivalent of Muslims' *Shab-e-baraat* (15 days before the start of Ramadan), Christians' All Souls' Day (2nd November) and the Parsees' *Farwadin Roj* (September-October) is *Pitrupaksh*, which takes place in September-October, when the dead are honoured with prayers and offerings of food.

CLUBS

Social and sports clubs exist throughout India. It's said that Victorian England lives on in the gymkhana clubs of India – anglicised places where members play bridge, drink whisky and speak the Queen's English rather than Indian English. Gymkhana, cricket, golf and polo clubs offer temporary membership to foreigners, although a member must recommend you.

Clubs run by councils are subsidised for local residents and governed by rules and regulations, some of which have strict dress codes that forbid traditional Indian and casual Western attire. However, such clubs provide one of the best opportunities to establish contacts in government and business circles, besides friendships. They also save you the hassle involved in wining and dining business associates.

Clubs are also organised by international associations, such as Rotary International.

POPULAR CULTURE

Individualism is foreign to Indians – collectivism is innate. Indians live, work, fight, mourn, rejoice and play in groups. Whether eating out, camping or picnicking, they will gather together not only the extended family (from great-grandparents to toddlers) but often also one or more other families, making it a social occasion.

Picnic fare isn't of the cheese-sandwich-and-coffee type – whatever the location. Innumerable lunch baskets containing a variety of food, mostly vegetarian, vie for space on the palm mats spread on the ground along with fruit and the inevitable ice box containing soft drinks for the women and beer for the men. It isn't uncommon for Indians to cook at a picnic spot and then leave the leftovers and litter behind.

Festivals & Fairs

Festivals (*utsav*) and fairs (*mela*) are integral part of the country's socio-cultural fabric. Given the number of religions and regional identities in India, it isn't surprising that a festival is being celebrated or a fair being held somewhere every day of the year, whether in a city or in a remote village.

If there's a religious festival, a fair usually comes with it, although a fair can also be held by itself. These events herald themselves with a display of gaudy colours – streamers, banners, banderols, sweets, ices and wares – accompanied by a cacophony of exploding firecrackers and music blaring

from loudspeakers at distortion levels. You can pick up unbeatable bargains, but quality is far from the best. Food and drinks (non-alcoholic) are left exposed to the dust and flies and are best avoided.

Festivals last several days and everyone can join in, foreigners included; there's rarely any crime except pick-pocketing. However, the fear of bomb blasts always hangs in the air, particularly in cities, and the presence of a large number of armed security personnel is a constant reminder of the threat of terrorist attack.

India's largest festivals are shown below (in chronological order):

- **Makar Sankranti:** Although 14th January is the official date of the festival, it begins on the 13th and lasts a week. The festival is associated with kite-flying, and since 1989 Ahmedabad in Gujarat has hosted the three-day (13th to 15th January) International Kite Festival, where kite-flyers and kite-makers from countries such as Japan, the US and UK (among others) display their skills along with the local talent. People fly kites from terraces and rooftops from dawn until night, when illuminated box kites called *tukals* dot the sky. There are paper kites as well as self-propelled fibreglass kites in various shapes and sizes, flown on lines coated with a mixture of glue and ground glass – traditional 'cutting-edge' technology used in duels between rivals trying to cut each other's lines at the point of intersection of two 'necking' kites.

- **Holi:** A Hindu festival, though observed by most Indians, *Holi* takes place around the time of the spring equinox (the exact date varies from year to year). On the first evening, huge bonfires are lit at night to celebrate the end of winter and to welcome spring, and on the following morning family, friends and neighbours sprinkle each other with coloured powder (*gulal*). Adolescents usually fling little balloons filled with coloured water, which burst on impact, while small children use water pistols to shoot jets of coloured water at each other. People wear old clothes, for obvious reasons. Come dusk, everyone's in the bathroom – futilely trying to scrub the pigments off their skin.

In cities in particular, natural colourants extracted from flowers have given way to toxic chemical pigments, resulting in an increasing number of cases of skin and eye damage.

Holi Festival

Singing and dancing to the rhythm of drums (*dholak*) while indulging in sweets and *thandai* (a drink made from milk, nuts and spices – 'unofficially' laced with cannabis for adults) is also part of the day's festivities.

- **Ganesh Chaturthi:** Most popular in Goa, Gujarat and Maharashtra, this is a celebration in honour of Ganesh, the elephant-headed God of wisdom who removes obstacles and brings prosperity. The ten-day festival, usually in September, is marked by displays of clay images of Ganesh in various styles and sizes to the accompaniment of recorded or live music. The images are immersed in rivers or the sea, usually on alternate days.

- **Onam:** Held in Kerala in the south of India, *Onam* celebrates the end of the monsoon, usually in September, and takes the form of a regatta, in which 'snake boats' are paddled by as many as 40 men.

- **Navratri:** A nine-day festival, celebrated in most of western and northern India in around October, to mark the end of the monsoon (which takes several weeks to cross the country from the southwest) and is considered auspicious for new beginnings. It's particularly colourful in Gujarat and Western India, where men and women dress in traditional costumes and dance the *Garbha* and *Dandiya-Rasa* (see box) at night to traditional songs accompanied by the rhythmic beating of sticks held by the dancers themselves, as well as drums and folk instruments, or even to music from modern bands.

- The Garbha is a group dance involving both men and women, but not necessarily in pairs, who rhythmically clap their hands while dancing in a circle. The Dandiya-Rasa is similar to the Garbha, but the men form an outer circle and the women an inner circle, and the dancers strike a stick instead of clapping.

- **Dussehra** – A ten-day festival in October, commemorating the slaying of the buffalo-headed demon Mahishasur by Durga (wife of Shiva). On the tenth day, effigies of Ravana, the demon king of Lanka, are burned to celebrate the victory of good over evil.

- **Diwali** – Diwali is the main Indian festival (October-November), when it's traditional for the whole family to gather for lunch (see **Family Occasions** above). The word Diwali derives from the Sanskrit dipavali meaning 'row of lights' and is therefore also known as the festival of lights. Gardens, parks and the exteriors of houses, shops, supermarkets and other buildings are decorated with flashing lights and traditional *diyas* (clay lamps with oil-soaked wicks). Displays of fireworks light up the night sky and firecrackers assault the eardrums from dawn to around 2am, despite the 10pm noise restriction. The festive season lasts a week.

> **Despite a ban on firecrackers after 10pm, noise and air-pollution levels are at their highest from 11pm to 1am during *Diwali*, prompting an exodus of asthmatics from smoked-filled cities, seeking refuge in hill resorts.**

Muslims celebrate Ramadan, *Id al-Fitr*, *Bakari Id* and *Muharram*; Christians celebrate Christmas, New Year and Good Friday. Local festivals are celebrated on saints' days.

Gambling

Although Indians believe in destiny, they seldom lose hope and often take chances with luck. (The interplay between luck and destiny is best portrayed in the 1981 Hindi film *Naseeb* (luck), which begins with a drunk winning a lottery.)

Legal forms of gambling include lotteries, casinos and horse-racing. Lotteries have the major share of the gambling market and are permitted in 13 states, while horseracing and casinos are confined to Goa. It's estimated that the lottery market is worth Rs350bn (US$7bn) and the annual turnover from horseracing is 'just' Rs10bn (US$200m). Lottery tickets are sold in the streets by disabled people, particularly the blind. As well as at kiosks at train stations, bus stations, bookshops and supermarkets.

Illegal gambling is also popular, includes single-digit lotteries (*patta*); betting on elections, cricket matches (particularly when India and Pakistan are playing) and card games. Card playing is common during some festivals, e.g. Janmashtami – a Hindu festival to celebrate the birth of Krishna, which was supposed to have taken place at midnight – when it's a means of staying awake!

The television game show *Kaun Banega Crorepati* (*KBC*), based on the UK's *Who Wants to Be a Millionaire?*, went on air in 2000 with a top prize of Rs10m (US$200,000), which was doubled for the second series.

Street Life

Indians practically live on the streets: hawkers and pedestrians fight for right of way during the day, while at around 5.30pm town and city streets begin filling with people doing grocery shopping before the affluent crowd head to the kiosks for food and drink (and the rest head home to cook). Clusters of plastic chairs provide makeshift sitting for a few while the rest stand and eat. Then, as night falls, the have-nots take over – eating their discards. The pavements are never deserted, as they serve as 'dormitories' for the homeless after the crowds have dispersed late in the night. Until then, many of these pavement dwellers, especially children, take up positions near traffic lights to beg.

Benches on streets and in parks are occupied in the evenings, as it's common for people aged over 30 – particularly those who are overweight – to go for a walk after dinner. This may be on doctor's orders (there's a high incidence of diabetes in India) or an attempt to lose weight, although many Indians feel guilty about trying to stay looking good as they get older and may pretend that their exercise regime is doctor-prescribed. In small towns and villages, people generally prefer to sit on their verandas and talk with their neighbours across the narrow streets.

Paan (shredded areca nut, lime and condiments, often with a pinch of tobacco and wrapped in fresh betel leaves) or *paan masala* (the same mixture in dry, powdered form, sold in sachets) is part of the 'taking to the streets' experience – highly addictive and mostly in the male domain. It's a vice that restricts your speech to mumbles while you chew and suck on it without swallowing the blood-red saliva – crimson streaks staining the walls of corridors and stairwells are testimony to the prevalence of this habit.

Spectator Sports

While watching television soap operas is the nation's favourite pastime,

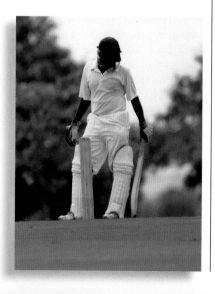

watching cricket comes a close second. Hockey may be the *de jure* national sport but cricket is the *de facto* national sport, and the main sport covered in dailies and on television.

Cricket

Most Indians are cricket fans and play the dual role of spectators and speculators. As well as official matches in India's 19 cricket stadiums, there are innumerable unofficial matches – on playing fields and in the streets – where players are oblivious to the traffic.

> **Indians are even more passionate about cricket than the British, who invented the game and brought it to India. Among the fans of all cricket-playing nations, Indians are known to be the most knowledgeable.**

Major cricket matches are televised spectacles, particularly One-Day International games and the World Cup. The domestic TV rights to such games have been sold for over US$600m. Giant screens are erected in shopping malls, pubs and restaurants, and even in the premises of some BPO companies to stave off absenteeism.

Endless radio and TV time and print media pages are devoted to predicting and analysing the outcome; all news bulletins include an item on cricket and the sports' section of most newspapers is devoted almost entirely to it. Only on the rare occasions when Indians achieve international prowess in a sport other than cricket (such as when Viswanathan Anand won the World Chess Championship in 2007 and 2008) does cricket take a temporary back seat.

Cricket stars enjoy equal celebrity status with Bollywood stars – sometimes even higher, Bollywood stars also being fans. Fans everywhere mob them and the leading players are brand ambassadors who endorse everything from soft drinks to shoes. Ask Indian boys what they want to be when they grow up and more often than not they want to be the next Sachin Tendulkar.

Hooliganism and violence at cricket matches isn't common, although effigies of players have been burnt after the Indian team has lost to Pakistan or after a string of dismal performances. Occasional displays of regionalism have occurred when certain states aren't represented in the national team.

India's national team, which is governed by the Board of Control for Cricket in India (BCCI), is currently the most highly sponsored national sports team in the world and has some of the world's best cricketers. Nevertheless, it last won the World Cup in 1983 and its ejection from the 2007 World Cup was a huge disappointment to fans. There's also a women's national team, which won the Women's Asia Cup of 2005-06, although it has a much lower profile, lower pay and less popular support than the men's team.

It's said that the India-Pakistan war is fought on the cricket pitch. Sporadic bursts of firecrackers call attention to the fact that the two countries are playing and non-stop firecrackers are an indication that India has won a game. 'Cricket visas' are issued to the tens of thousands of fans eager to cross the border to watch the two arch-rivals play.

Cricket is one of the most popular topics of conversation among Indian men, particularly when India is playing – talk at work, at parties, in bars, in shops and even in homes is about cricket. In the office, the internet is used for accessing live scores while in the streets the service is provided free on mobile phones – don't be surprised when total strangers ask you as casually as if asking for the time, "What's the score?"

> Indian cricketers have been nicknamed 'the men in blue' by the media on account of their sky-blue uniforms in one-day international matches.

Domestic Cricket Tournaments

The following domestic cricket tournaments are conducted under the aegis of the BCCI:

- **Ranjit Trophy:** The most important competition, in which two groups, Elite A and Elite B, play on a league basis;

- **Irany Trophy:** Played between the Ranjit Trophy champions of the previous year and a selected 'Rest of India XI', heralding the start of the new domestic season;

- **Deodhar Trophy:** Played on a league basis among the five zones: North, South, East, West and Central;

- **Duleep Trophy:** Also played on a zonal basis;

- **NKP Salve Challenger Trophy:** A one-day match featuring three teams, Seniors, India A and India B. The Seniors team comprises leading players of the national team and the other two teams are made up of India's most promising young players.

Other Sports

Although cricket is king, football, tennis, badminton and hockey are also popular. Fans of sports that aren't popular in India, e.g. rugby, needn't be disappointed as satellite television has proliferated in all cities and towns and even in many rural areas.

Football: The National Football league is under the aegis of the All India Football Federation. Enjoying a huge following, the best teams are based in Kolkata (Calcutta) and Goa. Other major clubs are the East Bengal Club and Mohun Bagan Athletic Club. There's a football league – the Street League – for homeless kids, set up by aid workers.

Tennis: Popular in urban India, the game's leading players currently include Mahesh Bhupathi, Sania Mirza and Leander Paes.

Sania Mirza

Badminton: Although the Indian team isn't a major player, badminton is a popular sport throughout India. Pullela Gopichand and Prakash Padukone have both won the All England Badminton Championships.

Hockey: Once the best team in the world, with eight Olympic gold medals and the 1975 World Cup to its name, the Indian men's hockey squad slid into obscurity when the International Hockey Federation introduced AstroTurf, a rare surface in India.

Major Sporting Events

The following annual sporting events are the most important in the Indian calendar:

Badminton – Senior National Championships (January); Yonex Sunrise India Open Gold (September)

Cricket – National Championship, Ranjit trophy (final match in February)

Hockey – National Championships (February); Premier Hockey League (finals in March); Beighton cup (finals in April)

Football – National Championship & Santosh Trophy (finals in October); Durand Cup (November); Federation Cup (finals in December); National Football League (deciding match in February)

Tennis – ATP Tournament in Chennai (January); WTA Tournament in Bangalore (February)

THE ARTS

In India, art and religion are inextricably interlinked – music and dance are considered as much a form of worship as sculpture and painting are part of temples of worship.

Booking

Tickets for cultural events can be bought in the following ways:

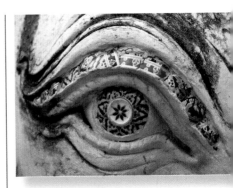

- **At music shops** – Most music shops sell tickets for cultural events. Booking is straightforward and you can usually choose your seat.

- **Online & by telephone** – Most theatres and cinemas in cities allow online and telephone booking. As elsewhere, phone booking lines are usually busy, making it difficult to get through – persistent redialling is the only option. Payment can be made by credit or debit card or online and there's often a booking fee of around 5 to 10 per cent. Tickets aren't sent to you and you need to arrive 30 minutes before the entry or start time to collect them – you don't have to queue with those wanting to buy tickets at the door, but you must show the credit card you used to pay for the tickets.

- **In person** – Depending on the popularity of an event, you may need to go early and queue for hours.

In appreciation of a good performance, Indians clap their hands and sometimes stamp their feet. Outstanding performances are rewarded with either shrill whistling or rhythmic, repetitive shouts of 'once more!'

Cinema & Theatre

When going to see a film or a play in India, bear in mind the following:

- **Security:** Metal/bomb-detecting devices and frisking are common in large cinemas in metropolitan cities due to the ever-present terrorist threat.

- **Disabled access:** A ramp is about all you can expect as a facility for disabled people in most theatres.

- **Late arrivals:** If you arrive late for a theatre or concert performance, you'll rarely have to wait for an interval or break before being admitted. Entrance to a cinema is allowed at any time.

- **Noise:** Theatregoers are usually quiet, but at cinemas many chat through trailers and adverts, and some even throughout the film. Late arrivals, inconsiderate teenagers and unruly children add to the disturbances, but mobile phones are becoming the biggest nuisance (Indians rarely switch them off).

- **Air-conditioning:** Air-conditioning is required all year round in India and is a welcome relief from the heat. However, air-conditioners often aren't switched on until the show begins.

- **Food:** Theatregoers rarely take food into the auditorium and at some theatres it's prohibited. Nevertheless, most cinemas have snack bars selling coffee, tea, ice cream, chocolate, pastries, sweets, hotdogs, popcorn and soft drinks – the last two, sold in plastic buckets, being the most popular (even in small towns).

Museums & Art Galleries

Until recently, all museums and galleries in India were state owned and, as most curators lack both training and relevant skills, displays are often dusty and explanations minimal, although in English. However, major museums offer detailed explanations of exhibits on their websites, therefore accessing the website before visiting the museum itself is recommended.

Indians are proud of their national heritage, and museums and art galleries display large collections of ancient artefacts and paintings, many of which (often housed in converted palaces) include royal memorabilia. The National Museum in New Delhi and the Heras Institute of Indian History and Culture in Mumbai (free to research scholars in Indian history and culture) are noteworthy.

> **The Devi Art Foundation in Delhi, which opened in September 2008, claims to be the country's first private museum of art.**

Museums and galleries are categorised as 'national' or 'district' institutions, the latter being intended to entertain and educate the public through lectures, training courses, seminars, competitions, exhibitions and research guidance, in addition to their traditional role of the preservation and display of artefacts.

Taj Mahal, Agra

- **Opening hours:** These vary but at large museums are usually from 9 or 10am to 5 or 6pm. Smaller museums may close at lunchtime, e.g. from 1 to 3pm. Museums close on different days of the week, in addition to public holidays. Last access is usually 30 minutes before closing time and visitors are asked to leave 10 or 15 minutes before the museum closes.

- **Entrance fees:** For Indians, entrance fees are around Rs5 (US10¢) for adults and Rs3 for children under 12. Reductions are available for students, who pay around Rs2. Foreigners, however, are charged extra (you may be asked to show your passport if you pretend you're Indian!) – usually around Rs100 (US$2) per person.

- **Security:** Most museums and galleries don't allow visitors in with belongings other than a handbag. Other bags, cameras and coats must be left in a locker if available or in the cloakroom. At major city museums you may be frisked as well as having to pass through an X-ray machine.

- **Disabled access:** As with cinemas and theatres, a ramp for a wheelchair may be the only provision, if any, for disabled people.

- **Cafés & shops:** Although there's usually a museum shop, cafés are rare and basic with a limited choice of food and higher prices than elsewhere. Few museums allow you to consume your own food on the premises unless it's in the gardens.

- **Noise:** Despite the usual 'Silence Please' signs, Indian museums aren't the quietest of places due to noisy school parties and tourists. However, these groups are usually in a hurry to move on, so you may soon have the place all to yourself – until the next batch arrives.

9.
RETAIL THERAPY

Talk about shopping in India and the word 'bazaar' comes to the mind of most Westerners. However, the rising buying power of the great Indian middle class is creating an ever-increasing demand for supermarkets, hypermarkets and shopping centres (mall or multiplex), which are competing with traditional family-run shops and markets. Shopping malls are particularly popular and they aren't exclusive to cities; they're sprouting in most large towns and in a number of small industrial towns.

According to a report by the McKinsey Global Institute, India's middle class will soon embark on a spending spree that will make it the fifth-largest consuming economy behind the US, Japan, China and the UK.

CUSTOMER SERVICE

Indian customer service ranges from the enthusiastic to the indifferent, most shop assistants falling into the former category – particularly in traditional shops, where the owner will welcome you as soon as you enter. If attending to other customers, the owner will excuse himself and enquire about your needs, after which he may assign an assistant to you and return to what he was doing. If you happen to be the first customer at opening time, the owner will want to make a sale, however small, even if he has to offer you a large discount, as he believes that it will bring him luck throughout the day.

In a non-traditional setting, the enthusiastic assistant cannot say 'no' and will show you a plethora of items, sometimes unrelated to your original request, and then make it difficult for you to say 'no'. However, you must hope that what you've bought works, as the assistant's enthusiasm won't extend to replacing or refunding it, even within a month of purchase (see **Consumer Rights** below).

Always ask for a receipt. In the event of a complaint, the first thing that will be asked of you by the shopkeeper is the receipt as proof of purchase.

If you receive indifferent service, go elsewhere. Competition from multinational retailers and the 'activism' of consumer forums is rapidly making Indian shop-owners believe in the sign they frequently display: 'The customer is king'.

OPENING HOURS

Shopping hours in cities are generally Mondays to Saturdays from 10am to 8pm, but although they remain open during lunchtime, you may not find more than one assistant on duty. Some supermarkets, hypermarkets and large department stores in busy cities remain open until 10pm. while shops in small towns are usually open from 8am to 8pm. While most shops close on Sundays, many also close on other days of the week (known as 'weekly offs'), Tuesdays being a favourite. Butchers and fishmongers follow the same routine but break for lunch from 2 to 4pm. In rural areas, where many businesses are independent concerns, shops may also close between 2 and 4pm.

QUEUING

There are various queuing 'systems' in India, but queue jumping, jostling and general chaos are a common sight:

- **Tickets:** Many shops and supermarkets have machines which dispense a numbered ticket, where customers are required to wait until their number is displayed. If you miss your number you'll have to start the process all over again.

- **Tokens:** similar to ticketing and mostly used in banks; you collect a copper token with a number on it and wait until your number is called.

- **Sex:** There are separate queues for men and women in India, the women's queue usually being shorter. It isn't uncommon to see men coming off long queues, particularly at railway stations, and asking women in the women's queues to buy tickets for them.

- **Single file:** Single file queuing is common in many banks and government offices, where the first person in the queue goes to the first available desk.

- **Enquiring:** When you enter a shop with neither a ticket system nor a discernible queue, common practice is to stand as near to the counter as possible without jostling and then try to catch an assistant's eye.

Rules are frequently broken in India, particularly in public places and in situations that call upon courtesy – often it seems as if not breaking the rules is the exception to the rule. There's always a bully or a so-called VIP or 'senior government official' arrogantly jumping queues as if it's his birthright. Protesting, even politely, can invite hostility – not least from the vendor, who wants to oblige such (self-) important people.

Most shops gift-wrap items at the counter but charge you for the paper and tag. In large stores you must carry the item to a dedicated gift-wrapping counter, where you can select the paper and tag of your choice.

PAYMENT

According to Visa research, less than 30 per cent of wealthy people in India have a credit card compared, for example, with over 90 per cent in Hong Kong; there are some 70m credit cards in use in the UK, while Indians, who are almost 20 times more numerous, possess a mere 22mn! Nevertheless, credit cards are widely accepted in all cities and most towns, and 'swipe' cards can still be used.

As an alternative to credit cards, many Indians use 'netbanking' – online payment direct from their bank account – and debit cards.

SALES

There are at least five annual sale periods in India:

- **March** – stock clearance, just before the closing of the financial year (31st March);

- **June–September** – to boost sales during the monsoons, a slack season;

- **March–May** & **October–December** (the peak buying periods) – sales may be limited to promotional offers on new products;

Sales are also linked with the three major festivals, *Diwali*, *Dusserah* and *Holi*, and increasingly with Christmas. Substantial discounts are offered on home appliances, while discounts on clothes and shoes are as high as 60 per cent. Indians shop most during the fortnight preceding *Diwali*, buying new cars, televisions, electronic gadgets and home appliances, besides the traditional sweetmeats and assortments of dried fruit and nuts.

TYPES OF SHOP

With the opening up of the economy, global giants such as Wal-Mart are taking over the retail trade in India, which is predicted to become the largest retail market in the world, and major brand names such as Calvin Klein, Gas, Tommy Hilfiger, Marks & Spencer and Hugo Boss are entering into joint ventures with Indian firms. India has around 70 hypermarkets and 1,300 supermarkets. Traditional family-run stores, although threatened by the large retailers, shopping malls and multiplexes, are finding innovative ways to survive. These include specialisation, the

recruitment of professional staff and the introduction of home-delivery services, although it's their convenience that ensures them a loyal clientele.

Typical Indian shops include the following:

- **Cloth shop** – a shop that sells material (cloth) for curtains, bed linen, table linen, towels and clothing;

- **Emporium** – run by state governments in major cities, emporiums sell indigenous fabrics such as *khadi* (hand-spun cotton), local handicrafts, paintings by Indian artists, etc. Quality is superior to that of similar items found elsewhere, but prices are fixed (a printed price list is available and is often displayed) and generally a little higher than what you can expect to pay in other shops.

- **General store** (*kirana* or *bazaar*) – sells cereals (known as 'food grains'), cooking oils, dairy products, nuts, dried fruit, toiletries, cosmetics, household cleaning products, bottled and canned foods, and over-the-counter medicines, but not meat or fish;

- **Kiosk** – a white plastic or plywood booth, selling essential food items such as bread, butter, cheese, milk, eggs, ice-cream, soft drinks and confectionery as well as toiletries, condoms and plastic toys;

- *Paan* **stall** – unique to India, these are little plywood kiosks wedged between shops and selling *paan*: chopped areca nut and various spices wrapped in a green betel leaf lined with slaked white lime. *Paan* stalls also sell tobacco and cigarettes.

- **Street hawkers** – these peddle fruit, vegetables, bread, pastries, condiments, nuts and even fresh fish, either from handcarts or a bamboo basket carried on their heads.

Condoms

Condoms come in only one size. Though this isn't large by Western standards, a 2007 survey by condom manufacturer Durex reported that over 60 per cent of Indian men experienced 'slippage'.

Markets

In India, people go to the market for two essential commodities – food and local news. For foreigners the compelling reason to shop at a market is the atmosphere: the crowds, aromas and colourful displays; the heat, dust and noise; the incessant haggling; the pickpockets and the beggars; the stray cows, goats and dogs; vendors vying for your attention; and the mounds of produce beckoning, while swarms of flies repel you. You will be either enchanted or repelled!

Food Markets

Food markets are held under cover but invariably spill out onto the roadside, with stalls sprawling all over the pavements. They're laid out in clearly defined sections – a whole floor of a building or a whole row of stalls on the pavement dedicated to a single commodity, e.g. meat, vegetables, fruit or fish. They are open Mondays to Saturdays, usually from 8 or 9am to 3pm, when any remaining perishable stock is sold off cheaply.

you can make special orders or ask them to keep items for you.

Street Markets

Street markets are held once a week in most Indian towns and cities, starting at around 8am and finishing at 2pm. Stalls generally sell spices, grains, sweets, fruit, vegetables, flowers, pickles, livestock, ceramics, CDs, craftwork, cheap jewellery, clay pottery, clothes, shoes and other items. Haggling is expected and although you can get a substantial discount, the quality of goods is generally low.

Beware of the bystander who offers to exchange your high denomination currency note for small change. It may be the last you see of him – and your money.

FOOD

Indians not only cook just before each meal, they use fresh produce – not frozen or even refrigerated – which necessitates daily shopping for food. Indians haven't developed a taste for Western food and this is understandable, given the immense variety of Indian cuisine. However, imported foods such as cheeses, tinned fish, olive oil, broccoli, celery, kiwi fruit and grapefruit are available in the major cities in India. Ready-to-eat, frozen, canned and junk foods are (unfortunately) also finding a ready market with the entry of McDonald's, Baskin Robbins and KFC.

Most non-packaged food is bought in multiples of 100g, although bananas are sold in dozens. Most fresh food is weighed and priced at the counter and not at the checkout.

Food markets are popular and the best place for variety and freshness. Food is usually cheaper than in supermarkets, particularly if you buy what's in season and grown locally. Butchers and fishmongers at markets will prepare meat and fish exactly to your specification – a service that isn't offered in many supermarkets – but you need to make sure that it's fresh.

You're free to touch and select fruit and vegetables yourself and will often be offered a sample to taste, particularly of sweets, pastries and fruit.

Shopping at markets isn't for those in a hurry – queues at stalls often move slowly as each customer has a chat with the stallholder to catch up on the local gossip – but an experience to be savoured. If you shop regularly at food markets and get to know stallholders,

Meat

Most Indians are vegetarians, but even meat eaters are squeamish about meat

Metric/Imperial Conversion			
Weight			
Imperial	**Metric**	**Metric**	**Imperial**
1 UK pint	0.57 litre	1 litre	1.75 UK pints
1 US pint	0.47 litre	1 litre	2.13 US pints
1 UK gallon	4.54 litre	1 litre	0.22 UK gallon
1 US gallon	3.78 litres	1 litre	0.26 US gallon
Capacity			
Imperial	**Metric**	**Metric**	**Imperial**
1 UK pint	0.57 litre	1 litre	1.75 UK pints
1 US pint	0.47 litre	1 litre	2.13 US pints
1 UK gallon	4.54 litres	1 litre	0.22 UK gallon
1 US gallon	3.78 litres	1 litre	0.26 US gallon

Note: An American 'cup' = around 250ml or 0.25 litre.

being displayed on a supermarket counter. Not so in a market, where chickens are displayed alive, hanging from hooks over the chopping block. When you buy one, the butcher cuts off the head and claws, plucks the feathers and cleans out the innards but leaves the skin on, unless you instruct otherwise. Chicken is the most common meat and usually has a market section to itself. Goat meat is almost as fresh, and carcasses are hung from hooks over the chopping block.

Pork isn't popular, except in Goa and the northeast. Goa pork sausages are famous not only for their taste but also for their spiciness. Frozen ham, bacon, salami and frankfurters are sold in supermarkets in most cities. Any dish on a restaurant menu detailed as mutton in likely to be goat meat.

Dairy Products

Fresh milk and other dairy products are readily available. You can buy milk in 500ml 'pouches' (transparent, square polythene bags – as used for blood) or in cartons, but you won't know whether it's cow or buffalo milk. If you specifically want one or the other, you can buy it 'unpackaged' from the dairy but it's often watered down. Milk in India should always be boiled, even if the package says it's pasteurised. *Paneer* is a fresh cheese similar to cottage cheese, which is widely used in Indian cooking.

As people are becoming more health conscious, the demand for probiotic food is increasing, with companies such as Yakult Danone India and Amul launching probiotic products.

Eggs

Eggs are sold (by the dozen) everywhere, from the neighbourhood kiosk to the supermarket. In the latter, they come in boxes, but elsewhere you'll need to take your own box or take them home in a plastic bag. Demand for eggs is seasonal, dropping as the mercury rises.

Fruits & Vegetables

The bazaar (market) is the most popular place to buy fresh, locally grown fruit – mangoes, bananas, chickoos (sapodilla), guavas, oranges, papayas, custard apples, pineapples, grapes and strawberries. Imported fruit, such as kiwi fruit and grapefruit, are now available in most cities. Similarly, locally grown vegetables such as potatoes, onions, carrots, cucumbers, cabbages, cauliflowers, aubergines, green peppers and spinach are sold alongside imported asparagus and broccoli.

Herbs & Spices

Foreign herbs such as oregano, basil, rosemary and thyme are sold in dried form in some cities. Indian herbs and spices are sold everywhere – fresh or dried, whole as well as powdered or puréed.

Garam masala **is an assortment of spices (***garam* **is Hindi for hot,** *masala* **for spice mix, although they're pungent rather than hot) – cinnamon, cloves, nutmeg, cardamom and black pepper – widely used in Indian cuisine. Add chopped onions and garlic, grated ginger, a few green chillies and curry leaves (***kaddipatta***) and you have an authentic curry mix.**

Bread & Pastries

Bread and pastries are sold by some bakeries (not all sell to the public) and other shops. Bread usually comes in small loaves – more like Western rolls – of which an Indian may eat four or five with a meal. These can be bought loose or sliced in plastic packets. Most of the bread produced is white, and 'brown bread' is usually just coloured white bread. Whole-grain breads are sold in bakeries in some large cities catering to foreigners and the new breed of health-conscious Indians.

A variety of pastries are available in cities – cakes, doughnuts, croissants, Danish pastries, tarts, and pies.

Pizzas are popular in cities and towns, where a home-delivery service is offered by chains such as Dominos and Pizza Hut.

Organic Food

Organic foods are only just beginning to be appreciated and therefore rarely have a section of their own. Free-range eggs and chickens aren't easy to find in cities, and are double the price of battery produce.

DRINK

Soft Drinks

Besides Pepsi and Coca Cola, there's a variety of non-alcoholic bottled drinks, including fruit juices such as mango, orange, pineapple, chickoo and apple. Fresh coconut milk is sold in the shell on street corners and on beaches.

Alcoholic Drinks

Alcohol is generally available in India. However, Gujarat in the west and Mizoram and Nagaland in the northeast are 'dry' states (where no alcoholic products may be produced or consumed) while Tamil Nadu, Kerala and Andhra Pradesh, all in South India, have partial prohibition, i.e. one or more types of liquor, usually *arrack*, the local firewater, is prohibited. Outside urban areas, liquor stores are 'hole in the wall' type establishments where alcohol is sold through a metal grille. Generally, it isn't advisable for women to buy alcohol from such premises as they're likely to attract the unwanted attention of drunks.

Foreigners can obtain a 'liquor permit' for any dry or semi-dry state or an All-India permit from visa-issuing authorities such as Government of India tourist offices in India and Indian embassies, high commissions and tourist offices abroad. The permit allows you to drink in designated 'permit rooms' in certain hotels.

There are also occasional national and regional 'dry days', e.g. when there's an election, but those with a liquor permit can drown their sorrows 365 days a year.

Beer

Beer is widely available, although annual per capita consumption is 0.8 litres, a mere 3 per cent of the global average. Beer is mostly sold in 650ml bottles but cans are slowly gaining in popularity with the young, while draught beer is sold only in big-city pubs; prices vary from state to state. Kingfisher is India's favourite beer – a lager beer which is highly drinkable (especially when you're dying of thirst).

Wine

Surprisingly, India also produces wine, which, although not among the best in the world, is steadily improving as its popularity increases. Domestic wine production is around 10mn litres (comparable with that of Albania) and consumption 15mn litres, the latter figure growing at 30 to 40 per cent per year.

India's main wine-producing areas are in Andhra Pradesh, Karnataka and Maharashtra states, the last producing half of the country's wine. The top three Indian wine producers are Grover in Karnataka, and Sula and Indage in Maharashtra. Other top wineries include Bluestar Agro and Winery, Costa & Company, Dajeeba and ND Wines.

> **Grover, whose vineyards are in the Nandi Hills outside Bangalore, claims that, unlike other Indian winemakers, it uses only French wine grape varieties. Its prestigious 'La Reserve' red (80 per cent cabernet sauvignon and 20 per cent syrah) was recently voted 'Best New World Red Wine' by** *Decanter* **magazine.**

Foreign wines are also available and, in accordance with India's commitment to the World Trade Organisation (WTO), the government recently reduced import duty on wines from 150 per cent to 100 per cent. In a supermarket, wine generally ranges from US$2 to US$15 per bottle.

Spirits

India's only indigenous spirit is *fenny* (made from coconut or cashew nuts), which is made in Goa. Local imitations of foreign spirits are labelled 'Indian Made Foreign Liquor' (IMFL) and are of generally poor quality. Foreign spirits bottled in India (labelled 'BII'), such as Seagram's Hundred Pipers scotch, cost far more and those 'bottled in origin' ('BIO') are prohibitively expensive owing to 150 per cent import duty.

CLOTHES

Clothing you can buy in India varies from the mediocre to the high-quality, with both local labels and international brands on offer in shopping malls. (Indians are no less label-obsessed than Westerners.) Cities and large towns have a choice of clothing to suit all budgets and tastes, and even small towns may have several clothes shops. Indian style tends to be smart-casual, but if you're looking for cheap-and-cheerful clothes, try the stalls on city streets – 'Fashion Street' in Mumbai is an excellent place for cheap but trendy clothes.

You'll find an abundance of fabric shops, tailors and dressmakers and if opting to wear *salwar kameez*, you'll probably have more choice by selecting your material and asking a tailor to make the garment. This will probably be no more expensive, and may even be cheaper, than buying 'off the peg'. As a rule of thumb, you'll need two metres of material for the *salwar* and the same for the *kameez*.

In small clothes shops, you should always 'barter', i.e. ask for a reduction. Most Indian shop-owners quote a price in accordance with the apparent affluence of the customer. As a foreigner, you'll be

perceived as rich, so the price will be high. A counter-offer of 50 per cent of the asking price is a good starting point; if you drive a hard bargain, you may end up with a 25 per cent 'discount'.

Sizes

Men's shirts are classed like most other garments, by body, rather than collar, size, i.e. 'S' for small, 'M' for medium, 'L' for large and 'XL' for extra large. Indian sizing tends to be smaller than in Western countries, so if you're very large you'll need to look out for XXL clothes.

Shoes

Although shoes for men with large feet are available in all shoe shops, few shops stock women's shoes larger than around UK size 7.

Children's Clothes

Children's clothes can be expensive and elaborate, even carrying designer labels. Long shorts with fancy shirts for boys and dainty dresses with patent shoes for girls are common.

Alterations

Most clothes shops provide an extensive alteration service – trousers can be taken up or in, sleeves shortened and waists reduced, usually at no extra charge. The shop assistant pins the garment for you and a simple alteration usually takes a couple of hours at most.

MAIL-ORDER SHOPPING

In general, Indians aren't keen on buying goods other than in shops – some people are suspicious of paying money for a product they haven't seen and most are reluctant to leave delivery of goods in the unreliable hands of the post office, which has a reputation for damage, delay, loss and sometimes theft. The majority of mail-order retailers therefore use courier companies for delivering goods – which means that catalogue shopping isn't popular in India due to the high delivery and return costs.

Nevertheless, CDs and other products can be purchased by post from Reader's Digest (💻 www.rd-india.com).

Internet

Online shopping has been slow to take off in India, due more to slow internet speeds than to worries about security, although Indians are reluctant to use credit cards online, even via a secure site. However, with the introduction of broadband connectivity in most cities and large towns in 2007, the number of net shoppers rose by over 75 per cent, resulting in an increase in the number of large retailers offering internet shopping

services, taking the market to Rs23bn (US$460m). Travel products top the list of online items being purchased by Indians, followed by jewellery, books, accessories, apparel, gifts, CDs and DVDs.

Some large supermarkets offer online shopping, although it has yet to take off as there's a limited delivery area, e.g. within a 10km (6mi) radius, and sometimes a minimum spend (see below).

Home Delivery

Most large supermarkets and even traditional shops offer free home delivery within a 5km radius, provided the value of purchases is above a certain amount, usually Rs100 (US$2). Furniture and domestic appliance stores usually deliver free to your home, and many companies include the installation of an appliance, such as a fridge or washing machine, in the purchase price.

CONSUMER RIGHTS

As in Western countries, consumers in India have extensive rights. The difference is that most people are unaware of them and the official complaints and redress system is slow and corrupt. Retailers take advantage of this – and their customers.

Refunds

You hardly ever receive a refund in India. If you're lucky, you may be offered a replacement or alternative item. If a refund is made on an item bought with a credit or debit card, it's made electronically as a credit and not in cash.

Guarantees

Most electronic items and appliances have a one-year warranty and you're entitled to free repair during this period, subject to a number of conditions (detailed in very small print).

> **When you buy an appliance, ask for a warranty card and check that it has been completed, date-stamped and signed by the dealer.**

Complaints

Printed on most receipts in India are the words 'Goods once sold will not be taken back.' Sometimes shopkeepers will make a fuss even if you return spoiled food products, leaving you to take your complaint directly to the manufacturer or the courts.

The principal government consumer protection agency – in respect of both products and service – is the National Consumer Disputes Redressal Commission (NCDRC), whose offices are at Janpath Bhawan (A Wing, 5th Floor, Janpath, New Delhi, 11-237 12109, 🖳 www.ncdrc.nic.in). Complaints must be filed in accordance with the Consumer Protection Act, with the nearest district forum. If you aren't satisfied by the decision of the district forum, you can challenge it before the state commission and, if you still aren't satisfied, before the national commission. However, the machinery is very slow.

A much faster and more effective avenue for consumer redress is provided by the Consumer Education and Research Cell (CERC, Thaltej, Sarkhej-Gandhinagar Highway, Ahmedabad – 380054, Gujarat, 79-7489945, 🖳 www.cercindia.org), which uses the media to publicise consumer complaints. To become a member of the CERC and be entitled to use its services, you must subscribe to its monthly magazine, *Insight*, at an annual fee of Rs250 (US$5). More often than not, just a letter or an email to the defaulting party, copied to the CERC, will get your dispute settled in a matter of weeks, if not days.

Hawa Mahal (Palace of Winds), Jaipur

10.
ODDS & ENDS

A country's culture is influenced by various factors and reflected in myriad ways. Among the principal influences are its climate, geography and religion, which are considered here along with various cultural manifestations, including crime, the national flag and anthem, government and international relations, pets, tipping and toilets.

> Everything in India is of biblical proportions: floods, droughts, earthquakes, relief camps, pests and the Constitution – the world's longest.

CLIMATE

India is a country of climatic extremes: from freezing winters in the Himalayan north to year-round heat and humidity in the tropical south; from places which must manage with just 10cm (4in) of rain in a year to those which must cope with 70cm (28in) in a single day. The wettest place on earth is Mawsynram in northeast India, where almost 1,200cm (470in) of rain falls each year – 20 times more than in London.

Except in the hills, March to July is generally hot, though the southwest monsoon brings relief from June, when it begins lashing southern and western India. The monsoon takes around two weeks to reach Goa, another two weeks to arrive in Mumbai and two more to get to Gujarat, retreating around mid-September in a series of thunderstorms that diminish in intensity each day and, as it does so, showering much of central India. A second, weaker, monsoon, the northeast monsoon, which travels down the east coast, makes its brief appearance in October and lasts until the end of November.

The monsoons not only bring relief from the heat but also, more importantly, determine the annual harvest. Too much rain and there are floods, damaging crops. Too little rain and there will be droughts, leading to famine.

Most of India is at its best from December to February, when it's dry and relatively cold. Nights are cool and days pleasant in Delhi and the rest of North India. There's snow in the far north, while the south is bearably warm.

India has the following 'seasons':

Winter – December, January, February

Summer – March, April, May

South-west monsoon – June, July, August

North-east monsoon – October, November

Heat

Because India is so vast, temperatures vary from region to region. While Delhi is blistering in summer heat of between 26°C and 41°C (75°F to 106°F), the snow is yet to melt in the mountains in Jammu, Kerala in southwest India is being drenched by the first monsoon showers, and Darjeeling on the lower slopes of the Himalayas in the east feels like the tropics.

In the dry, unrelenting heat of summer, from March to May, temperatures on the plains climb to 45°C (113°F) and a hot wind raises dust storms. Tempers also rise, and murder, suicide and motor vehicle accident rates soar.

Scientists have predicted that climate change due to global warming will hit India hard from the third decade of the 21st century by way of extreme heat waves, a drop in per capita water availability (from around 1,900 cubic metres to 1,000 cubic metres by 2025), and floods and mudslides due to glacial meltdown in the Himalayan region, followed by a retraction of glacier-fed rivers.

Extreme Weather

The cliché 'It never rains, but it pours' couldn't be truer when it comes to India. Rivers which have dried up during droughts swell in a couple of days of torrential rain and overflow, causing floods, which result in loss of life (human and livestock), crops and property. Hundreds of people die every year during the monsoons as a result of drowning, house collapses, landslides and electrocution. Diseases such as cholera, typhoid, malaria and diarrhoea then follow. Flash floods are more common in the Himalayan regions. The cold wave in winter takes its toll mostly on the elderly and the homeless in northern India, while elsewhere many die of heat stroke in the summer.

As a foreigner, you should protect yourself from the sun, using sunscreen on all exposed parts of the body, and drink plenty of water (eight glasses a day is

the recommended minimum) to avoid dehydration. Fruit juice is also beneficial, especially the juices sold from roadside stalls, which have added salt, sugar and spices – the last believed to act as body coolants! Many foreigners attempt to combat the heat by leaving most of their bodies bare, but this exposes the skin to the damaging rays of the sun. Instead, light and loose-fitting white cotton clothes are the best choice for keeping cool.

> 'In tropical climes there are certain times of day
> When all the citizens retire, to tear their clothes off and perspire.
> It's one of those rules that the biggest fools obey,
> Because the sun is much too sultry and one must avoid its ultra-violet ray.
> The natives grieve when the white men leave their huts,
> Because they're obviously, absolutely nuts ...
> In Bengal, to move at all, is seldom if ever done,
> But mad dogs and Englishmen go out in the midday sun.'
>
> Noël Coward, English playwright & composer

During the monsoon season, always wear rubber footwear (though not gumboots) rather than leather and carry an umbrella or a raincoat, as the weather forecast is unreliable. Most importantly, beware of open manholes, which are concealed by floodwater: every year people fall into these and drown.

If you get soaked, make sure that you wash your feet and apply an antiseptic to prevent infection from the contaminated water flowing out of drains and sewers. If waterborne diseases such as cholera and typhoid break out, avoid eating fresh fruit and vegetables; cholera germs are carried by the house fly, which abounds in Indian bazaars during the monsoons.

CRIME

Despite widespread crushing poverty and a chasm-like, rich-poor divide, India is a fairly 'safe' country (by international standards) with a crime rate of just 170 per 100,000 population per annum, compared, for example, with over 8,000 per 100,000 in the UK and US. However, crime is on the rise, particularly in urban areas.

While hold-ups at gunpoint are rare, petty theft of the snatch-and-run type and minor fraud are common. Bejewelled women are usually the victims of 'chain-snatchers', while petty scammers include touts at railway stations who offer to buy your ticket, order a taxi for you or take you to a hotel and take a 'commission', and 'freelance currency exchange agents', who run off with your money.

'White collar' crimes such as tax evasion, corruption and bribery aren't just commonplace but are taken for granted – as explained elsewhere in this book.

Violent crimes against foreigners receive a lot of exposure in the media but are rare and usually speedily dealt with by the normally sluggish courts.

Security

India is a very security conscious nation. Security searches are common at major religious sites and tourist attractions, and you may have to deposit your bag in a cloakroom or locker on entry. Mobile phones, pocket knives, lighters, etc., may also be confiscated if you try to enter a site with them; wallets and cameras are often the only items you'll be permitted to carry. When buying a mobile phone or SIM card in India, you must complete an application form, produce your passport and visa, a passport photo and a letter from your employer confirming your residence and employment.

Maoist terrorists (including Naxals) operate in rural and hill areas of Bihar, Jharkhand, Chhatisgarh, Andhra Pradesh and, to a lesser extent, Orissa. These groups have never attacked foreigners – their targets are government officials and institutions and the police. However, if you're visiting any of these states it's advisable to exercise caution and avoid remote areas when travelling alone. Bihar, in particular, has an unfortunate reputation for lawlessness and travellers are warned of possible attacks by bandits. Bandhs (protest rallies) and curfews can be declared at short notice and should be observed.

As a foreign national you'll be quite conspicuous and your inadvertent presence at a political protest or *bandh* could bring you to the attention of the local police, which may cause complications for any future visa extension. The best approach is to ask your colleagues and neighbours to advise you if a strike is called, or subscribe to the free SMS (text) news service in your locality. When travelling to a destination within 50km (31mi) of a land border you need a designated area permit unless there's an immigration gate. Military and government buildings and TV and radio stations all have protected area status and photography is strictly prohibited.

FLAG & ANTHEM

Flag

The national flag is a horizontal tricolour of deep saffron at the top, white in the middle and dark green at the bottom, in equal proportion, with a 24-spoke navy-blue (*ashoka*) wheel centred on the white band. The saffron band symbolises renunciation (on the part of the country's leaders, who are expected to be indifferent to material gain and dedicated to their work); the white band represents light (the path of truth that guides one's conduct); and the green the land itself, on which all life depends.

The Ashoka Wheel denotes the law of *dharma* (virtue), the controlling principle of Indian life, and represents motion, the dynamism of peaceful change.

Anthem

The poem *Jana-gana-mana* (Thou Art the Ruler of The Minds of All People), composed in Bengali by Nobel laureate Rabindranath Tagore in 1911, was set to music by Ram Singh Thakur, an Indian freedom fighter, and adopted in a Hindi translation by the Constituent Assembly as the National Anthem of India on 24th January 1950.

Indian National Anthem

O! Dispenser of India's destiny, thou art the ruler of the minds of all people.

Thy name rouses the hearts of Punjab, Sindh, Gujarat, the Maratha country, the Dravida country, Utkala and Bengal;

it echoes in the hills of the Vindhyas and Himalayas,

it mingles in the rhapsodies of the pure waters of Yamuna and the Ganges.

They chant only thy name.

They seek only thy auspicious blessings.

They sing only the glory of thy victory.

The salvation of all people waits in thy hands,

O! Dispenser of India's destiny, thou art the ruler of the minds of all people.

Victory to thee, victory to thee, victory to thee,

victory, victory, victory, victory to thee!

GEOGRAPHY

Despite having a population that's second in size only to China's (and expected to overtake it before the middle of the century), India is only the seventh-largest country in the world, with an area of 3,287,623km² (1,269,219mi²) – a mere third of the size of the US, whose population is less than half of India's.

India's neighbours are China (Tibet), Bhutan and Nepal to the north, Pakistan to the northwest, and Myanmar (Burma) to the northeast. To the east, almost surrounded by India, is Bangladesh. Near India's southern tip, across the Palk Strait, is Sri Lanka.

Although technically part of Asia, India is described as a 'subcontinent', set apart from the rest of Asia (along with Bangladesh and Pakistan) by the Himalayas, the youngest and highest mountain chain on the planet. A triangular peninsula, it's bounded by the Arabian Sea to the west and the Bay of Bengal to the east, making its coastline not only among the world's longest, but one with the greatest variety of beaches.

To Indians, the country is a goddess ('Mother India'), her head crowned by the Himalayas, her arms stretching towards Pakistan and Bangladesh, her life-giving heart the fertile Indo-Gangetic plain and her feet bathed by the Indian Ocean.

Regions

India has a huge variety of landscapes, even within each of its four regions (see below) and sometimes within a state. The regions are divided into 28 states, some as large as France, and there are also seven union territories, some as small as a city.

North India

The country's largest region begins in the north with Jammu & Kashmir, with their snow-capped Himalayas, lakes and forests. The Great Indian (Thar) Desert is located in the northwest. Further south, along the Indus River, the land becomes flatter and more hospitable, widening into the fertile plains of Punjab to the west and the Himalayan foothills of Uttar Pradesh to the east along the Ganges river valley.

West India

West India extends from Gujarat in the north down to Maharashtra and Goa, and eastwards to Madhya Pradesh. The coastline has some of the country's best beaches, backed by lush rainforests. Low-lying, rounded hills known as the Western Ghats separate the verdant coast from the Vindya Mountains and the dry Deccan plateau further inland.

East India

East India stretches from Madhya Pradesh to Bihar and Orissa. It also contains an area known as the eastern triangle, which extends beyond Bangladesh to the Naga Hills along the Burmese border and is only joined to the rest of the country by a narrow strip of land. It includes the states of Arunachal Pradesh, Assam, Manipur, Meghalaya, Mizoram, Nagaland, Sikkim and Tripura.

South India

South India consists largely of a huge plateau called the Deccan, bounded by the Eastern and Western Ghats (mountains) to the north and reaching the sea at Cape Comorin in the south. The Ghats run parallel to the east and the west coasts, meeting at the Nilgiri Hills in the south.

Earthquakes

India is divided into five zones – I to V – with respect to earthquake risk, Zone V being seismically the most active, where earthquakes of eight or more on the Richter scale could occur. Many areas along the Himalayan range, including the entire north-eastern triangle, the Andaman & Nicobar islands in the Bay of Bengal and Kutch in north-western Gujarat, are categorised as Zone V.

> **The Bhuj earthquake (Richter 7.7) in Kutch on 26th January 1926 was the most disastrous earthquake in India's history; at least 20,000 people were killed, over 200,000 injured, and almost 400,000 houses were destroyed and twice as many damaged.**

Due to the frequency of earthquakes, recent legislation makes it mandatory for all high-rise buildings under construction to be made earthquake-resistant.

You will never hear a warning of an earthquake and most people die or are injured when buildings collapse, which is why people in India rush out of their houses and even jump off top floors the moment they feel a tremor. Your best protection is to choose a bungalow or low-rise building. If you must live in a high-rise building, you should choose one that has been built after 2002, as most older buildings aren't earthquake resistant.

GOVERNMENT

India is a secular, socialist, sovereign democratic republic with a federal form of government, which has adopted a British-style parliamentary system.

The government exercises its broad administrative powers in the name of the president, whose duties are largely ceremonial. Real national executive power is centred in the Council of Ministers (Cabinet), led by the Prime Minister. The Constitution of India, the longest written constitution in the world, came into effect on 26th January 1950.

The Judiciary

Modelled on the British form of jurisprudence, the judiciary is independent of the executive and the legislative arms of the government. The Supreme Court is the apex court consisting of 25 judges headed by the Chief Justice, all appointed by the president on the advice of the Prime Minister. At the state level there are high courts with a hierarchical system of judges and magistrates.

President

Elected by members of an electoral college, the president must be a citizen of India, of not less than 35 years of age and qualified for election as a member of the Lok Sabha (House of the People or lower house).

The president appoints the Prime Minister, who is designated by legislators of the political party or coalition commanding a parliamentary majority in the Lok Sabha. The president then appoints subordinate ministers on the advice of the Prime Minister. Pratibha Patil became the first woman to be elected president of India on 21st July 2007.

Vice-president

Similarly elected, the vice-president is the *ex-officio* chairman of the Rajya Sabha (Council of States or upper house). He takes on the role of president when the president is unable to discharge his functions or, if he resigns or dies, until the election of a new president (held within six months).

Parliament

India's bicameral parliament consists of the Rajya Sabha (Council of States or upper house) and the Lok Sabha (House of the People or lower house). The legislatures of the states and union territories elect 233 members to the Rajya Sabha, and the president appoints another 12. The members of the Rajya Sabha serve six-year terms, with one-third being elected every two years. The Lok

Vidhana Soudha State assembly, Bangalore

Sabha consists of 545 members, who serve five-year terms; 543 are directly elected, and two are appointed. The Lok Sabha is the more powerful of the two houses and can overrule the Rajya Sabha in certain matters.

At state level, some legislatures are bicameral, patterned after the two houses of the national parliament. The states' chief ministers are responsible to the legislatures in the same way that the Prime Minister is responsible to parliament.

Each state also has a governor, appointed by the president, who may assume certain broad powers when directed by the central government. The central government exerts greater control over the union territories than over the states, although some territories have gained more power to administer their own affairs.

Political parties

The Indian National Congress or INC, headed by Sonia Gandhi, and the Bharatiya Janata Party or BJP, headed by Rajnath Singh, are the two main parties. Other major parties include Bahujan Samaj Party (BSP), Biju Janata Dal (BJD), Communist Party of India (CPI), Dravida Munnetra Kazagham (DMK), Janata Dal United (JDU), Jharkhand Mukti Morcha (JMM), Lok Jan Shakti Party (LJSP), Marumalarchi Dravida Munnetra Kazhagam (MDMK), Marxist Communist Party of India (CPIM), Nationalist Congress Party (NCP), Pattali Makkal Katchi (PMK), Rashtriya Janata Dal (RJD), Samajwadi Party (SP), Shiromani Akali Dal (SAD), Shiv Sena (SS), Telangana Rashtra Samithi (TRS) and Telugu Desam Party (TDP).

As neither of the main parties can command a clear parliamentary majority, the balance of power is held by a coalition. This currently consists of United Progressive Alliance (UPA), whose main constituent parties are included in the list above (half a dozen smaller parties are also included).

INTERNATIONAL RELATIONS

Unlike many developing countries in Asia, India has never bowed to major foreign powers, most notably the US. Its size, strategic location, military strength, scientific and technological sophistication, growing industrial base and huge manpower give it a prominent voice in international affairs.

India is a member of the Commonwealth, the United Nations, the World Trade Organisation, the South Asian Association for Regional Co-operation (SAARC), the Non-Aligned Movement (NAM) and the Association of Southeast Asian Nations (ASEAN).

The Commonwealth

The Commonwealth is an association of 53 countries, 60 per cent of whose people are Indian. The countries consult and cooperate in the common interests of their peoples and in the promotion of international understanding and world peace. Among other things, it stresses the need to foster international peace and security; democracy, liberty of the individual and equal rights for all; the importance of eradicating poverty, ignorance and disease; and it opposes all forms of racial discrimination.

India & the UK

Relations between India and the UK are currently excellent, which is reflected in a number of areas including international policy and cooperation in trade and education. The New Delhi Declaration, formally endorsed by the Prime Ministers of the two countries in January 2002, commits India and the UK to continuing to work closely together in areas such as security, development, education, trade and investment.

The India-UK Round Table brings together senior UK and Indian opinion-formers to work out practical suggestions for enhancing bilateral activity and cooperation on global issues. The UK has expressed its support for India to have a permanent seat on the UN Security Council and has agreed to work with India to achieve this.

The British Council's India operation is one of its largest, with offices in the four major Indian metropolitan cities and British libraries in seven other cities, including an online service to reach a wider audience of young Indians.

India & the USA

India and the US have a common interest in breaking down barriers to commerce, in fighting terrorism and creating a politically and economically stable Asia. In July 2005, President Bush played host to Prime Minister Man Mohan Singh in Washington DC, when the two leaders announced the successful completion of the 'Next Steps in Strategic Partnership' (NSSP) agreement, as well as other agreements aimed at enhancing their cooperation in the areas of civil nuclear and space development and high-technology commerce. President Bush made a return visit to India in March 2006, during which these

agreements were strengthened and new initiatives launched.

In December 2006, Congress passed the historic Henry J. Hyde United States-India Peaceful Atomic Cooperation Act, which allowed direct civilian nuclear commerce with India for the first time in 30 years, clearing the way for India to buy US nuclear reactors and fuel for civilian use. Since then, the two countries have sought to extend their cooperation to counter-terrorism, defence, education and democracy.

Despite the fact that the British ruled India as recently as 1947, most Indians are favourably disposed towards them; in fact, among the many Westerners who come to live and work in India, Britons take pride of place. The US, on the other hand, is viewed as a country seeking world domination and constantly interfering in the internal affairs of other countries, and Americans are widely perceived as 'suckers' – not in the American sense but literally, i.e. as sucking in the resources of other peoples.

India & Pakistan

The dispute over the status of Jammu & Kashmir, which has raged since India's Independence in 1947, remains the major stumbling block to harmony between India and Pakistan. While India maintains

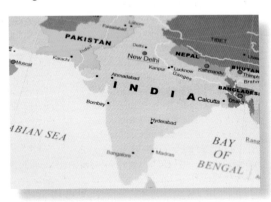

that the entire former princely state is an integral part of the Indian union, Pakistan insists upon the implementation of UN resolutions calling for self-determination for the people of the state. The dispute triggered wars between the two countries in 1947 and 1965 and provoked the Kargil conflict in 1999, which almost resulted in a full-scale war.

> In May 1998, Pakistan followed India in conducting nuclear tests.

PETS

India is home to around 4m pets, the great majority of them dogs. White Pomeranians are by far the most popular dog, followed by German shepherds and Dobermans. Pedigree dogs are expensive, a Chihuahua costing as much as Rs120,000 (US$2,400). Cats are believed to bring bad luck and therefore aren't   popular as pets in India.

Among birds, parrots are the most popular, followed by lovebirds, despite legal protection. Home aquariums with exotic fish are also gaining in popularity. Some people even keep turtles, although this requires permission from wildlife authorities.

Anyone entering the country can import two pets at one time, subject to certain requirements. You must apply for a 'No Objection Certificate' (NOC) to the Animal Quarantine Station in India (through a local clearing agent, as it must be obtained in person) before entering the country, for which you must provide the animal's vaccination records and details of how it will be travelling to India. If you're accompanying your pet, you must carry a copy of the NOC; if not, a copy of the NOC must be attached to the crate in which it travels.

The import of more than two pets requires an 'Import Sanitary Permit' issued by the Department of Animal Husbandry and Dairying. No quarantine is required, but pets must have had a rabies vaccination no less than 30 days and no more than a year prior to travel.

Pets require a municipal licence as well as regular vaccinations against rabies. Pet insurance plans are available, covering premature death and public liability claims.

RELIGION

The Indian Republic has no official religion and the Constitution states that India is a secular state. However, Hinduism is by far the dominant religion, being practised by over 80 per cent of the population, and the Hindu way of life is synonymous with Indian living. Other religious groups include Muslims (11 per cent), Christians (2.5 per cent), Sikhs (2 per cent), Jains (less than 1 per cent), Buddhists (less than 1 per cent, although the religion was founded in India) and Parsees.

Like most countries, India has its religious fanatics. The Bharatiya Janata Party (BJP), which leads the opposition, advocates the 'Hindutva' philosophy, an ideology that defines Indian culture in terms of Hindu values as against the secular policies of the Indian National Congress. The party was directly involved in the movement that culminated in the destruction of the Babri Masjid, a Muslim mosque, which was replaced by the Ram Janmabhoomi Hindu temple in December 1992. This fuelled Hindu-Muslim riots throughout the country, from which the BJP benefited by way of support from millions of 'devout' Hindus.

Extremist Hindu groups – principally the Bajrang Dal and the Vishwa Hindu Parishad – are also responsible for the persecution of Christians, and reports of violence appear intermittently in the national newspapers. One of the most heinous religious crimes in recent years was the murder of the Australian missionary Graham Staines and his two young sons, who were burnt alive in their jeep in 1999. Fortunately, Christians are rarely the subject of harassment or discrimination on a day-to-day basis.

As a general rule, footwear must be removed and you must dress modestly when entering any place of worship in India. Some temples, including the Jagannath Temple in Puri, Orissa, don't permit entry to non-Hindus.

TIME

Indian Standard Time (IST) is observed throughout the country and throughout the year; there's no ' daylight saving' or other seasonal adjustment. IST is 5.5 hours ahead of Greenwich Mean Time and 4.5 hours ahead of British Summer Time.

Times are usually written using the 12-hour clock format and the suffixes 'am' for morning and 'pm' for afternoon. Note that *kal* in Hindi means both 'yesterday' and 'tomorrow'. Indian Standard Time (IST) is jokingly referred to as 'Indian Stretchable Time'.

The time difference between Delhi and cities elsewhere in the world at noon in winter is shown below:

TIME DIFFERENCE						
DELHI	J'BURG	LONDON	NEW YORK	SINGAPORE	SYDNEY	TOKYO
12 noon	8.30am	6.30am	1.30am	2.30pm	5.30pm	3.30pm

TIPPING

There are no hard and fast rules about tipping in India, where tipping isn't widespread. In India, tipping is often referred to as *baksheesh* or money for tea or coffee. Usually, tipping is done after a service has been rendered but in certain places tips are given beforehand to ensure prompt service. For example, in a good restaurant, a tip of around 10 per cent of the bill is usual, while in cheap restaurants waiters won't expect one, although some people leave some small change. In a top class restaurant or hotel there may be a service charge, in which case you shouldn't tip or only tip if you receive exemplary service.

While no tips are usually given to taxi and rickshaw drivers, if you hire a guide or a car with a driver, it's normal to tip him Rs50-100 (US$1-2) per day. At railway stations, porters usually receive around Rs10 (US20¢) per bag, which is usually decided beforehand. Staff in hair salons and spas are tipped around 10 per cent. You may wish to tip staff in a hotel, when Rs20-50 (US40¢ to $1) is sufficient for most services (such as room service).

Government employees expect 'tips' (i.e. bribes) for just about everything, although you need to ensure that a tip isn't mistaken for a bribe!

TOILETS

Toilets in India are of three types: Western, Indian (a ceramic platform at floor level with a foot rest on either side and a keyhole-shaped bowl sunk into the floor, over which you squat – Turkish style) and Anglo-Indian – a clumsy compromise between the two 'pure' styles which has the two footrests up on the rim of the (otherwise Western-style) bowl – a precarious, not to say compromising, position for both types of user and hence not popular.

Toilet paper is seldom available as Indians use water rather than toilet paper for cleaning themselves (so make sure you take a toilet roll when travelling). However, there's usually a nozzle built into the rear of Western-style toilets that squirts a jet of water at the appropriate angle at the press of a button. Other toilets may have a contraption resembling a hand-held showerhead, which serves the same purpose.

Public toilets aren't just few and far between in India, they're notorious for being among the filthiest in the world. In fact, in many small towns and rural areas, it's hardly possible to gain access to a public toilet because of the human waste surrounding it. Men's urinals in public places are usually in full view of passers-by.

Toilets in bus and railway stations, as well as on trains, are best avoided – unless it's an emergency! Toilets in bars, cafés, restaurants, hotels, department stores, supermarkets, shopping centres and cinemas are generally cleaner – and free.

There are no modern, coin-operated public toilets in cities, but there are some where you pay an attendant and obtain a key to the toilet, which is generally of a relatively high level of cleanliness. Sulabh International is a social service organisation that operates attended toilets in all major cities. Charges are Rs2 (5 cents) for what the Indians call a 'number one,' and Rs5 (10 cents) for a 'number two'. There's even a Sulabh International Museum of Toilets in Delhi.

Toilet Signs

Ladies' – *Pooroosh* (in *Devanagari* **script) with the silhouette of a woman (usually in a sari) or the profile of a woman's face with her hair in a bun.**

Gents' – *Mahila* (in *Devanagari* **script) with the silhouette of a man (usually in shirt and trousers) or the profile of a man's face with short-cropped hair.**

Bengal tiger

APPENDICES

APPENDIX A: EMBASSIES & CONSULATES

In India

Listed below are the contact details for the embassies of the main English-speaking countries, in Delhi. A list of embassies and consulates in India is available from the Directory of Indian Government websites (🖳 www. goidirectory.nic.in – click on 'Intergov. Organisations in India' under 'International Presence').

Australia: High Commission: 1/50 G Shantipath, Chanakyapuri, New Delhi (☎ 4139 9900, 🖳 www.ausgovindia.com). Consulates are also located in Chennai and Mumbai.

Canada: High Commission: 7/8 Shantipath, Chanakyapuri, New Delhi (☎ 4178 2000, 🖳 www.newdelhi.gc.ca). Consulates are also located in, Chandigarh, Chennai, Kolkata and Mumbai.

Ireland: Embassy: 230, Jor Bagh, New Delhi (☎ 2462 6733, 🖳 www. irelandinindia.com). Consulates are also located in Bangalore and Mumbai.

New Zealand: High Commission: Sir Edmund Hillary Marg, Chanakyapuri, New Delhi (☎ 2688 3170, 🖳 www.nzembassy.com/India). Consulates are also located in Chennai and Mumbai.

South Africa: High Commission: B-18, Vasant Marg, Vasant Vihar, New Delhi (☎ 2614 9411, 🖳 www.sahc-india.com).

United Kingdom: High Commission: Shantipath, Chanakyapuri, New Delhi (☎ 2687 2161, 🖳 www.ukinindia.org). Consulates are also located in Chennai, Kolkata and Mumbai.

United States of America: Embassy: Shantipath, Chanakyapuri, New Delhi (☎ 2419 8000, 🖳 http://newdelhi.usembassy.gov). Consulates are also located in Chennai, Kolkata and Mumbai.

Abroad

L isted below are the contact details for Indian embassies in the main English-speaking countries. A list of Indian embassies is available from the Directory of Indian Government websites (⌨ www.goidirectory.nic.in – click on 'Indian Missions Abroad' under 'International Presence').

Australia: 3/5 Moonah Place, Yarralumla, ACT 2600 (☎ 61-2 6273 3999, ⌨ www.hcindia-au.org).

Canada: 10, Springfield Road, Ottawa K1M 1C9 (☎ 613-744 3751, ⌨ www. hciottawa.ca).

Ireland: 6, Leeson Park, Dublin 6 (☎ 01-497 0843, ⌨ www.indianembassy.ie).

New Zealand: 180, Molesworth Street, PO Box 4045, Wellington (☎ 64-4473 6390, ⌨ www.hicomind.org.nz).

South Africa: 852 Schoeman Street, Arcadia, Pretoria-0083 (☎ 12-342 5392, ⌨ www.india.org.za).

United Kingdom: India House, Aldwych, London WC2B 4NA (☎ 207-836 8484, ⌨ www.hcilondon.net).

United States of America: 2107, Massachusetts Avenue NW, Washington DC 20008 (☎ 202-939 7000, ⌨ www.indianembassy.org).

> The business hours of embassies vary and they close on their own country's holidays as well as on Indian public holidays. Always telephone to confirm opening hours before visiting.

APPENDIX B: FURTHER READING

English-language Newspapers

The Asian Age (☎ 11-2653 0001, 🖳 www.asianage.com). Daily newspaper with various Indian editions plus one published in London.

Business Standard (☎ 22-2497 8456, 🖳 www.business-standard.com). India's leading business daily newspaper.

The Economic Times (☎ 11- 2349 2057/162, 🖳 www.economictimes. indiatimes.com). Free daily online business and economics newspaper.

The Financial Express (☎ 11- 2370 2100, 🖳 www.financialexpress.com). Leading finance and business newspaper.

The Hindu (☎ 44-2857 6300, 🖳 www.hinduonnet.com). India's national newspaper.

Hindustan Times (☎11-2336 1234, 🖳 www.hindustantimes.com). Popular daily newspaper.

The Indian Express (☎ 011-2370 2100, 🖳 www.indianexpress.com). Leading Indian national newspaper.

Mid Day (☎ 22 2419 7171, 🖳 www.mid-day.com). Daily Mumbai newspaper whose motto is 'make work fun', now with Delhi and Bangalore editions.

The Statesman (☎ 11- 2331 5911, 🖳 www.thestatesman.net). Free daily online newspaper published in Kolkata.

The Telegraph (☎ 33-2234 5374, 🖳 www.telegraphindia.com). Daily newspaper published in Kolkata.

The Times of India (☎ 011-2331 2271, 🖳 www.timesofindia.com). India's best-selling national newspaper.

The Tribune (☎ 172-265 5066, 🖳 www.tribuneindia.com). One of Indian's oldest newspapers, established in Lahore in 1881, now published in Chandigarh.

English-language Magazines

Business Today (☎ 011-2368 4800, 🖳 www.business-today.com). Fortnightly magazine from the *India Today* Group.

Business World (☎ 011-2370 2170, 🖳 www.businessworld.in). Free online weekly magazine.

Frontline (☎ 044-2858 9060, 🖥 www.flonnet.com). Fortnightly magazine from the publishers of *The Hindu* newspaper.

India Today (☎ 011-2368 4848, 🖥 www.india-today.com). Fortnightly – India's leading magazine.

Indian Life & Style (☎ US 510-383 1140, 🖥 www.indianlifeandstyle.com). Published in the USA.

Outlook India (☎ 011-2619 1421, 🖥 www.outlookindia.com). Free online weekly magazine.

Woman's Era (☎ 011-2352 9557, 🖥 www.womansera.com). Fortnightly magazine on women's issues.

Books

The books listed below are just a selection of the hundreds written about India. The title is followed by the author's name and the publisher's name (in brackets).

Culture

An ABC of Indian Culture: A Personal Padyatra of Half a Century into India, Peggy Holroyde (Mapin Publishing)

The Age of Kali: Travels and Encounters in India, William Dalrymple (Flamingo)

The Argumentative Indian: Writings on Indian History, Culture and Identity, Amartya Sen (Picador)

Being Indian: Inside the Real India, Pavan K Varma (Arrow Books)

Holy Cow: An Indian Adventure, Sarah Macdonald (Broadway)

No Full Stops in India, Mark Tully (Penguin)

In Spite of the Gods: The Strange Rise of Modern India, Edward Luce (Little, Brown)

History

Armies of the Raj: From the Great Indian Mutiny to Independence, 1858-1947, Byron Farwell (W. W. Norton & Co Inc)

A Brief History of India, Alain Daniélou (Inner Traditions)

A Concise History of Modern India, Barbara D. Metcalf & Thomas R. Metcalf (CUP)

The Dynasty: Nehru-Gandhi Story, Jad Adams & Phillip Whitehead (Penguin)

Early India: From the Origins to AD 1300, Romila Thapar (University of California Press)

Freedom at Midnight, Larry Collins & Dominique Lapierre (Harper Collins)

History of India: Vol. 1, Romila Thapar (Penguin)

History of India, Vol. 2, Percival Spear (Penguin)

India: A History, John Keay (Grove Press)

India After Gandhi: The History of the World's Largest Democracy, Ramachandra Guha (Pan)

India: From Midnight to the Millennium, Shashi Tharoor (Harper Collins)

India's Unending Journey: Finding Balance in a Time of Change, Mark Tully (Rider)

The Mughal Empire, John F. Richards (CUP)

A New History of India, Stanley Wolpert (OUP)

Language

Beginner's Hindi Book/CD Pack, Rupert Snell (Teach Yourself Books)

Hindi Made Easy: For Beginners, J. S. Nagra (Nagra Publications)

Hindi, Urdu and Bengali, Richard Delacy (Lonely Planet Publications)

Learn Hindi in a Month, I. Datt (Readwell Publishers)

Say It in Hindi, Veena T. Oldenburg (Dover Publications)

Teach Yourself Beginner's Hindi Script, Rupert Snell & Simon Weightman (Teach Yourself Books)

Teach Yourself Hindi Dictionary, Rupert Snell (Teach Yourself Books)

Living & Working in India

Bangalore: An Expat Survival Guide (Chillibreeze)

Doing Business in India, Rajesh Kumar (Palgrave Macmillan)

India (Living In...), Rachel Thomson (Franklin Watts)

Mumbai: An Expat Survival Guide (Chillibreeze)

What's This India Business? Offshoring, Outsourcing and the Global Services Revolution, Paul Davies (Nicholas Brealey Publishing)

Miscellaneous

50 Great Curries of India, Camellia Panjabi & Peter Knab (Kyle Cathie)

The Complete Kama Sutra: The First Unabridged Modern Translation of the Classic Indian Text, Mallanaga Vatsyatana & Alain Danielou (Inner Traditions)

The Far Pavilions, Mary Margaret Kaye (Penguin)

India (DK Publishing)

The Jewel in the Crown, Paul Scott (Arrow)

Madhur Jaffrey's Ultimate Curry Bible, Madhur Jaffrey (Ebury)

Midnight's Children, Salman Rushdue (Vintage)

A Passage to India, EM Forster (Penguin)

In Spite of the Gods: The Rise of Modern India, Edward Luce (Anchor)

Simple Indian: The Fresh Tastes of India's New Cuisine, Atul Kochhar & David Loftus (Quadrille)

A Suitable Boy, Vikram Seth (Harper Perennial)

Trekking Holidays in India (Outlook)

White Mughals: Love and Betrayal in Eighteenth Century India, William Dalrymple (Harper Perennial)

The White Tiger, Aravind Adiga (Atlantic)

Tourist Guides

Alastair Sawday's Special Places to Stay India, Laura Kinch (Alastair Sawday Publishing)

Fodor's India (Fodor's Travel Publications)

India Eyewitness Travel Guide (D K Travel)

India - Footprint Travel Guide, Annie Dare & David Stott (Footprint Handbooks)

India: Pocket Guide (Berlitz Pocket Guides)

Lonely Planet India, Joe Bindloss, Sarina Singh, etc al (Lonely Planet)

India by Rail, 3rd, Royston Ellis (Bradt Travel Guides)

Picture of India: Journey Through the Eyes of a British Tourist, Chris Boyes (Amit Atwal)

The Rough Guide to India, David Abram (Rough Guides)

A South Indian Journey, Michael Wood (Penguin)

APPENDIX C: USEFUL WEBSITES

This appendix contains a list of some of the most popular websites dedicated to India and the Indian people.

Business

Business India (💻 www.business-india.in). Business directory.

Business Online India (💻 www.businessonlineindia.com). A searchable online Yellow Pages and *business* directory.

Business Today (💻 http://businesstoday.digitaltoday.in). India's number one business magazine.

Businesses for Sale (💻 www.businessesforsale.com/Business-Region/business-for-sale-in-India.aspx).

India in Business (💻 http://indiainbusiness.nic.in). Comprehensive information from the Ministry of External Affairs.

India Catalog (💻 www.indiacatalog.com). Marketplace for Indian business.

India Government - Business (💻 http://india.gov.in/business.php). Comprehensive business information from the Indian government.

UK India Business Council (💻 www.ukibc.com). Promotes bilateral business between the UK and India.

Culture

Culture of India (💻 www.cultureofindia.net). General information on culture, cuisine, history, religion and fashion.

Cultural India (💻 www.culturalindia.net). Yet another excellent culture website.

Culturopedia (💻 www.culturopedia.com). Encyclopaedia of India's culture, art, architecture, heritage, customs and music.

Indian Culture (💻 www.indiaculture.net). Indian culture, customs and history.

Indian Culture Online (💻 www.indiancultureonline.com). Yet another excellent culture site.

Indian Heritage (🖥 www.indian-heritage.org). Comprehensive heritage and cultural information.

Indian Mirror (🖥 www.indianmirror.com). Excellent cultural website.

Government

Delhi Government (🖥 http://delhigovt.nic.in/index.asp).

Government of India Directory (🖥 www.goidirectory.nic.in). Directory of official websites of the Government of India.

Indian Government (🖥 http://india.gov.in/govt.php). How the government works.

National Portal of India (🖥 www.india.gov.in). A comprehensive, accurate and reliable one-stop source of information and services provided by the Indian government.

Parliament of India (🖥 http://parliamentofindia.nic.in).

Rajya Sabha (🖥 http://rajyasabha.nic.in). Official website of the upper house of the Parliament of India.

Language

Bengali (🖥 www.omniglot.com/writing/bengali.htm). Omniglot guide to Bengali.

Hindi Learner (🖥 www.hindilearner.com). Learn Hindi online.

Indian Languages (🖥 www.indianlanguages.com). Excellent resource for Indian languages.

Languages Home (🖥 www.languageshome.com). Learn Indian languages online.

Let's Learn Hindi (🖥 www.letslearnhindi.com).

Urdu (🖥 www.omniglot.com/writing/urdu.htM). Omniglot guide to Urdu.

Living & Working

Allo' Expat India (🖥 www.india.alloexpat.com). A one-stop information and service centre for expatriates living in India.

Bangalore Best (🖥 www.bangalorebest.com). The number one website for Bangalore.

Bangalore Expat Club (🖥 www.bangalore-expatriate-club.com). A place to have fun and meet people who live and work in Bangalore.

Career India (🖥 www.careerindia.com). Jobsite.

Indax (🖥 www.indax.com/living.html). Extensive information for foreigners in India.

India Property (🖥 www.indiaproperty.com). One of the best websites on property with up-to-date and useful information about buying and renting property in the major cities.

Kolkata (🖥 www.kolkata.net). The web guide to Kolkata.

Monster India (🖥 www.monsterindia.com). Monster job site India.

Mumbai on the Net (🖥 www.mumbainet.com). The most comprehensive Mumbai site.

Naukri (🖥 www.naukri.com). India's 'no.1 job site.'

Surfing India Online (🖥 www.surfingindiaonline.com). Indian lifestyle magazine.

Times Jobs (🖥 www.timesjobs.com). Jobs from *India Times*.

Top India Jobs (🖥 www.topindiajobs.com). One of India's leading job sites.

UK in India (🖥 www.ukinindia.com). The British Embassy's official site including useful information about many aspects of living and working in India.

Media

All India Radio (🖥 http://allindiaradio.org).

India.com (🖥 www.india.com). Indian news and current affairs.

India Today (🖥 www.india-today.com). Fortnightly magazine – India's number one magazine.

Mega Indian TV (🖥 www.megaindiantv.com). Watch all the Indian TV channels free.

Online Newspapers (🖥 www.onlinenewspapers.com/india.htm). Online access to dozens of India's English-language newspapers.

The Times of India (🖥 www.timesofindia.com). The worlds best-selling English newspaper.

Miscellaneous

Indian Child (🖥 www.indianchild.com/culture). A parent's guide to internet safety.

India Forums (🖥 www.india-forums.com). Indian entertainment portal.

Indian Food Forever (💻 www.indianfoodforever.com). Everything you ever wanted to know about Indian food.

Indian History (💻 www.indhistory.com). Excellent history site.

India Net Zone (💻 www.indianetzone.com). The largest free encyclopaedia about India.

India.org (💻 www.india.org). Portal site for information about India.

I love India (💻 www.iloveindia.com). One of the most exhaustive websites on India with information about culture, crafts, cars, sports, festivals, travel, housing, insurance, pets, etc.

Maps of India (💻 www.mapsofindia.com).

Spices of India (💻 www.spicesofindia.co.uk). More mouth-watering Indian food.

Surf India (💻 www.surfindia.com). Indian web directory.

Wikipedia (💻 http://en.wikipedia.org/wiki/India). Wikipedia pages for India.

Travel & Tourism

Air India (💻 www.airindia.com). India's national airline.

Delhi Tourism (💻 www.delhitourism.com).

Incredible India (💻 www.incredibleindia.org). The Official Tourism Website of the Ministry of Tourism.

India Mike (💻 www.indiamike.com). India travel forum.

India Rail (💻 www.indianrail.gov.in). India rail passenger reservation site.

Lonely Planet (💻 www.lonelyplanet.com/India). Where Lonely Planet started life …

Palace on Wheels (💻 www.palaceonwheelsindia.com). Information about the luxury train journey from Delhi through the historical cities of Jaipur, Jaisalmer, Jodhpur, Sawai Madhopur, Chittaurgarh, Udaipur, Bharatpur and Agra.

Tour India (💻 www.tourindia.com). General information about travelling in India.

Travel Mart India (💻 www.travelmartindia.com). India's first eCommerce travel portal.

Pushkar camel fair, Rajasthan

APPENDIX D: MAP OF INDIA

India is divided into 28 states and seven Union territories, which are listed below and shown on the map opposite. The capital, New Delhi, lies within the federally-administered Union Territory known as the National Capital Territory (NCT) of Delhi.

States

Andhra Pradesh
Arunachal Pradesh
Assam
Bihar
Chhattisgarh
Goa
Gujarat
Haryana
Himachal Pradesh
Jammu and Kashmir
Jharkhand
Karnataka
Kerala
Madhya Pradesh
Maharashtra
Manipur
Meghalaya
Mizoram
Nagaland
Orissa
Punjab
Rajasthan
Sikkim
Tamil Nadu
Tripura
Uttarakhand
Uttar Pradesh
West Bengal

Union Territories

Andaman and Nicobar Islands
Chandigarh
Dadra and Nagar Haveli
Daman and Diu
Lakshadweep
National Capital Territory of Delhi
Puducherry

APPENDIX E: USEFUL WORDS & PHRASES

This appendix includes a list of everyday words and phrases that you may need during your first few days in India. They are, of course, no substitute for learning the language, which you should make one of your priorities if you plan on staying for a few years.

However, English isn't just widely spoken in India but is so popular with the masses that many Hindi-speaking people use English words without ever knowing their Hindi counterparts, for example most don't know the Hindi word for 'station', which is such a long phrase that it's too cumbersome for common usage. Similarly, the word for 'mobile phone' is simply 'mobile.' English words are also used for days of the week, months, numbers, greetings, etc.

The polite *aap* form of addressing has been used below and, where applicable, the feminine form of verbs has been included in brackets after the masculine form – you should use these when addressing a woman or if you're a woman. The Hindi phrases have been written in the Roman script (instead of the '*Devanagari*' script) for readers' convenience – in fact, Hindi written in the Roman script is called 'Roman Hindi' and is used in the Indian army.

It should be noted that spoken Hindi is phonetic and the translations below should be pronounced exactly as they are spelt. As you'll notice, there are no capital letters in Hindi.

Asking for Help

Do you speak English?	*kya, aap angreji bol sakte (sakti) ho?*
I don't speak Hindi	*mai hindi na-hinh bol sakta (sakti) hunh*
Please speak slowly	*kripya dhireh-dhireh boliye*
I don't understand	*mai na-hinh samjha*
I need ...	*muzeh .... zaroorat hai*
I want ...	*muzeh .... chaahiye*

Communications

Telephone & Internet

landline	*sthaniya 'phone'*
mobile phone	*mobile*
no answer	*uttar na-hinh*
engaged/busy	*vyaast*

internet	*internet*
email	*email*
broadband connection	*broadband/ADSL*
internet café/wifi spot	*cyber café/hot spot*

Post

post office	*dak ghar*
postcard/letter/parcel	*postcard/patr/parcel*
stamps	*tickat*
How much does it cost to send a letter to Europe/North America/Australia?	*yoorope/amrika/astralia patr bejne ke liye, kitni kimmat lageggi?*

Media

newspaper/magazine	*samachaar patr/samachaar patrika*
Do you sell English-language media?	*kya, aap angreji samachar ko betch-te hai?*

Courtesy

yes	*haanh*
no	*nahin*
excuse me	*shama karenh*
sorry	*maaf kijiye*
I don't know	*muzeh nahin patta*
I don't mind	*muzeh parva nahin*
please	*kripya*
thank you	*dhanyavad* or *shukriya*
you're welcome	aapka swaagat hai

Days & Months

Monday	*somwar*
Tuesday	*mangalwar*
Wednesday	*budhwar*
Thursday	*guruwar*

Friday	*shukarwar*
Saturday	*shaniwar*
Sunday	*raviwar*
January	*janwary*
February	*farwary*
March	*march*
April	*april*
May	*maye*
June	*joon*
July	*julaye*
August	*agust*
September	*sitember*
October	*actuber*
November	*navamber*
December	*desember*

Driving

car insurance	*gaadi ka bima* (common usage, 'motor vehicle insurance')
driving licence	*gaadi chalaani ka adhikar patr* (common usage, 'driving licence')
hire/rental car	*kirayi ki gaadi*
How far is it to ...?	*idhar se kitni duur hai ...?*
Can I park here?	*kya, mai idhar gaadi khadi kar sakta (sakti) hunh?*
unleaded petrol (gas)/diesel	*sishaa rahit 'petrol'/'diesel'*
Fill the tank up, please	*kripya, taanki pura bhar dho*
I need Rs: 100 of petrol (gas)	*muzeh ek sow rupaiya ka 'petrol' chahiyeh*
air/water/oil	*havaa/paani/tael*
car wash	*gaadi dhona* (common usage, 'car wash')
My car has broken down	*meri gaadi kharab ho gayi hai*
I've run out of petrol (gas)	*meri gaadi menh 'petrol' khatam ho gaya hai*
The tyre is flat	*'puncture' ho gaya hai*
I need a tow truck	*muzeh ek 'tow truck' chahiyeh*

Emergencies

Emergency!	*aapatkaleen!*
Fire!	*aag!*
Help!	*bachao!*
Police!	*surakshakari!* (common usage, 'Police!')
Stop!	*thehero!*
Stop thief!	*chor roko!*
Watch out!	*dekhna!*

Health & Medical Emergencies

I feel ill/dizzy	*mai asvasth mehsoos kar raha (rahi) hunh*
I need a doctor/ambulance	*muzeh ek chikitsak'/'ambulance' ki jaroorat hai* (common usage, 'doctor/ambulance')
doctor/nurse/dentist	*chikitsak/paricharika/dant chikitsak* (common usage, 'doctor/nurse/dentist')
surgeon/specialist	*shailya chikitsak/viscsagya* (common usage, 'surgeon/specialist')
hospital/healthcentre/A&E	*aspataal/swaasth kendra/aappatkaleen kamra* (common usage, 'emergency room')
chemist/optician	*davaiiyon ki dookaan/chasmaa ki dookaan* (common usage, 'medical store/optician')
prescription	*nuskha*

Other phrases for medical emergencies are shown in **Chapter 3**.

Finding your Way

Where is ...?	*.... kahanh hai?*
Where is the nearest ...?	*nazdik menh .... kahanh hai?*
How do I get to ...?	*mai kaise .... pahunch sakta (sakti) hunh?*
Can I walk there?	*kya, mai udhar chal sakta (sakti) hunh?*
How far is ....?	*.... kitni duur hai?*
A map please	*kripya, ek manchitr dijiye*
I'm lost	*mai kho gaya (gayi) hunh*

left/right/straight ahead	*baaya/daaya/seedhe aagae*
opposite/next to/near	*vepreet/aglaa/aaspaas*
airport	*hawai adda*
bus/plane/taxi/train	*'motor' gaadi/vimaan/'taxi'/'rail'-gaadi*
bus stop	*'bus' adhaa*
taxi rank	*'taxi-stand'*
train/bus station	*rail-gaadi 'station'/'bus depot'*
When does the ... arrive/leave?	*.... kub aayegi/jaayegi?*
one-way/return ticket	*ek taraf se/vapsi ka tickat*
bank/embassy/consulate	*'bank'/dootavaas* (common usage, 'embassy/consulate')

Greetings

Hello	*namaskar*
Goodbye	*alvida*
Good morning	*soobh prabhat*
Good afternoon	*namaste*
Good night	*soobh raatri*

In a Bar or Restaurant

Waiter!	*sewadar!* (common usage, 'Waiter!')
menu	*bhojan ki soochi* (common usage, 'menu')
bill	*lekha* (common usage, 'bill')
well done/medium/rare (for meat/fish)	*poori taruh/aadha pakana/thoda sa pakana*
vegetarian	*shakaharee* (common usage, 'veg')
meat/fish	*maanhs/machhi*

Numbers

one	*ek*
two	*doh*
three	*teen*
four	*char*
five	*paanch*

six	*chh*
seven	*saat*
eight	*aath*
nine	*nau*
ten	*dus*
eleven	*gyarah*
twelve	*bara*
thirteen	*tera*
fourteen	*chowdha*
fifteen	*pandhra*
sixteen	*solah*
seventeen	*satrah*
eighteen	*athrah*
nineteen	*oonice*
twenty	*biss*
thirty	*tiss*
forty	*chaalice*
fifty	*pachaas*
sixty	*saath*
seventy	*satar*
eighty	*assi*
ninety	*nabhe*
100	*ek sow*
200	*doh sow*
500	*paanch sow*
1,000	*ek hajar*
100,000	*ek lakh* (written as 1,00,000 and pronounced, 'lac' in Indian English, e.g. one 'lakh')
10,000,000	*ek crore* (written as 1,00,000,000 and pronounced, 'ka-roar' in Indian English, e.g. one 'crore')

Paying

How much is it?	*ye kitni kimat ka hai?*
The bill, please	*kripya, laikha dijiyeh/ kripya, 'bill' dijiyeh*
Do you take credit cards?	*kya, aapke yahaanh 'credit' card chalega?*

Socialising

Pleased to meet you	*Aapse milker kooshi huii*
My name is ...	*mera naam .... hai*
This is my husband/wife/ son/daughter/colleague/friend hai	*yeh mera pati hai/ meri patni hai/mera beta hai/meri beti hai/mera (meri) mitr*
How are you?	*aap kaise ho?*
Very well, thank you	*bahoot achhaa, aapka dhanyavad*

Shopping

What time do you open/close?	*aap kiss samay kholte (kholti)/bandh karte (karti) ho?*
Who's the last person (in the queue)?	*iss katar menh aakhri vyakti kaun hai?*
I'm just looking (browsing)	*mai seerf dhek raha (rahi) hunh*
I'm looking for ...	*mai .... khoj raha (rahi) hunh*
Can I try it on?	*kya, menh isse pehen kar dek sakta (sakti) hunh?*
I need size ...	*muzeh .... naap ka chaaiye*
bigger/smaller/longer/shorter	*isse badhaa/isse chota/isse lamba/isse chota*
A bag, please	*kripya, ek thailee dijeeye*
How much is this?	*yeh kitne ka hai?*

Kathakali dancer, Cochin, Kerala

INDEX

Survival Books

Essential reading for anyone planning to live, work, retire or buy a home abroad

Survival Books was established in 1987 and by the mid-'90s was the leading publisher of books for people planning to live, work, buy property or retire abroad.

From the outset, our philosophy has been to provide the most comprehensive and up-to-date information available. Our titles routinely contain up to twice as much information as other books and are updated frequently. All our books contain colour photographs and some are printed in two colours or full colour throughout. They also contain original cartoons, illustrations and maps.

Survival Books are written by people with first-hand experience of the countries and the people they describe, and therefore provide invaluable insights that cannot be obtained from official publications or websites, and information that is more reliable and objective than that provided by the majority of unofficial sites.

Survival Books are designed to be easy – and interesting – to read. They contain a comprehensive list of contents and index and extensive appendices, including useful addresses, further reading, useful websites and glossaries to help you obtain additional information as well as metric conversion tables and other useful reference material.

Our primary goal is to provide you with the essential information necessary for a trouble-free life or property purchase and to save you time, trouble and money.

We believe our books are the best – they are certainly the best-selling. But don't take our word for it – read what reviewers and readers have said about Survival Books at the front of this book.

Order your copies today by phone, fax, post or email from:
Survival Books, PO Box 3780, Yeovil, BA21 5WX, United Kingdom.
Tel: +44 (0)1935-700060, email: sales@survivalbooks.net,
Website: www.survivalbooks.net

Buying a Home Series

Buying a home abroad is not only a major financial transaction but also a potentially life-changing experience; it's therefore essential to get it right. Our Buying a Home guides are required reading for anyone planning to purchase property abroad and are packed with vital information to guide you through the property jungle and help you avoid disasters that can turn a dream home into a nightmare.

The purpose of our Buying a Home guides is to enable you to choose the most favourable location and the most appropriate property for your requirements, and to reduce your risk of making an expensive mistake by making informed decisions and calculated judgements rather than uneducated and hopeful guesses. Most importantly, they will help you save money and will repay your investment many times over.

Buying a Home guides are the most comprehensive and up-to-date source of information available about buying property abroad – whether you're seeking a detached house or an apartment, a holiday or a permanent home (or an investment property), these books will prove invaluable.

For a full list of our current titles, visit our website at www.survivalbooks.net

Living and Working Series

Our Living and Working guides are essential reading for anyone planning to spend a period abroad – whether it's an extended holiday or permanent migration – and are packed with priceless information designed to help you avoid costly mistakes and save both time and money.

Living and Working guides are the most comprehensive and up-to-date source of practical information available about everyday life abroad. They aren't, however, simply a catalogue of dry facts and figures, but are written in a highly readable style – entertaining, practical and occasionally humorous.

Our aim is to provide you with the comprehensive practical information necessary for a trouble-free life. You may have visited a country as a tourist, but living and working there is a different matter altogether; adjusting to a new environment and culture and making a home in any foreign country can be a traumatic and stressful experience. You need to adapt to new customs and traditions, discover the local way of doing things (such as finding a home, paying bills and obtaining insurance) and learn all over again how to overcome the everyday obstacles of life.

All these subjects and many, many more are covered in depth in our Living and Working guides – don't leave home without them.

The Expats' Best Friend!

Other Survival Books

The Best Places to Buy a Home in France/Spain: Unique guides to where to buy property in Spain and France, containing detailed regional profiles and market reports.

Buying, Selling and Letting Property: The best source of information about buying, selling and letting property in the UK.

Earning Money From Your French Home: Income from property in France, including short- and long-term letting.

Investing in Property Abroad: Everything you need to know and more about buying property abroad for investment and pleasure.

Life in the UK - Test & Study Guide: essential reading for anyone planning to take the 'Life in the UK' test in order to become a permanent resident (settled) in the UK.

Making a Living: Comprehensive guides to self-employment and starting a business in France and Spain.

Renovating & Maintaining Your French Home: The ultimate guide to renovating and maintaining your dream home in France.

Retiring in France/Spain: Everything a prospective retiree needs to know about the two most popular international retirement destinations.

Running Gîtes and B&Bs in France: An essential book for anyone planning to invest in a gîte or bed & breakfast business.

Rural Living in France: An invaluable book for anyone seeking the 'good life', containing a wealth of practical information about all aspects of French country life.

Shooting Caterpillars in Spain: The hilarious and compelling story of two innocents abroad in the depths of Andalusia in the late '80s.

For a full list of our current titles, visit our website at
www.survivalbooks.net

CULTURE WISE
JAPAN

The Essential Guide to Culture, Customs & Business Etiquette

★ vital reading for visitors who want to understand how Japan really works

★ helps newcomers quickly find their feet and settle in smoothly

★ reduces the anxiety factor in adapting to Japanese culture

★ explains how to behave in everyday situations in order to avoid cultural and social gaffes

★ helps you make friends and establish lasting business contacts

★ enhances your understanding of Japan and its people

Culture Wise Japan will help you adapt to the Japanese way of life and enable you to quickly feel at home.

Culture Wise
JAPAN

The Essential Guide to Culture, Customs & Business Etiquette

Edited by David Leaper

Culture Wise - The Wisest Way to Travel

PHOTO

CREDITS

Culture Wise Series

Current Titles:

America
Australia
Canada
England
France
Germany
India
Japan
New Zealand
Spain
Turkey

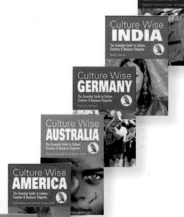

Coming soon:

Cyprus
Dubai
Greece
Holland
Hong Kong
Ireland
Italy
Switzerland

Culture Wise - The Wisest Way to Travel